KEW
GARDENS BOOK OF

INDOOR
PLANTS

KEW
GARDENS BOOK OF
INDOOR
PLANTS

GENERAL EDITOR
JOHN SIMMONS O.B.E. V.M.H.
CURATOR OF THE ROYAL BOTANIC GARDENS

GEORGE
PHILIP

British Library Cataloguing in Publication Data

The Kew Gardens book of indoor plants.
1. House plants
I. Simmons, John, *1937*–
635-9'65   SB419

ISBN 0–540–01129–0

Published by George Philip & Son Ltd
27A Floral Street, London WC2E 9DP

Designed by Derek St Romaine
Picture Research by Anne-Marie Ehrlich
Original artwork copyright © Lynn Cawley 1988

Filmset by Tameside Filmsetting Ltd
Ashton-under-Lyne, Lancashire

Printed and bound in Italy

CONTENTS

THE AUTHORS

Tender bulbs
Kenneth A. Beckett is a general plantsman with a keen interest in greenhouse subjects. Formerly Assistant Curator of Glasgow Botanic Garden and Deputy Editor of the *Gardeners' Chronicle*, since 1969 he has been a freelance writer and technical adviser, and has written thirty publications on plants and gardening.

Carnivorous plants
Ken Burras has been Superintendent for thirty-five years of the University Botanic Garden at Oxford, which is well known for the excellence of its collection of carnivorous plants.

Cacti and other succulents
Brian Fearn has been a cactus enthusiast for forty years. In 1956 he founded the Abbey Brook Cactus Nursery and is a member of the International Organisation for Succulent Plant Study. He recently received the Award of Merit from the British Cactus and Succulent Society for exceptional services.

Gillian Fearn is a lecturer in Applied Biology at Sheffield City Polytechnic with a PhD in plant taxonomy and is co-proprietor of the Abbey Brook Cactus Nursery with her husband, Brian.

Useful plants
Jim Keesing is Senior Scientific Officer at Kew who, in addition to his responsibilities for plant exchange and quarantine work, deals every year with thousands of requests from the public for information on the cultivation of plants.

Tender flowering climbers
Sue Minter is Supervisor of the Palm House at Kew with previous experience in both commercial horticulture and publishing and a special interest in threatened plants of the tropics.

Bromeliads
Dave Philcox, recently retired from the post of Principal Scientific Officer in the Herbarium at Kew, has a lifetime's special interest in the taxomony of Bromeliaceae.

Orchids
Joyce Stewart is Sainsbury Orchid Fellow at Kew, where she is co-ordinating research, conservation and cultivation of orchids, after many years studying them, including assembling and growing a large personal collection.

Tender ferns
John Woodhams is Assistant Curator of the Tropical Section at Kew, for many years Supervisor of Kew's extensive living fern collection and an authority on their cultivation. He has travelled to Papua New Guinea, New Zealand and South America in search of plants from the wild.

Publisher's note
For the convenience of the home gardener, the Latin plant names used in some sections such as *Cacti and other succulents* are those under which the plants are likely to be purchased or already known, and these do not necessarily reflect the latest taxonomic understanding. Cross reference to the new name is given where appropriate to encourage recognition of these revisions.

Acknowledgements
The Publishers would like to thank the following for their help in compiling this book: Susyn Andrews, Mark Flanagan, Lynn Foss, Vicki Mathews, Michael Maunder, Dave Philcox and Marilyn Ward.

INTRODUCTION

THERE IS a paradox between the decline of the once large collections of tropical plants, the reduced numbers of species available commercially, the loss of these species in their natural habitats worldwide, and the rising popularity of all tropical house plants. The ease of foreign travel and the frequency of natural history and gardening programmes on television have brought these plants into greater familiarity, while in the home and office central heating creates opportunities in which to grow plants, although the risk of lower night temperatures along with the lack of light and humidity can constrain the range to an all too familiar few.

The attached conservatory is happily a relatively economic way of adding space to a home. Not only can it be a delightful space for sitting and dining, but it has the advantage of literally double-glazing that part of the house, trapping warmth on cold days. But gardening in warmer climates has quite different rhythms.

In warm sunlit Mediterranean zones, as in a heated greenhouse, a greater range of plants is available, literally thousands more species. The richly diverse floras of Australia and southern Africa, for example, each possess more than 20,000 species, many of which are of great beauty, allowing an almost unusable choice, and when parts of Central and South America, the oceanic islands and Asia are added, the range is indeed vast. Some of the most enjoyable of such gardens have been formed on the ragged south-facing Mediterranean coast, where France, Monaco and Italy join, with an azure sea and sheltered inlets; the exotic displays of Kew's Temperate House grown out of doors with no roof to inhibit their luxuriance. The dark blue pea blossoms of a great climbing *Mucuna* at Cap Ferrat, brightly coloured gerberas at Menton, rarities at La Mortola, and cacti too thrive as splendidly grown and displayed by the Jardin Exotique in Monaco.

Move closer to the tropics, and the experience intensifies yet further – this is the richest of the floral regions. Some two-thirds of the world's plant species exist in the tropics, where luxuriant growth never stops but pests increase all year round; with riotous colours and forms, there is an immense palette of design opportunities scarcely exploited. Instant gardening. Within twenty years there can be a grown garden of trees and blossoms that would take more than a lifetime's work in cool temperate climates, but it is much harder work, with no respite for a winter to plan and develop, and hot, very hot, conditions in which to labour love upon the land.

Although containing but a fragment of this exciting flora, the popularity of Kew's great greenhouses remains undiminished and its visitors find them a focus for their attention. Such greenhouses distil the essence of the flowering tropics, for rarely are natural displays so colourful. In the Amazon forests the apparent greenness masks the real diversity of the many species involved, with a great wealth of trees, climbers, epiphytes, and ground cover, so that in an area not much greater than that covered by one of Kew's conservatories there may be as many as seventy, or even eighty, different species of orchids. Their flowers are not easily seen because they are so well in tune with their pollinators, while the many climbers in the trees flower high in their canopies away from our earth-bound view. But the diversity is immense and one of different species in different areas. The contrast can be seen in a desert where a floral spectacle may occur after rains with the flowering of many annuals, but the number of species involved is relatively few.

From this floral diversity of the tropics botanic gardeners select the most exotic species and place them in the forefront of their greenhouse displays, training climbers down to dip the heads of visitors, selecting yet further the particular type of plant, for few homes or conservatories can accommodate trees of any size. In many homes the list reduces yet further to those that will tolerate a dusty, shady dryness.

Fortunately many tropical climbers, such as the Central and South American philodendrons and monsteras, and the many epiphytic (perching on trees) orchids and bromeliads which leave the soil and use the forest trees to reach the light, are designed to cope with reduced water supplies. This adaptation produces plants capable of withstanding extreme conditions which makes them suitable for cultivation in the home.

Structurally Kew's greenhouses are a curious admixture of historic and horticultural pragmatism and of a commensalism between architect and engineer, resulting in a great collection of plant houses within which is shoehorned a distillation of the

world's exotic flora. Generations of plantsmen have laboured to form these collections, travelling in remote regions, struggling through dark forests, scaling moisture sodden mountains, gathering and lovingly caring for pieces of these floral gems that are carried back, with often even greater difficulty, their life sustained to reach Kew's nurseries, where yet another succession of botanical gardeners has given long and careful nursing to their establishment. The seeds, or propagules, need warmth, moisture and free-draining composts to encourage healthy new roots. For some perhaps even a year's wait in quarantine is necessary if the health of the plant is in doubt, but all need constant attention, care and understanding.

Some will thrive, others fail, as they prove unable to cope with the artificial conditions of a greenhouse. For the Victorians success lay in growing any new plant in their grand structures, and certainly both the Palm and Temperate Houses at Kew failed to provide the best growing conditions for many of the species required, so that the purpose of their planners and designers was not fully achieved when only the most robust plants succeeded. While the dark, dank conditions of Kew's Temperate House killed off its once prestigious collection of proteas and their relatives from Australia and the Cape, so too the Palm House's unavoidable winter chill prevented the growth of plants even as common as coconut and cocoa until the heating was improved in the 1960s. Its cold outer faces still continue to chill the benches and cause the winter death of all but the commoner palms. In restoring these two great Victorian greenhouses the opportunity to solve their problems and advance the range of plants grown within has been taken, at the same time making the houses yet more durable, with the result that once again the proteas in the Temperate House have flowered after 125 years. These structures now more nearly meet their designers' intentions. To this have been added new houses, such as the Alpine House with its refrigerated bench for arctic-alpines, and the Princess of Wales Conservatory which provides for an increased range of plant habitats from Namib desert to mangrove swamp, cloud forest to dry tropical forest, giving Kew almost unrivalled conditions for its successful cultivation of a great variety of the plants of this world.

The necessity to propagate and maintain many endangered species at Kew has been reflected in the Gardens' great concern to simulate several of the world's natural environments. The advances now made have resulted from greater field experience by its horticultural staff which has been put into effect by architects and engineers, using newly developed systems to give a long wished for, almost precise, control over heating and the cooling of both air and growing media. These, along with automatic humidification and water treatment, have produced greatly improved growing conditions for a wider variety of species. Add to this the recently acquired ability to propagate many difficult and rare plants under test tube conditions, and part of the reason for Kew's recent successes with endangered species can be explained. Currently Kew is working with twice as many endangered species as the most active of any of the other botanic gardens engaged in this field.

The loss of species worldwide is a matter of concern to us all, and in promoting the cultivation of tropical plants we are conscious that we could be aiding their exploitation and destruction. Unlike animals, however, plants can be propagated from their component parts, and so it is perfectly feasible for all saleable plants to be produced by nurserymen from plants already in cultivation. Many countries are now signatories to international agreements aimed at controlling the trade in endangered species, but by various means these rules are broken. It is thus very important now for gardeners to be aware of the possible origin of the plants they purchase, since rare species such as orchids from, say, tropical Asia or America, bulbs and cyclamen from Asia Minor, or cacti from Central America are all still stripped from their native habitats to be sold in Europe and North America.

Each section of this compendium has a separate author, well experienced in his or her subject. Each, too, has a differing view of the plants involved since some of the writers are taxonomists (who name plants), others curate botanical collections and one is a nurseryman who produces plants. The blending of these many contributions has been undertaken by Ken Beckett as Technical Editor and Joanna Roughton as General Editor, and this has brought together an unusual gathering of experience.

Whilst seeming to cover some common points of cultivation each specialist draws from his or her own experiences, picking out the subtle points that are critical to the success of the different plant groups. Like master chefs, some specialists may savour each nuance of change to a compost mixture but, as ever with plants, success is about having a sympathy with their living processes, gained by careful observation and an understanding of their interactive relationship with their environment.

Sound information on the cultivation of many tropical plants is not easily found, and it is hoped that this work will enable many more people to enjoy the successful cultivation of their house and conservatory plants. As already indicated, Kew is currently celebrating the restoration of its period greenhouses and the creation of new and interesting houses, the most important of which is the Princess of Wales Conservatory. Already public delight in this house is well evident and in concentrating this book on its plants, although of course many occur elsewhere at Kew, this publication may be seen as a celebration of the regeneration of Kew's greenhouses.

John B. E. Simmons
Royal Botanic Gardens, Kew, 1987

CACTI AND OTHER SUCCULENTS

A SUCCULENT IS a perennial plant which has evolved adaptations such as the ability to store water, which enable it to survive under conditions where very little water is available for long periods. When water is available it is taken up very rapidly and stored. Its subsequent loss is restricted by various features such as reduced or absent leaves, or a waxy covering over the plant. There are three principal ways in which a plant can store water: inside a swollen stem, swollen underground rootstock, or inside fleshy leaves. In addition, many succulent plants photosynthesize by a special method called crassulacean acid metabolism (CAM) which enables them to make organic compounds nocturnally while conserving water. A cactus is a succulent with a particular structure called an areole, which resembles a cushion on the swollen stem from which spines are produced. This felted structure only occurs in the cactus family (Cactaceae).

There are many plants within a large number of families which have succulent characteristics. Jacobsen (1977) lists fifty-one different plant families which contain succulents, although not all of these are suitable for growing indoors. The most important succulent families from a horticultural point of view, apart from the Cactaceae, are the Aizoaceae (Mesembryanthemaceae), Agavaceae, Asclepiadaceae, Crassulaceae, Euphorbiaceae and Liliaceae (now split to include Aloeaceae and Dracaenaceae). Altogether, there are about 5000 species of succulents and about 1500 species of cacti.

Cacti as a family are almost exclusively restricted to the New World –

(Above) The fascinating structure of a melocactus.   (Opposite) *Trichocereus candicans*

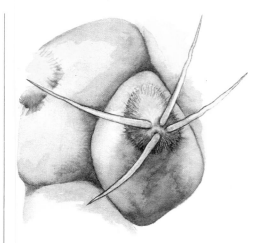

The areole of a cactus, from where flowers, sideshoots and offsets develop.

North, South and Central America. If they are found anywhere else they have been introduced; opuntias, for example, have been widely introduced into Africa, the Mediterranean region and Australia where they were once a serious pest.

Other groups of succulents are also confined either to the Old World or the New World in their native distribution. *Agave*, like the cacti, occurs naturally only in the Americas, although widely introduced elsewhere. *Aloe* and *Stapelia* are restricted to the Old World, with succulent euphorbias found in both Africa and South America. Southern Africa is the home of more species of succulents than anywhere else. The Crassulaceae is the only common family of succulents which has a worldwide distribution, occurring in North and South America, Africa, Europe and Asia.

Basic cultivation

Cultivation of the majority of cacti and other succulents should present few problems as they are, in the main, plants which can exist even when neglected. Over many years diverse methods and techniques have been developed for the cultivation of cacti and succulents, some of these seemingly contradictory.

Though succulent plants are indigenous across the continents they have developed under broadly similar environmental patterns. Knowledge of natural habitat conditions can be helpful, although it is impossible to provide the high light intensity, low humidity and reduced rainfall under which these plants normally grow, many will accept an approximation of these conditions.

In general cacti and succulents are tolerant plants when their basic requirements are met; species from the Old and New Worlds will grow happily together. However there are many difficult species which require more individual attention in cultivation.

Watering: As a general rule, for horticultural purposes, the growing season is from spring until autumn for the majority of species (although there are exceptions, such as *Aeonium*, *Conophytum* and some crassulas, which grow in the winter), and during this period frequent watering is required – at least once a week. In hot sunny weather watering two or three times a week may be required, especially for large leafy succulents. The compost should not be allowed to become waterlogged since the plants are then prone to rot and to infestations of sciarid fly. Watering can be done from overhead using a watering can with a fine rose, preferably in early morning or evening. Ideally, unpolluted rainwater should be used since in many areas tap water is too alkaline.

Resting: In the winter the majority of species are not growing. At this time a complete rest in cool dry conditions appears to be essential for cacti (but not for succulents, which require higher temperatures), and a period when the temperature is near to freezing appears to promote flowering, especially in *Lobivia*,

Rebutia and some *Echinocereus*. Most cacti and other succulents need plenty of light and a good sunny position is essential, whether it is a window sill, greenhouse or conservatory.

Compost: Although these plants can be grown in virtually any growing medium, a soilless compost consisting of three parts peat-based compost to one part coarse lime-free grit is recommended. Alternatively a loam-based compost with an added one-quarter part of coarse sand can be used. During the growing season, in good weather, plants can be given a balanced liquid fertilizer once a fortnight at the normal recommended strength.

Repotting: It is only necessary to repot when the plants have outgrown the container. With slow-growing species this should be done every two years. Repotting is best done in the spring.

Some species are difficult to cultivate successfully and are not recommended for beginners. These species are indicated in the text. A particularly porous compost is normally required for them, consisting of equal parts of compost and sand. They require full sun and very little water, even during the growing season. For some species a minimum winter temperature of $10°-15°$C $(50°-59°$F) is required. Reference to the native distribution will give a clue as to the winter temperature requirements; for example plants from the West Indies, Madagascar and India all require much higher winter temperatures than those from high in the Andes of Peru or Bolivia.

Propagation

Most cacti are best propagated from seed, but other succulents can often be propagated by removing offsets or cuttings in the summer; these must be left exposed to the air for a few days for the cut surface to heal. They can then be planted in moist compost. New roots should form within two to three weeks. Sometimes offsets root while still attached to the parent plant and these grow on very quickly.

Euphorbias: These plants are very difficult to propagate vegetatively since the white latex bleeds copiously from any damaged surface. Dipping the cut surface in dry sand helps to arrest this and the cuttings should be left out in the air for a minimum of seven days before planting. A hormone rooting powder should then be applied and the cutting supported on top of a layer of sand overlying compost without the cut end being buried. New roots should start to grow within two to three weeks. Light spraying rather than watering is advisable during this period, as is bottom heat from an electric propagator.

Leaf cuttings: Many species of succulents, particularly those in the Crassulaceae, can be propagated from detached leaves. A complete leaf can be removed from the plant and laid on the surface of a sandy compost. After a few weeks, new roots followed by a miniature plant will appear at the base of the old leaf.

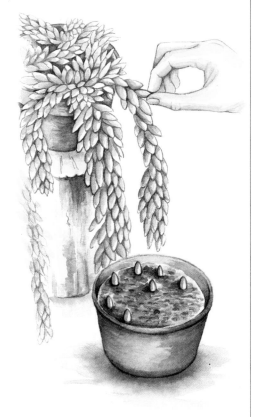

Propagation of *Sedum morganianum* by leaf cuttings. A new plant will form from the base of each succulent leaf.

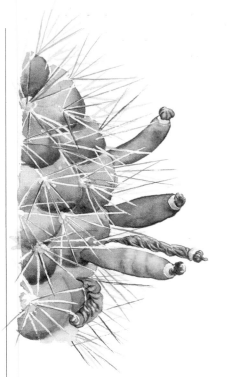

The elongated fruits of *Mammillaria*. The older more shrivelled pods are ready for collection.

Sowing seeds of *Mammillaria* from a ripe seed pod.

Layering: Trailing plants, such as the rat's tail cactus, can be propagated by layering. The long stem can be trailed across sandy compost and, after the adventitious roots have grown into this, the rooted stems can be detached.

Stem cuttings: Other epiphytic cacti such as *Epiphyllum* and Christmas cacti can be propagated from stems cut into segments with a sharp knife. Care should be taken to plant these cuttings the right way up – the serrated margins of the stems can be used as a guide here. A simple way of ensuring that these cuttings are correctly named is to write the name on the plant with a waterproof felt-tip pen.

Seeds: Cacti can be grown quite easily from seed on a warm window sill, *not* in the airing cupboard, since light is required immediately after germination. Seed is best sown in the spring, unless a heated propagator is available. A compost consisting of equal parts of a peat-based potting compost and coarse lime-free sand is recommended. Shallow seed trays or pots should be filled to within 1cm ($\frac{2}{5}$in) of the top with moist compost, and the seed scattered thinly on the surface. The seeds should be pressed lightly into the surface if they are large and should not be covered with further compost. A temperature of about 20°C (68°F) is required for germination, but once the seedlings are two or three weeks old this can be reduced to about 16°C (61°F). Watering should preferably be done from above using a fine spray. The seed tray or pot can be covered with a clear plastic lid fitted with a ventilator. Seedlings should start to appear within two weeks. The young seedlings should be sprayed regularly with water, but care should be taken not to let the compost become waterlogged, or else the plants will rot. The lid can be removed after a while, but the young plants must be shaded and must not be exposed to bright sunlight until they are at least nine months old – even in the wild, young cacti are shaded by a 'nurse' plant. Seedlings need not be transplanted until they are at least one or even two years old.

Pests and diseases

Pests: Mealy bugs are the most common pests of cacti and other succulents. They look like tiny woodlice covered in a white waxy coat, and the young insects are hidden under white cotton-wool like material. They usually aggregate in areas which are difficult to reach, e.g. around the base of tubercles. A severe attack will stunt the growth of affected plants. A spray with dimethoate, a systemic insecticide, is recommended. Malathion can be used on cacti but must never be used on other succulents. Pyrethrinoid insecticides are normally less effective. Root mealy bugs also occur and usually remain unseen until the plants are repotted, when they are visible as whitish grey cottony masses around the roots. They can be eradicated by watering with a systemic insecticide. The dose should be repeated after seven to ten days.

Red spider mite can be a serious pest in dry conditions and causes dry reddish brown disfiguring marks to occur on the plants, which stop growing. The tiny red-brown mites are just visible to the naked eye. Spraying with systemic insecticide is recommended. The spray should be repeated after ten days.

Scale insects are occasional pests and attach themselves to the plants like miniature limpets. They can be treated in the same way as red spider mite.

Sciarid fly is a relative newcomer. These small black flies lay their eggs in moist peaty compost, but it is the larvae which do the damage when they hatch out and feed on the bases of the plants. They particularly affect young seedlings, and cause them to collapse. A layer of grit or granite chippings 1cm deep on the soil around the plant will deter the adults from laying the eggs. Watering with a systemic insecticide will eradicate them.

Aphids are not an important pest, but do occasionally occur on flower buds and other young growth. A pyrethrinoid insecticide will usually control them.

Diseases: Cacti and other succulents are not usually prone to disease because they are normally kept under fairly dry conditions. Young seedlings grown in a very moist environment may suffer from damping off, which can be controlled with a fungicide.

Guide to purchasing

There are many ways of building up a collection of cacti and other succulents. Probably the best way is to start with a few easily grown, widely available species. Gradually the space available for them starts to become full and a choice has to be made as to which plants to collect and which to discard. Often the choice is already made in that some species will thrive and some will not under particular conditions.

Many people find it interesting to collect plants of one particular genus. Among the most popular are *Lithops*, *Gymnocalycium*, *Mammillaria* and *Rebutia*. These genera contain a large number of species which are easy to collect, including a number of rare and more difficult species, so that there is a sense of achievement when a complete set is acquired. Other people prefer to collect large-flowering species such as *Epiphyllum* or *Echinopsis*. A different and interesting way is to build a collection of all the plants discovered by a particular plant-hunter, such as Alfred Lau or Friedrich Ritter, collecting not only the plants but also all the literature and background information about each person. Another idea is to collect plants distributed by the International Succulent Institute, an organization in California which distributes uncommon species and new introductions which are supplied with their field collectors' numbers. A good specialist nursery should be able to supply many of these plants and also provide extra information and advice on plant care.

Pricking out one-year-old cactus seedlings into trays. (With spinier species, the use of a glove or finger pads is recommended.)

Recommended genera

Cacti

The following list of genera is not intended to be exhaustive but is a selection of genera and species chosen for their suitability for indoor cultivation. As mentioned previously, the majority of these plants need high light conditions, and a south-facing window (or north-facing in the southern hemisphere), conservatory or greenhouse are essential for successful cultivation. This is particularly important if the plants are to flower regularly. A number of genera are also included which do not require such high light conditions.

ACANTHOCALYCIUM (from the Greek *acantha*, a thorn or spine, and *kalyx*, a bud)

This genus of one species is native to northern Argentina on the lower slopes of the Andes. The flowers are large and showy: white or pink. It is closely related to *Lobivia* and *Echinopsis* but is characterized by the brown scales and spines on the flower tube and fruit.

A. spiniflorum has long yellow flexuous spines and lilac-pink flowers.

APOROCACTUS (from the Greek *aporos*, impenetrable)

There are two species of *Aporocactus*, which are native to Mexico. These plants are commonly known as rat's tail cacti and have been in cultivation for a long time. For example, *A. flagelliformis* was known to Linnaeus in 1744 at Uppsala Botanic Garden. Both species have pendulous spiny stems which are often over 1m (3ft 3in) long. In their natural habitat, the plants grow as epiphytes on tree branches or rocks.

(Below) × *Aporophyllum* 'Helena'
(Right) *Astrophytum ornatum*

× APOROPHYLLUM A bigeneric cross between *Aporocactus* and *Epiphyllum*, also known as × *Aporepiphyllum*

An increasing number of *Aporocactus* hybrids are being produced. They are less spiny than *Aporocactus* species and the flowers are usually larger and trumpet-shaped, more like the *Epiphyllum* parent. The colours of their flowers are very variable. Some of the best are 'Orange Queen' (narrow, deep-orange flowers), 'Pink Duchess' (inner petals pale pink, outer petals deep pink), 'Temple Fire' (large, brilliant red flowers), 'Tracy' (very large bronze-orange-pink flowers) and 'Wisewood' (the first cultivar and probably still one of the best, with magenta outer petals and pink inner petals; it is very free-flowering, often blooming in late spring and again in early winter).

ASTROPHYTUM (from the Greek *astron*, a star, and *phyton*, a plant)

This is a small genus of four species from Mexico. They are attractive plants which are very popular and widely cultivated. The flowers are large (up to 8cm/$3\frac{1}{4}$in in diameter) and very striking, with yellow petals and often with a red centre. There are several cultivars and hybrids, all characterized by the curious greyish-white flakes of hair on the surface of the plants, the quantity of which varies between the varieties and forms. All of

them can be grown indoors but high light intensity is essential and a well-drained compost is required.

A. asterias is a very attractive dark green spineless plant resembling the sea urchin. It is not easy to grow; a porous compost and careful watering are essential. Rare in the wild, this plant is not an ideal one for a beginner.

A. myriostigma usually has five or more strong ribs, but four-ribbed forms occur ('Quadricostata' – the bishop's mitre). All are spineless and densely covered with white flecks, except 'Nudum', which is wholly green.

A. ornatum is heavily armoured with brownish-yellow spines, and will flower only when 10–20cm (4–8in) in diameter. They live to a great age and in the wild can grow to over 1m (3ft 3in) in height.

BORZICACTUS (named after Antonino Borzi, 1832–1921, an Italian botanist)
Now more correctly placed under *Cleistocactus*, this genus of some seventeen Andean species is native to Peru, Bolivia and Ecuador. It is a difficult group to classify because the flowers are similar to those of several other genera. All the species are interesting, attractive plants, which are easy to flower and are well worth cultivating.

Borzicactus aureispinus

B. aureispinus is a superb species for a hanging pot. It has several thick branching stems, densely covered with golden-yellow spines, and orange flowers which are freely produced near the ends of the stems. They are different from other cactus flowers in having a double corolla – an outer ring of long expanded petals and an inner ring of short, erect petals.

Another species, *B. samaipatanus*, produces branching stems which are erect at first, but become decumbent when the stems are more than 30cm (1ft) long. Its flowers are deep crimson and contrast with the numerous dark purple filaments of the stamens.

CARNEGIEA (named after Andrew Carnegie, the American steel magnate and philanthropist)
This genus is represented by only one species, *C. gigantea*, the giant saguaro, which is native to Mexico and the south-western USA. It is extremely slow-growing – the giant branched plants seen in cowboy films are over 100 years old. The seedlings produce attractive spiny plants with strong ribs developing when the plants are over ten years old. Its white, bat-pollinated flowers are rarely produced in cultivation.

CEPHALOCEREUS (from the Greek *kephale*, a head)
These are columnar plants characterized by the production of copious hair. Only one well-known

(Above left) *Cephalocereus senilis*
(Above) *Chamaecereus silvestrii*

species is in cultivation, *C. senilis*, the old man of Mexico, which is a native of central Mexico. The young plants are densely covered with long white hair which masks the short sharp spines underneath. Older plants in the wild lose the hair except in the flowering zone (cephalium) which is not produced until the stems are more than 6m (20ft) in height. The cephalium is formed on one side of the columnar stem. Unfortunately it is not a very easy species to grow successfully as it is extremely sensitive to excess moisture. It is also slow-growing and unlikely to flower in cultivation. High light conditions, a minimum winter temperature of 15°C (59°F), a porous compost and little water are essential for successful cultivation.

CHAMAECEREUS (from the Greek *chamai*, on the ground; the plants in this species are prostrate or low-growing)

This small plant from Argentina forms clusters of finger-thick stems, 10cm (4in) or more in length. The only species is *C. sylvestrii*, the peanut cactus, which has orange flowers. This species has also been hybridized with *Lobivia*, giving bigger plants with larger, brilliantly coloured flowers. *Chamaecereus silvestrii* is now included in the genus *Echinopsis* as *E. chamaecereus*.

CLEISTOCACTUS (from the Greek *kleistos*, closed)

This genus has thirty to forty species of attractive, free-flowering columnar cacti, with dense spines, from Peru

and Bolivia. The flowers are red or orange, tubular, with the petals barely opening at the end and a protruding stigma. They are typical of flowers pollinated by humming birds. All the species are easy to cultivate in a sunny position. The plants flower when they are 30cm (1ft) or more in height.

C. strausii is one of the most attractive of all cacti with tall stems, dense white spines and very long, purplish-red flowers.

See also *Borzicactus*.

ECHINOCACTUS (from the Greek *echinos*, a hedgehog)

These are giant barrel-shaped plants in a genus of two species from Mexico. They are distinguishable from the genus *Ferocactus* by their woolly calyces and fruits. Both species are well-known in cultivation, *E. platyacanthus* (*E. ingens*) and *E. grusonii*; the latter is the best-known species, popularly known as the golden barrel cactus or mother-in-law's chair. It grows into a beautiful, yellow-spined globe up to 80cm (2ft 8in) in diameter. It is extremely rare in the wild. In cultivation flowers are rarely produced, because to flower the plants need to be over 50cm (1ft 8in) in diameter (which means they are at least thirty years old) and kept in a very sunny position. The flowers are small, 3cm (1¼in) wide and yellow.

ECHINOCEREUS (from the Greek *echinos*, a hedgehog)
This genus has about forty-five species and a variety of forms, but most of its species have spectacularly large flowers in brilliant colours. One species has highly scented green flowers. There are two basic habit forms in this genus: one consists of small plants with spines in flattened rows like a comb and includes *E. pectinatus*, which has large purple flowers almost 10cm (4in) wide; the plants of the other group form very large clumps often 1m (3ft 3in) wide with long straight spines – *E. pentalophus* is a clump-forming species with finger-thick prostrate stems and large lilac flowers 12cm (4¾in) across. Many species are frost-hardy if kept under dry conditions. Cold dry conditions also promote flowering. *E. rigidissimus* is often called the rainbow cactus on account of its rings of different coloured spines. It has beautiful large pink flowers.

ECHINOFOSSULOCACTUS (from the Greek *echinos*, a hedgehog, and *fossula*, a little ditch, referring to the grooves between the stem ribs)
These plants are now correctly assigned to the genus *Stenocactus*. There are about ten species which are native to central Mexico. Most are characterized by numerous, thin, wavy ribs, in one species up to 120 in number. The flowers are produced near the stem apex and are usually pink or yellowish, surrounded by broad papery scales. They are not difficult to cultivate in a bright sunny position.

ECHINOPSIS (from the Greek *echinos*, a hedgehog)
This genus of about forty-five species from South America is grown mainly for its large flowers. These are usually long-tubed, funnel-shaped, scented and nocturnal, each flower lasting for about twenty-four hours. Flower colour is variable.

This genus is similar to other closely related genera such as *Lobivia*. Species of *Echinopsis* are easily hybridized with each other and also with species of *Lobivia*. Most of the plants in cultivation are hybrids which are noted for their colourful displays of pink, orange, lilac, red, yellow or white flowers.

These plants are easy to grow and, provided that they are kept cool and dry in winter, a superb display of flowers can be expected in summer.

Several nurseries have been engaged for many years in producing new hybrids and from hundreds of crosses

Echinocactus grusonii

many new cultivars have been introduced, a large number of which are improvements on the parent species. For example, *E. calorubra* produces superb multicoloured flowers of orange, red and pink, but unfortunately only one or two flowers are produced per plant each season. By hybridizing this with other more free-flowering species, hybrids have been produced which are free-flowering and with an enhanced colour range.

See also *Chamaecereus* and *Trichocereus*.

EPIPHYLLUM (from the Greek *epi*, upon, and *phyllon*, a leaf, referring to the flowers which are borne on leaf-like stems)

Popularly known as orchid cacti, these are epiphytes from the rain forests of Central and South America. Most of the cultivated forms are hybrids, often with related genera such as *Heliocereus* and *Nopalxochia*. They have extremely large, brightly coloured flowers, up to 20cm (8in) in diameter, which are often scented. The plants are shade tolerant and require plenty of water in the summer and a humid atmosphere all the year round. They are easy to grow and are very popular cottage window-sill plants. The genus contains fewer than ten species.

Epiphyllum 'Pegasus' has massive flowers with purple petals with an orange mid-stripe, and 'Reward' bears beautiful yellow flowers, whereas 'Wedding Anniversary' has scented white flowers. *Nopalxochia phyllanthoides* produces masses of shell-pink flowers in early summer; *N. ackermannii* has similarly shaped orange flowers.

The brightly coloured flower of a hybrid *Epiphyllum*.

ESPOSTOA (named after N. E. Esposto, a Peruvian botanist)

These are columnar cacti from Peru and Ecuador. Thirteen species have been described. The plants are very attractive because of their white woolly covering. Young plants resemble balls of cotton wool, but later long needle-like spines grow through. They need to be kept reasonably warm in winter with a minimum temperature of about 12°C (54°F). A porous compost and full sun are recommended. In cultivation, plants rarely mature to flowering size. As in *Cephalocereus*, flowers are eventually produced from a dense woolly lateral cephalium.

When small the plants of *E. melanostele* look like tufts of cotton wool, but older plants become columnar and develop long central spines. They are always densely covered with soft white hair.

FEROCACTUS (from the Latin *ferox*, or ferocious, referring to the sharp spines)

This genus of twenty-three species is native to Mexico and the south-western states of the USA. In North America they are called barrel cacti because of their large size and shape, although there are a number of smaller or clump-forming species in Mexico. Most species possess strong colourful spines which are often ribbed and hooked. A few species reach maturity as relatively small plants, 10cm (4in) across, but the majority start to flower only when they are considerably larger than this. The flowers are large and attractive, in shades of red, yellow or purple, but are produced only under favourable conditions. Bright sunlight is essential to develop the full colour and strength of the spines. Ample water in the summer will promote growth, but dry conditions are necessary in the winter.

F. glaucescens grows up to 50cm (1ft 8in) in diameter and is blue-green with yellow spines and flowers.

F. latispinus grows to the size of a flattened football and is characterized by very robust spines which are ribbed and strongly hooked; the flowers are purple or yellow.

GYMNOCALYCIUM (from the Greek *gymnos*, naked, and *kalyx* a bud; the flower buds lack hair and spines)

This is a genus of about forty species from South America. The plants are globular with rounded ribs and varied forms of spines. One widely available form of *G. mihanovichii* ('Rubrum') is scarlet, and as it completely lacks chlorophyll must be grown grafted on to another species.

Gymnocalycium flowers are very striking, produced from the stem apex, and remain open for several days. The outer parts of the flowers are covered with smooth green scales and lack the spines or bristles characteristic

Lobivia backebergii

of some cacti. The colours are usually white or pale pink, but some species have red or yellow flowers.

These are undemanding plants to grow and are recommended because of their ease of cultivation and their free-flowering nature. Protection from blazing sun is advisable, so an indoor window sill is satisfactory. The majority of species rarely grow more than 10cm (4in) in diameter, although one or two can grow into large specimens over 30cm (1ft) in diameter.

G. baldianum is a small plant with red or occasionally pink or white flowers.

G. buenekeri is a relatively recent introduction with few ribs and spines and large delicate pink flowers; it will eventually form large clumps.

G. damsii is a small species with a purplish-bronze colour. It is extremely free-flowering, producing its pale pink flowers for most of the year.

LOBIVIA (an anagram of Bolivia, the main country of origin)
These plants originate from the high Andes, often growing at altitudes of over 4000m (13,000ft), and many species can withstand temperatures below freezing. Most species are easy to grow and flower, and many produce large flowers in a wide range of colours. About thirty-five species have been described, plus a large number of flower colour variants. These plants are closely related to the genus *Echinopsis*, with which they are often hybridized, but are distinguished from that genus by diurnal flowers, the short tubes of which are covered with black woolly hairs. In the summer, these plants require a sunny position with plenty of water. In winter, a dry very cool place is essential. Only then will the reward be a beautiful display of flowers in summer.

L. backebergii is an easily grown clump-forming plant from Peru; *L. b.* var. *binghamiana* has bright tomato-red flowers, whereas var. *wrightiana* produces lilac flowers. Older plants sometimes produce long flexuous central spines.

L. haematantha ssp. *densispina* has spines which grow close to the stem; its flowers grow up to 8cm ($3\frac{1}{4}$in) in diameter in white, yellow, orange or red.

LOPHOPHORA (from the Greek *lophos*, a crest, and *phorein*, to bear, referring to the tufts of hair on the areoles)
This easily recognizable, blue-green, spineless globular plant comes from Mexico and Texas. *L. williamsii*, the most common species, is the famous peyote or mescal button which contains alkaloids including mescaline which is used by some Mexican Indian tribes in their religious rites.

Mammillaria gracilis

MAMMILLARIA (from the Latin *mammilla*, a nipple, referring to the teat-like tubercles characteristic of the genus)
There are approximately 160 species in this genus distributed throughout the south-west USA, Mexico and south to northern South America. It is one of the most popular of all cactus genera, represented in most collections, and *M. zeilmanniana* is probably the most popular species, being grown literally by the million for sale around Easter time.

Growth forms vary from small clustering types, such as *M. prolifera*, to large clumps of more than 1m (3ft 3in) in *M. compressa*. There are also single-headed plants 30cm (1ft) or more in diameter, such as *M. gigantea*, or tiny single-headed plants perhaps only 2cm ($\frac{3}{4}$in) across even when mature. The spination is just as variable; for example, *M. plumosa* is completely obscured by feathery spines; other species, such as *M. sheldonii*, bear long hooked spines; *M. melanocentra* bears very long straight spines and *M. pectinifera* bears groups of small flattened spines that look like miniature woodlice.

The majority of species flower easily even as small plants, most having small white, red or pink flowers produced in a ring around the upper part of the plant in early summer. Other species such as *M. guelzowiana* and *M. longiflora* have much larger pink flowers.

Cultivation of most species is easy apart from a few exceptions such as *M. tetrancistra* and the *M. wrightii* complex which tax even the most skilled growers. Most other species can be easily grown in well-drained compost, with plenty of water in the growing season and a minimum winter temperature of about 6°C (43°F), with little or no water required. When grown in a warm, centrally heated house at higher temperatures, regular winter watering once a month is required. *M. bombycina*, one of the most attractive species, eventually forms very large clumps with glossy white radial spines and a strongly hooked red central spine; the flowers are pink.

M. longimamma (*Dolichothele longimamma*) is a distinctive species with very large tubercles up to 4cm (1$\frac{1}{2}$in) long and large yellow flowers 6cm (2$\frac{1}{2}$in) across.

M. spinosissima is a tall-growing cylindrical species with abundant, straight brown spines and rings of purple flowers.

M. zeilmanniana is one of the most abundantly flowering of all cacti. It is a globular plant with hooked central spines and hairlike radial spines, it eventually forms clumps and produces pinkish-purple flowers in summer. A white-flowered form is also in cultivation.

MELOCACTUS (from the Latin *melo*, a melon, referring to the shape of the plant)

These plants have an extensive geographical distribution in Central America, occurring on islands in the Caribbean as well as in Mexico and South America, particularly Brazil. Over 300 species have been described, but many of these may only be varieties or synonyms and there are probably only about twenty true species. They are very interesting globular plants with distinctly ribbed melon-shaped bodies. After five to ten years or more, depending on species and conditions, the plants cease vegetative growth and develop a bristly cephalium, or flowering zone, at the apex, from which small pink or purplish flowers are produced. Later, red, pink or white berry-like fruits push out through the cephalium as they ripen. The plants are mostly self-fertile and the black seeds germinate readily.

Melocacti are not recommended for the beginner because considerable care and skill is needed to cultivate them successfully. Warm conditions, with a minimum of $15°C$ ($59°F$), are essential all the year round, as well as high light conditions and high relative humidity. The species from the West Indies, such as *M. broadwayi*, are the most difficult, whereas the Brazilian species, such as *M. glaucescens*, are the easiest.

MYRTILLOCACTUS (from the Latin *myrtillus*, a small myrtle, referring to the similar fruit)

These are large-growing, many-branched, treelike cacti from Mexico which eventually reach about 4m (13ft) in height. The young seedlings of *M. geometrizans*, which are five-ribbed, spineless and a bright blue-green colour, make very attractive house plants. They require a minimum winter temperature of $10°C$ ($50°F$) as cold causes unsightly brown marks on the plants. This genus contains four species.

Nopalxochia see *Epiphyllum*.

NOTOCACTUS (from the Greek *notos*, south; the species are all South American)

This genus consists of about eighty species from South

Notocactus leninghausii

America, in particular Argentina, Paraguay and Brazil. It has now, however, been absorbed into the genus *Parodia*. Species vary from small globular plants to tall cylindrical columns or large many-headed clumps. Most species are strongly ribbed with attractive coloured spines. The flowers are large, usually yellow, but sometimes orange, red or purple and are freely produced during the summer months. Cultivation is easy for the majority of species.

N. haselbergii is a white-spined species with orange-red flowers which remain open for up to two weeks.

N. leninghausii is one of the most popular and widely grown cacti. Becoming columnar with age and freely offsetting from the base, its golden-yellow spined columns are very attractive. The large lemon-yellow flowers remain open for up to seven days.

N. magnificus is a species which lives up to its name, the blue-green globular plants having strong ribs and golden-yellow spines. The yellow flowers are produced from the apex when the plants are about 10cm (4in) in diameter.

N. scopa, first described in 1825, has remained a favourite with collectors. It has white radial spines and red central ones. The flowers are yellow. There are also wholly white- or yellow-spined forms of this species in cultivation.

OPUNTIA (named in 1754 after an ancient name for a thistle growing around Opus, a town in Greece inhabited by the Locri Opuntii tribe)

Opuntia, which includes the prickly pear, is a very large genus with approximately 250 species. It is native to North and South America and the Galapagos Islands, but has been introduced to many other parts of the world. The plants vary considerably in size with some species forming low-growing clumps and others producing large bushy plants which are frequently planted in arid parts of the world as hedges or windbreaks. The largest group of plants in the genus are characterized by having jointed stems in the form of large flat pads which grow out of one another. Another group is the chollas (pronounced choyas) which have branched cylindrical stems and vicious sheathed, barbed spines. All opuntias have either single spines or clusters of short fine spines (glochids) which easily penetrate the skin but are not easily removed. For this reason, they should be handled with care.

Opuntias are tough, resilient plants, many of which can withstand very cold conditions in the winter. In cultivation the large, rapidly growing species, such as *O. ficus-indica*, may soon outgrow the space available.

O. microdasys is the popular bunny's ears cactus. It has rounded pads with golden-yellow glochids and yellow flowers. There is also a white-spined form in cultivation and a monstrose form with wavy pads. It should be kept warm and dry in the winter, otherwise the pads become disfigured with brown marks.

(Left) *Opuntia microdasys* 'Albata'
(Below) *Parodia nivosa*

O. monacantha has a variegated monstrose form which makes an interesting and unusual pot plant.

See also USEFUL PLANTS.

PARODIA (named after Dr L. R. Parodi, 1895–1966, a botanist from Argentina)

This genus of small-growing globular cacti, which produce clusters of large brightly coloured flowers from the apex, originates from northern Argentina and Bolivia, where it often grows at high altitudes, and at lower elevations in Uruguay, Paraguay and Brazil. There are about fifty species which are not difficult to grow. High light conditions, a well-drained compost, and the avoidance of excess water are the main cultural requirements.

P. chrysacanthion is a yellow-spined plant with yellow flowers produced in early spring.

P. mairanana is a small clump-forming species with brown or blackish spines and deep orange-yellow flowers.

P. microspermum (P. sanguiniflora) is a hook-spined species with yellow or blood-red flowers produced in early summer.

See also *Notocactus*.

Rebutia krainziana

REBUTIA (for the Frenchman, P. Rebut, a dealer in cacti around 1900)

The genus is native to Argentina and Bolivia where some species grow at altitudes of over 3600m (11,700ft). Most species are thus tolerant of low temperatures and must be given a cold, dry dormant period during the winter to promote flowering in the following year. The classification of this genus is controversial and some plants which are now included here have formerly been placed in *Aylostera*, *Mediolobivia*, *Digitorebutia* and other genera.

This is a popular genus of dwarf globular cacti which have short spines and often form clumps. They are extremely free-flowering and will produce flowers when the plants are as small as 2cm ($\frac{3}{4}$in) across. Flower colour is mainly brilliant orange or red, but in a few species it is yellow, white, pink or cerise.

R. fiebrigii was one of the first of the rebutias to be discovered and cultivated. The plants are densely covered with brown-tipped white spines and have flame-red flowers.

R. krainziana is a striking plant with large dark red or orange flowers and pure white spines growing close against the plant.

R. minuscula is one of the easiest and most widely grown species. It will produce large bright red flowers

when only one year old. It was the first *Rebutia* to be discovered and was first described in 1895.

R. pygmaea is a distinctive species with pectinate spines; the large flowers are often multicoloured.

RHIPSALIS, HATIORA, SCHLUMBERGERA (from the Greek *rhips*, wickerwork, Thomas Hariot, a sixteenth-century botanist, and Frederick Schlumberger, a Belgian horticulturist, *c*1900)

These genera are considered together as they are all related plants, having similar cultural requirements. There are many hybrids and cultivars and they are commonly known as Christmas and Easter cacti, according to the time of flowering. *Hatiora* and *Schlumbergera* originate from tropical rain forests in Brazil; *Rhipsalis* is also found in Africa, Madagascar and elsewhere in South America.

These plants consist of jointed leaflike segments often with a notched or serrated margin, and the flowers are borne from the ends of the segments. They like moist humid conditions and a rich compost. Bathroom or kitchen window sills with indirect light are ideal places to grow these plants which dislike full sun and dry atmospheric conditions.

The Christmas cactus (*Schlumbergera* × *buckleyi*, also known incorrectly as *Zygocactus truncatus*), has cerise flowers and a serrated margin on the stem segments. The Easter cactus, *Hatiora gaertneri* (*Schlumbergera gaertneri*), has orange-red flowers and acute serrations on the stem segments. There are various hybrids in this group which have increased the range of flower colours and length of the flowering period. *Hatiora rosea* (*Rhipsalidopsis rosea*) is a most attractive small pink-flowered species.

SELENICEREUS (from the Greek *selene*, the moon; these cacti bloom at night)

This genus of ten to fifteen species is found from Texas south to Colombia in South America. These are climbing, thin-stemmed, mostly jungle plants with aerial roots, producing gigantic nocturnal flowers – some of the largest in the plant kingdom. They are fast-growing and can be trained up a trellis. *S. grandiflorus* (the queen of the night) has spectacular white flowers 25cm (10in) in diameter. The long buds take several weeks to develop and when mature start to open during late evening and become fully open at midnight. By the following morning they have closed and withered. These plants require copious water and spraying during the summer growing season. Regular applications of a high potash fertilizer will encourage the production of flowers.

Stenocactus see *Echinofossulocactus*

(Opposite) *Schlumbergera* × *buckleyi*

TRICHOCEREUS (from the Greek *trichos*, a hair, referring to the hairy tubes of the flower)

This genus of thirty to forty species originates from the Andes of Chile and Argentina. They are all robust columnar plants reaching over 1m (3ft 3in) in height with very large flowers. Several species, such as *T. pachanoi*, are fast-growing and are often used as grafting stocks. The flowers are large, nocturnal and usually white, up to 15cm (6in) across. Culture is easy but plenty of sun is necessary for the plants to flower. There are many hybrids between *Trichocereus*, *Lobivia* and *Echinopsis* with large multicoloured flowers. The species listed here are now placed under the genus *Echinopsis*.

T. candicans forms golden-spined plants when young and produces white flowers when large.

T. fulvilanus is an attractive plant with orange-felted areoles and long brown spines.

T. thelegonus is a relatively small species which will flower when only 20cm (8in) tall; it has large white flowers.

Zygocactus see *Schlumbergera* under *Rhipsalis*

Other Succulents

AEONIUM (from an ancient name first used by Dioscorides for a plant similar to *A. arboreum*)

The genus includes about forty species, the majority of which are native to the Canary Isles, but with a few species from Morocco, Ethiopia, the Middle East and Madeira.

Most species are bushy, often with bare woody stems which produce a terminal rosette of leaves and ultimately a large pyramidal inflorescence. Many species are monocarpic, dying after they flower. The plants grow most actively in the winter when they should be kept at a minimum temperature of about 12°c (54°F) and watered regularly (about once a week). Most species grow best in bright conditions, but not in direct sunlight, and many are tolerant of shade or semi-shade. Plants can be propagated from cuttings.

A. arboreum is a bushy species up to 1m (3ft 3in) high with rosettes of bright green shiny leaves and large plumes of yellow flowers. A number of variegated and coloured forms exist, such as 'Albovariegatum' with green and white striped leaves; 'Atropurpureum' has dark purple leaves and 'Schwartzkopf' has almost black leaves.

A. domesticum (*Aichryson domesticum* is now the correct name) is a small, regularly branched plant with pubescent leaves, which looks like a miniature tree and is often grown for this reason in indoor decorative gardens. A more attractive green and yellow variegated form is also available.

A. tabuliforme is one of the most attractive and characteristic succulents in cultivation. It produces a flat dinnerplate-sized rosette of closely overlapping leaves on a very short stem. In its natural habitat this species grows on vertical, north-facing, clay cliffs and even in cultivation it will often hang vertically out of the side of its pot. It needs to be grown in semi-shade and requires regular watering throughout the year.

AGAVE (from the Greek *agauos*, noble or admirable) There are about 300 species of Agave from South and Central America and the southern states of the USA, but most species are native to Mexico. They have been widely introduced elsewhere as ornamental plants of warm dry climates. Several species are important commercially for the production of alcoholic beverages such as pulque and tequila, or for their fibre (sisal) which is made into rope or carpet. The most widely cultivated species is *A. americana*, commonly known as the century plant because it was erroneously supposed to flower only when it was 100 years old.

Many species grow to a large size and are suitable only for planting outdoors in warm climates, but there are also a number of smaller species which make admirable indoor pot plants. Flowering is fortunately rare as the plants are monocarpic – they die after flowering unless

Agave victoria-reginae

offsets have been formed around the base. They are easily propagated from seed or offsets.

A. americana is the most popular cultivated species, eventually getting very large. Several variegated forms with white- or yellow-striped leaves are grown.

A. victoria-reginae is a striking slow-growing species which eventually reaches about 50cm (1ft 8in) in diameter, having short, very rigid, dark green leaves with prominent white stripes.

See also USEFUL PLANTS.

Aichryson see *Aeonium*

ALOE (from the Arabic word *alloeh*, the name for this genus)
There are about 300 species in the genus, which is native to southern and central Africa, the Middle East and Madagascar. Most species have a basal rosette of fleshy pointed leaves, often with spiny teeth along the margins. A spike of red, orange or yellow flowers is produced from near the centre of the rosette. A few species, such as *A. arborescens*, are woody and can grow into small trees. Several species have been hybridized with one another and also with related genera such as *Gasteria* to produce modern cultivars.

Aloes are grown in many parts of the tropics as

(Above) *Aloe variegata*
(Above right) *Conophytum cupreiflorum*

ornamental garden plants or for medicinal purposes. The most important medicinal aloe is *A. vera* (*A. barbadensis*), also known as the burn plant. The gelatinous sap from the leaves of this species rapidly relieves the pain from burns and has antibiotic properties which promote healing. Preparations of the plant have also been used internally, mainly as a purgative. Most species are easy to cultivate, growing best in indirect light or semi-shade. They can be propagated from offsets produced around the base of the plant.

A. aristata is another easily grown species which is frost-hardy and will survive the winter in an unheated conservatory or greenhouse. This species produces clusters of rosettes which are individually about 8–10cm (3¼–4in) across. The leaves are numerous, relatively thin and soft, and end in a finely attenuate point. The best cultivated form is 'Cathedral Peak'.

A. variegata is the partridge-breasted aloe, a common and attractive species which has dark green leaves with abundant white spots and streaks. It is one of the easiest house plants to grow, being tolerant of shade, drought and overwatering.

A. vera (the Mediterranean aloe or burn plant) grows to a height of about 30–40cm (12–16in). The leaves are pale greyish-green (reddish-brown in strong sun),

slightly spotted with white and with widely toothed margins. Unlike most aloes, the flowers of this species are usually yellow.

See also USEFUL PLANTS.

CEROPEGIA (from the Greek *keros*, wax, and *pege*, a fountain, referring to the trailing inflorescence of waxen flowers)
This is a genus of trailing vinelike plants which often have interesting parachute-shaped flowers pollinated by flies.

C. woodii, the most commonly cultivated species, has spotted heart-shaped leaves arranged widely apart on the threadlike stems. It produces small spherical tubers and is shade tolerant.

CONOPHYTUM (from the Greek, *konos*, a cone, and *phyton*, a plant)
These are small clump-forming succulents similar to *Lithops*, and come from the south-western part of South Africa. About 300 species have been described. The plant consists of pairs of leaves fused together, often the tiny fissure at the centre being the only external indication that there are two leaves. The daisylike flowers grow up through this fissure and are white, pink, purple, yellow, orange or red. Some species are delightfully scented.

These plants grow and flower in the winter. They require watering from autumn to early spring but very little water for the rest of the year.

COTYLEDON (from the Greek *kotyle*, a cavity or cup)
This genus of about forty species was named by Linnaeus in 1753 for a group of plants with opposite leaves and showy, usually hanging, five-parted flowers. They are native to southern Africa and parts of north-east Africa and the Middle East. The flowers are

Cotyledon ladismithiensis

produced on long stalks which arise from the centre of the plant. Plants are easily grown either from seed or from cuttings. They require a position in full sun with a minimum winter temperature of about 5°C (41°F). Some species have a tendency to become leggy. If so, fresh plants should be restarted from cuttings.

C. ladismithiensis is an attractive plant with brownish-red flowers and hairy leaves which are dentate at the apex.

C. orbiculata has oval red-edged leaves with a thick white floury (powdery) covering. Large pendulous orange-pink flowers are produced in midsummer.

C. undulata is an interesting plant similar to *C. orbiculata* but with wavy leaf margins like clam shells.

The name *Cotyledon* was originally used by Linnaeus to describe *Cotyledon umbilicus*, a plant with a central hollow in the circular leaves, but now reclassified as *Umbilicus rupestris*, a temperate succulent native to Europe, and commonly found growing on walls.

CRASSULA (from the Latin *crassus*, thick, referring to the fleshy succulent leaves)

This is a large genus of about 300 species mostly from southern Africa. There are also a number of hybrids and modern cultivars. Most species are low-growing, being less then 10cm (4in) in height, although a few species, such as *C. arborescens*, *C. ovata* and *C. obliqua*, may grow into bushes more than 2m (6ft 6in) in height. The majority of species are winter-flowering and produce sprays of white or pink (occasionally red) flowers which make an attractive show in January and February when little else is in bloom. Many of the smaller species are very neat plants with closely overlapping leaves. This growth habit reaches its most extreme form in *C. quadrangula* and *C. pyramidalis*. Plants can be propagated from stem cuttings or offsets which root easily in the summer months. They will grow in full sun or semi-shade. Watering should be carried out sparingly all through the year, but with more in summer, applied as soon as the compost dries out.

C. falcata is a species with large, sickle-shaped, overlapping, blue-green leaves and large clusters of scarlet flowers. A more compact form, *C.f.* var. *minima*, is also available.

C. 'Jade Necklace' develops into a spreading plant with small fleshy leaves in pairs, united at the base and spaced out along the stem like beads in a necklace.

C. lactea is a species with relatively large leaves, producing large plumes of creamy-white flowers in winter.

C. ovata, often sold as *C. argentea* or *C. portulacea*, is the jade or money plant and is one of the most widely grown house plants. It has probably achieved these popular names on account of its smooth rich green leaves and the supposition that it will bring its owner wealth. Variegated forms are also available, as is the strange monstrose form 'Coral'.

C. 'Springtime' forms a compact plant with overlapping dark green leaves and clusters of attractive pink flowers in early spring.

ECHEVERIA (named after the eighteenth-century Spaniard Athanasio Echeverria y Godoy, a botanical artist who accompanied an expedition to Mexico)

Echeverias are some of the most beautiful of all leaf succulents and a collection of these rosette plants can exhibit a wonderful range of pastel colours. There are over 130 species which are principally native to Mexico but also occur in the USA and a few countries in South America. There are innumerable hybrids in cultivation, many of recent origin. The flowers are pink or orange, waxy and long-lasting, and can occur at any time of year.

With age, the plants lose their lower leaves and can become leggy. Such a plant can be decapitated in the spring and the top dried for a few days before being planted in fresh sandy compost.

The chief pests of echeverias are mealy bugs. The insecticide malathion should *never* be used on these plants as it will at best cause damage to the leaves and at worst kill the plant. A systemic insecticide containing dimethoate carefully watered on to the compost is usually effective. All echeverias make very attractive window-sill plants and develop their best leaf colours in full sun. A few species, such as *E. carnicolor*, prefer indirect light.

E. derenbergii is one of the most popular species and the parent of many hybrids. The pale grey-green rosette leaves are tipped with red; the flowers are yellow.

E. 'Doris Taylor' (*E. pulvinata* × *E. setosa*) is a very attractive hybrid with hairy spathulate leaves and orange flowers.

E. harmsii was formerly called *Oliveranthus elegans*. It is characterized by its very large 2.5cm (1in) long, scarlet and yellow campanulate flowers.

E. 'Paul Bunyon' is a hybrid which has large blue-green leaves with extraordinary blister-like growths on their upper surfaces.

E. pulvinata is a beautiful species with hairy leaves and orange flowers in the winter. *E. p.* 'Rubra' has red leaves. *E. p.* 'Frosty' has its leaves densely covered with soft white hairs.

EUPHORBIA (King Juba of Mauretania discovered an unknown species, probably *E. resinifera*, growing on the

Euphorbia millii with *Opuntia subulata* (left)

slopes of the Atlas Mountains. According to Pliny, the king wrote a treatise on the plant and named it after his favourite physician, Euphorbus.)

Euphorbias have a world-wide distribution and the genus is very large, containing over 2000 species, of which about 500 are succulent.

All the species are characterized by the production of a milky latex and by a curious floral structure called a cyathium. This consists of a flower (or flowers) surrounded by a series of bracts which are often brightly coloured. Some species are dioecious, male and female flowers occurring on separate plants. Attempts have been made to produce commercial quantities of rubber from the milky latex. In some species, such as *E. virosa*, the latex is extremely poisonous, but fortunately none of these is common in cultivation. The latex of all species should, however, be treated with caution and particular care should be taken to keep it away from the eyes. It can also cause skin irritation.

These plants are extremely variable in growth form, varying from small globular plants, such as *E. obesa*, to trees, such as *E. antiquorum*. Cultivation is not difficult for the majority of species, providing that a minimum temperature of 10°C (50°F) can be maintained. However,

some species are extremely difficult and tax the skill of the most experienced grower. In the summer months euphorbias can be watered frequently, but they must be kept warm and dry in winter. Plants can sometimes be propagated from cuttings, but most species are best raised from seed.

E. grandialata has attractive green and yellow striped stems producing brown thorns along the wavy margins.

E. obesa is a popular, globular plant, grey-green with attractive criss-cross markings; it is dioecious.

E. millii (E. splendens) is the crown of thorns, a thorny, thin-stemmed plant from Madagascar with deciduous leaves and bright red bracts surrounding the flowers. Yellow-, white- and pink-bracted forms are also available.

FAUCARIA (from the Latin *faux*, a throat, referring to the leaves which resemble the open jaws of an animal) This is an interesting and distinctive genus in the Aizoaceae (Mesembryanthemaceae) family, containing about thirty species all from South Africa. They are dwarf compact rosette plants with opposite leaves, which are triangular in section with a single row of teeth along each edge, giving the plants the popular name of tiger's jaws. Some species have raised tubercles on the upper sides of the leaves. The flowers are yellow, up to 5cm (2in) in diameter, and open in afternoon sunshine. Cultural requirements are similar to the genus *Lithops*.

F. tigrina and F. tuberculosa are two of the most commonly grown species.

GASTERIA (from the Greek *gaster*, belly or stomach, referring to the swollen base of the flowers) This is a genus of about seventy species of succulents from South Africa with long, thick leaves having rounded or oblique tips which are often arranged in two opposite ranks in young plants, but which usually form rosettes with age. The flowers hang down from a long stem and are pink and tubular with a swollen base. They are ideal indoor plants as they are shade tolerant and relatively small. They are easily propagated from offsets and have attractive flowers in winter and spring.

G. batesiana is a slow-growing species with dark green warty leaves attractively spotted with white.

GRAPTOPETALUM (from the Greek *graptos*, writing or painting with letters, referring to the marks on the petals) This genus of ten species resembles *Echeveria* and is also native to Mexico and the south-western USA. It is

Haworthia paradoxa

distinguished by its flowers which are star-shaped, open widely and have petals marked with red spots and lines. There are many intergeneric hybrids with *Echeveria*, *Pachyphytum* and *Sedum*.

G. *paraguayense* produces rosettes of thick white waxy-coated leaves. It is easy to grow.

See also *Tacitus*.

× *GRAPTOVERIA*

This is an intergeneric hybrid between *Graptopetalum* and *Echeveria*. It forms easily cultivated rosette plants which are very free-flowering. They can be propagated from detached leaves which readily root and grow new plants from the leaf base. They require full sun to develop their attractive leaf colours and can withstand cold dry conditions in winter.

× G. 'Titubans' is a hybrid between G. *paraguayense* and *E. derenbergii* which has compact rosettes of pale green heart-shaped leaves.

GREENOVIA (named after the geologist G. B. Greenough who died in 1855)

This small genus of about four species is related to *Aeonium* and is endemic to the Canary Islands. The plants look just like huge bluish-green rosebuds in the vegetative state. Eventually the rosette elongates into a terminal spray of yellow flowers, after which the plant dies. Cultural conditions are as for *Aeonium*, except that *Greenovia* is slightly hardier. G. *aurea* and G. *dodrentalis* are the commonest species.

HAWORTHIA (named after the Englishman Adrian Hardy Haworth, 1768–1833, an authority on succulent plants)

The genus is native to South Africa, and there are about seventy species with a number of hybrids and cultivars.

These are small-growing plants, admirable for growing indoors as they are tolerant of partial shade. They form compact rosettes of pointed leaves often with toothed margins. Some species have a transparent window in the leaf tips, such as *H. truncata*, and are among the most unusual of all succulents. All have whitish flowers carried on long stems and most are propagated from rooted offsets. Some of the rarer species seldom produce offsets and can be propagated only from seed.

H. *attenuata* is a popular plant with narrow, dark green, pointed leaves striped with white.

H. *truncata* is a rare and slow-growing species with windowed tips to the leaves which look as though they have been sliced through.

H. *maughanii* is similar to *H. truncata*.

HOYA (named after Thomas Hoy, who died in 1809, a former head gardener at Syon House)

Kalanchoe farinacea

This is a genus of about 200 species of trailing or climbing plants with succulent leaves from China, southern Asia and Australasia. Two species are commonly grown as indoor plants.

H. *bella* has slender pendulous stems and small pointed leaves. The flowers are white with pink or red centres.

H. *carnosa* is the wax plant. It has twining to trailing stems, sizeable oval waxy leaves and large clusters of pinkish flowers which are very strongly scented in the evening. Variegated forms are also available.

HUERNIA (named after Justin Heurnius, 1587–1652, a Dutch missionary and the first to collect plants in South Africa)

The thirty species within the genus come mainly from Asia, and southern and eastern Africa. These are interesting small plants with fascinating spotted, striped and sometimes papillate flowers. They are in the same family as *Stapelia* and have similar fly-pollinated flowers. In some species, such as *H. zebrina*, the brown and yellow flowers have a peculiar shiny ring inside the corolla. It is not an easy genus to cultivate since the plants are very prone to bacterial and fungal diseases.

KALANCHOE (derived from the native name of a Chinese species)

This is a large genus of over 100 species distributed in many countries of the Old World, particularly in Africa and Madagascar, but also found in the Middle East, India and the Far East.

There are many free-flowering species such as *K. blossfeldiana* which are commonly seen in cultivation, but there are many others which are well worth growing. Most can be propagated from stem cuttings or detached leaves. In addition, a number of species formerly belonging to the genus *Bryophyllum* produce small plantlets along the leaf margins. When mature the plants often produce beautiful flowers in shades of pink, orange or yellow. Cultivation of most species is easy, provided that they are given a minimum winter temperature of above 5°C (41°F). *K. blossfeldiana* requires a moderate amount of water and is tolerant of semi-shade. Most other species need less water and good light.

K. beharensis is called the felt bush. A robust species from Madagascar, it has soft, felted leaves to 15cm (6in) long.

K. daigremontianum (*Bryophyllum daigremontianum*) is the Mexican hat plant, an interesting species with rows of plantlets along the margins of its triangular leaves.

K. pumila is an attractive species with pale grey leaves and delightful mauve flowers in early spring.

K. tomentosa is popularly known as donkey's ears. Small-growing, it has delicately felted pale grey-green leaves which are edged with reddish-brown.

Lithops localis var. *terricolor*

K. tubiflora (*Bryophyllum tubiflorum*) has tall, unbranched stems and narrow, spotted leaves with groups of plantlets at their tips. At a height of about 1m (3ft 3in) it produces showy orange-pink flowers and is one of the easiest plants to grow.

LITHOPS (from the Greek *lithos*, a stone, and *ops*, like) The name was given to these plants in 1922 because of their resemblance in colour and appearance to the pebbles among which they grow. *Lithops* belong to the Mesembryanthemum family, and are commonly known as living stones or pebble plants. There are about thirty species and varieties which are widely distributed in southern Africa. In the wild they are often completely buried in sand and gravel with just the truncate tips of the thick fleshy leaves visible. Their leaf colour is variable and mimics the rocks among which they grow. The flat surface of the leaves is frequently ornamented with networks of lines and dots and some species have a transparent window in the centre of the leaf.

A single pair of leaves is produced each year. During the resting period (winter to spring) a new pair of leaves is produced underneath and at right angles to the old pair, which eventually shrivel. Flowering occurs in the late summer and autumn at the end of the growing season. The flowers are like white or yellow daisies. The

first species to flower is *L. pseudotruncatella* and its relatives, which flower in summer. The last species is *L. optica* which flowers in winter. A very sandy, well-drained compost is recommended for these plants which should be watered from spring through to autumn. No water must be given during the winter when the plants should be kept cool at about 4°C (39°F). They should be kept in the lightest possible position, otherwise the leaves tend to become elongated.

L. julii ssp. *fulleri* has greyish-brown leaves with variable markings but always with distinct reddish-brown radiating lines around the margins; the flowers are white.

L. dorotheae is light brownish-yellow with red dots and lines; the flowers are yellow.

L. pseudotruncatella is a very variable species from Namibia, with a large number of named varieties and forms. The plants are brownish, greyish or whitish with a variable number of dots and lines; yellow flowers appear in July.

L. turbiniformis was the first species to be discovered by Burchell in 1811. They are reddish-brown plants with a rugose and reticulate surface, and yellow flowers.

L. verruculosa is a distinctive species characterized by large raised red dots which are unlike any other species; the flowers are yellow to brownish-orange.

PACHYPHYTUM (from the Greek *pachys*, thick, and *phyton*, a plant)

This is a small group of Mexican plants related to *Echeveria*. The leaves are usually thick and glaucous. Cultivation is easy, but high light conditions are essential, otherwise the plants tend to become elongated and lose their colour.

P. oviferum, the sugared almond plant, has leaves which are the shape and white colour of sugared almonds. Careful handling is required so as not to remove accidentally the white waxy bloom on the leaves. The flowers are waxy with red and white petals.

SANSEVIERIA (named after R. de Sangro, an eighteenth-century Prince of Sanseviero)

This is a genus of African and Indian xerophytes with stout rhizomes and leathery, long-pointed flat or cylindrical leaves, popularly known as mother-in-law's tongue. Several species have been grown commercially for their fibre.

S. trifasciata and its variegated forms are popular and attractive foliage house plants. In winter they must be kept warm at a minimum of 10°C (50°F) and dry, otherwise they may rot at the base.

SEDUM (from the Latin *sedere*, to sit, alluding to the way some species grow on rocks)

This is a very large genus of about 600 species which

Pachyphytum viride

have a world-wide distribution. They grow in a wide range of habitats including alpine conditions. The main group of these plants which are grown as indoor succulents originates in Mexico and has very attractive leaf shapes and colours. Most are dwarf or prostrate plants but some, such as *S. frutescens* from Mexico, grow to a height of 1.5m (5ft). Like many other succulents, cultivation is easy but high light conditions are essential. Propagation is from stem cuttings or detached leaves. The following list is just a small selection of this very interesting genus.

S. hintonii is a beautiful species with pale grey-green leaves covered with white hairs. The white flowers are produced in winter. The plants must be kept dry at this time as they are prone to rot.

S. morganianum (burro's tail) is a very popular hanging-basket plant with trailing stems up to 1m (3ft 3in) long. The stems are covered with narrow, overlapping, pale green leaves, and small pink flowers are produced from the tips of the mature stems.

S. rubrotinctum resembles a massive version of the common stonecrop but with bright reddish-brown leaves. *S. r.* 'Aurora' is an attractive chimaera with pale green, pink and white leaves.

(Above) *Senecio rowleyanus*
(Above right) *Tacitus bellus*

SENECIO (from the Latin *senex*, old man, referring to the hoary pappus of the fruit)
This is one of the largest genera of flowering plants with well over 1500 species. A number of them has evolved fleshy leaves and/or stems and may be regarded as succulents. As in all members of the Compositae (daisy family), there is a capitate inflorescence which is usually yellow, white or red, and is followed by clusters of fruits with a silky pappus.

S. *articulatus* also goes under the name of candle plant. It has swollen, jointed, blue-green stems up to 60cm (2ft) high with purple markings. Triangular leaves are produced from the stem apex during the growing season.

S. *rowleyanus* is often called the string-of-beads plant because of the small spherical leaves strung out along the pendulous stems like a necklace. Small white flowers are produced, mainly in the winter but also at other times.

STAPELIA (named after J. B. van Stapel, a seventeenth-century Dutch physician)
This genus is a member of the family Asclepiadaceae and

FURTHER INFORMATION

Bibliography

Backeberg, C., *Cactus Lexicon* (Blandford Press, 1977)

Bayer, M. B., *The New Haworthia Handbook* (1982)

Cullman, W., Gotz, E. and Groner, G., *The Encyclopaedia of Cacti* (Alphabooks, 1986)

Fearn, B., *Lithops (National Cactus & Succulent Society Handbook* No. 4, 1981)

Fearn, B. and Pearcy, L., *Choice Mammillarias* (Abbey Brook Cactus Nursery Publication, 1986)

— *The Genus Rebutia* (Abbey Brook Cactus Nursery Publication, 1981)

Jacobsen, H., *Lexicon of Succulent Plants* (Blandford Press, 1977)

Martin, M. J. and Chapman, P. R., *Succulents and their Cultivation* (Faber & Faber, 1977)

Rowley, G., *Name that Succulent* (Stanley Thorne, 1980)

Societies

British Cactus and Succulent Society
BCSS Publicity Officer
43 Dewar Drive
Sheffield S7 2GR
England

Deutsche Kakteen-Gesellschaft (German Cactus Society)
Geschaeftsstelle
D-2860 Osterholz-Scharmbeck
West Germany

Cactus and Succulent Society of America
1675 Las Canoas Road
Santa Barbara, Calif 93105
USA

contains approximately forty-three species. They all have interesting and complex flowers which often smell of rotting meat and are pollinated by large flies such as bluebottles. They are commonly known as carrion flowers. Most species are not difficult to cultivate if warm dry conditions are provided in the winter. Related genera such as *Caralluma*, *Stapelianthus* and *Echidnopsis* are much more difficult and a real challenge to grow successfully.

S. gigantea is a species with giant flowers 25–35cm (10–14in) in diameter, dull yellow with reddish-brown stripes and scattered reddish hairs around the margins.

S. variegata (*Orbea variegata*) is a species with starlike flowers and unusual brown and yellow markings.

TACITUS (from the Latin *tacitus*, silent, referring to the 'close-mouthed' corolla tube)
This monotypic genus from Mexico is now correctly placed in the genus *Graptopetalum*.

T. bellus (*Graptopetalum bellum*) was only discovered as a wild plant in 1972 by Alfred Lau. The plant forms dense sessile rosettes of glossy greyish-green leaves tinged with lilac. The large flowers are a striking bright rose pink, the five petals opening flat like a star.

PLANTS FOR SPECIAL PURPOSES

EASE OF CULTIVATION

Suitable for beginners	Moderately easy	Fairly difficult
Aporocactus flagelliformis	Astrophytum ornatum	Astrophytum capricorne
Chamaecereus sylvestrii	Borzicactus aureispinus	Cephalocereus senilis
Echinopsis	Cleistocactus strausii	Espostoa melanostele
Epiphyllum (cultivars)	Echinocactus grusonii	Melocactus
Gymnocalycium	Echinocereus pectinatus	Mammillaria guelzowiana
Lobivia	Hatiora gaertneri	Notocactus buiningii
Mammillaria (most)	Lophophora williamsii	Opuntia basilaris
Notocactus leninghausii	Mammillaria candida	Parodia nivosa
Rebutia (most)	Notocactus scopa	Conophytum
Trichocereus candicans	Opuntia microdasys	Crassula barbata
Aeonium arboreum	Parodia chrysacanthion	Echeveria laui
A. domesticum	Rebutia fiebrigii	Euphorbia aeruginosa
A. tabuliforme	Agave victoria-reginae	E. obesa
Agave americana	Cotyledon orbiculata	Haworthia paradoxa
Aloe aristata	C. undulata	H. truncata
A. variegata	Echeveria 'Doris Taylor'	Kalanchoe farinacea
Ceropegia woodii	Euphorbia milii	Lithops
Crassula falcata	Faucaria tigrina	Sedum hintonii
C. ovata	Kalanchoe pumila	Senecio tomentosa
Echeveria derenbergii	K. tomentosa	
E. harmsii	Pachyphytum oviferum	
Graptopetalum paraguayense	Sedum morganianum	
Kalanchoe tubiflora	Senecio rowleyanus	
Sedum rubrotinctum	Stapelia gigantea	
Senecio articulatus	Tacitus bellus	
S. stapeliaeformis		
Stapelia variegata		

MINIMUM TEMPERATURE REQUIRED

The following are able to tolerate cold, dry winter conditions.

Echinocereus	Echeveria
Lobivia	Pachyphytum
Rebutia	Sedum
Aloe aristata	

The following do not tolerate temperatures below 10–12°C (50–54°F).

Cephalocereus senilis
Melocactus (all)
Euphorbia (most)
Kalanchoe (most and especially *K. farinacea*)

LIGHT REQUIREMENTS

The majority of cacti and succulents require conditions of full light. The following, however, are tolerant of shade

× Aporophyllum	Aeonium
Epiphyllum	Aloe
Hatiora	Gasteria
Rhipsalis	Greenovia
Schlumbergera	Haworthia
Selenicereus	Hoya

SHOWY IN FLOWER

Acanthocalycium	Mammillaria	Echeveria
Aporocactus	Notocactus	Faucaria
Borzicactus	Opuntia	Hoya
Chamaecereus	Parodia	Kalanchoe
Cleistocactus	Rebutia	Lithops
Echinocereus	Selenicereus	Sedum
Echinopsis	Aeonium	Stapelia
Epiphyllum	Conophytum	Tacitus
Gymnocalycium	Cotyledon	
Lobivia	Crassula	

ATTRACTIVE FORM OR FOLIAGE

Astrophytum	Trichocereus	Graptopetalum
Cephalocereus	Agave	Greenovia
Cleistocactus	Aloe	Kalanchoe
Echinocactus	Cotyledon	Lithops
Espostoa	Crassula	Pachyphytum
Gymnocalycium	Echeveria	Sedum
Mammillaria	Faucaria	
Opuntia	Gasteria	

Tender Bulbs

ANYONE WHO gardens outside in temperate countries is fully aware of the beauty of form and variety of colours and shades which bulbous plants can provide. Rare indeed are the gardens and window boxes which do not take advantage of this fact and contain at least a few daffodils, narcissi, hyacinths and tulips in spring, and gladioli in summer.

In warmer climates there are bulbs of equal attraction. One has only to think of the gorgeous amaryllis hybrids (*Hippeastrum*) now so freely available from Dutch nurseries, and the fragrant and colourful freesias, for proof of this. These and many more tender bulbs make splendid pot plants for the home, conservatory and greenhouse provided the frost can be kept at bay in winter and, ideally, a night minimum temperature of $10°-13°$C ($50°-55°$F) can be maintained.

Botanically, bulbs, corms, tubers and rhizomes are underground storage organs containing food supplies to tide the plant over during periods when growth is not possible, such as during winter cold and summer drought. A true bulb is formed of a very short thick stem, known as a base plate, and few to many fleshy scales derived from modified whole leaves or leaf bases. In the centre at the apex of the base plate is the growing point from which leaves and flowers develop. Sometimes buds develop in the axils of the scale leaves, eventually forming daughter bulbs or offsets. In this way clumps form. Corms are greatly enlarged stem bases, usually of a globular or thickened disc-like shape. Tubers may be swollen roots as in *Dahlia*, but are some-

(Above) *Haemanthus albiflos*   (Opposite) *Sprekelia formosissima*

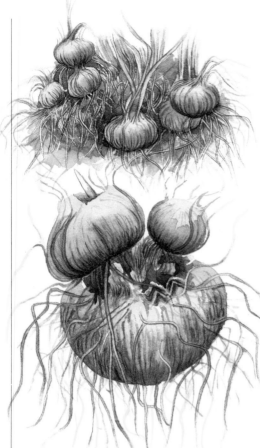

(Above) Bulbous plants naturally multiply by producing daughter bulbs. This affords a ready means of propagation. Clumps of bulbs can be lifted and divided up. The exhausted parent bulb should be discarded.

times swollen stems, such as in *Gloriosa*. Some corms and tubers are superficially alike. *Cyclamen*, for example, are described as cormous perennials, but technically, because they are largely of root tissue, they are tubers. Rhizomes may be comparatively thin, or thick and fleshy as in *Canna*. With their growing commercial popularity, the originally strict botanical definition of bulb is now widely applied by horticultural traders to all types of perennating organs and they are therefore also included here.

As was implied above, storage organs have arisen in response to climatic patterns. Most bulbous plants have evolved in areas where there is a cool, moist winter and a long, hot, dry summer. Basically this is a Mediterranean climate, which is found not only around the Mediterranean Sea, but also in California, Chile, southern Africa and southern Australia. In these areas growth starts as the weather cools and the rains begin in autumn. Leaves and flowers are produced during the late autumn to spring period and die away as the summer drought sets in. Familiar examples are *Colchicum*, *Freesia*, *Lachenalia* and *Hippeastrum*.

Bulbs have also developed in warmer areas where the winters are dry and fairly cool and the summers moist and warm. Tropical and subtropical regions with this pattern are found in parts of central and southern Africa and the Americas. Bulbous examples include *Crinum*, *Eucomis*, *Hymenocallis*, *Polianthes* and *Tigridia*.

There are of course variations within these climate types, some more extreme, others less pronounced. There are also bulbous plants in areas which do not seem to favour them, for example some *Crinum* species are aquatic and most lilies grow in climates which lack extremes.

It is obvious that plants which have evolved in extreme climates must have a cultural regime in the greenhouse or home

(Right) *Hymenocallis narcissiflora*

which approximates their natural growing and resting phases. Mediterranean species must be kept more or less dry in summer, started into growth in autumn and kept growing during the winter and spring. They are, however, disadvantaged when grown in higher latitudes by conditions of poor winter light. Many of the more tender bulbous plants discussed below come from summer rainfall areas. With sufficient warmth they are easily grown in the home or greenhouse, starting into growth in spring, growing through the summer when the light is good and resting or becoming completely dormant in winter.

Cultural requirements

Conditions in the home: Nowhere in the wild are conditions so basically inimical to plant growth as in the home and yet, despite no free exchange of air, no rain, almost no humidity and sunlight reduced in effectiveness as it passes through glass, a surprising number of plants grow well. It is of course necessary to choose the most suitable species, varieties and cultivars for these poor conditions, but this presents no great difficulty. Increased humidity can easily be provided by placing pot plants on trays of gravel flooded with water to just below the top of the stones. Alternatively, use trays or larger containers of moist peat and plunge them up to their rims. A further aid is the small pneumatic hand sprayer which delivers water in mist-fine droplets.

Put bulbs which grow in winter, such as *Freesia* and *Lachenalia*, in a south-facing (north-facing in the southern hemisphere) window, or, if this is not possible, an east- or west-facing one to make the best of the low light intensity of that time of year. Where winter light is poor it is worthwhile installing an artificial lighting unit which can be free-standing or suspended from above, the light source being one or more fluorescent tubes.

Conditions in the greenhouse: Compared with the home, the greenhouse or conservatory has a much greater potential for plant cultivation. Ventilation is freely available and water can be used to mimic rain and provide humidity. There is now a variety of sophisticated equipment to provide overhead watering and mistlike humidity. The glass is still a limiting factor but the all-round access to light partially compensates for this. To make the most of light conditions, make sure that any new greenhouse is aligned east-west and, if possible, has an unobstructed skyline either to the north or south depending on the hemisphere. Light is all important to plants which grow during winter.

Heating: If the bulbs described in the pages which follow are to be grown in a greenhouse or conservatory, a heating source, at least for the colder months, will be needed. A minimum night temperature of $7°-10°$C ($45°-50°$F) will suffice for most tender bulbs, and even the tropical species tolerate $13°-16°$C ($55°-61°$F).

Many tender bulbs can be grown in the home providing the

Where additional tubers have been produced by *Gloriosa superba* they can be separated when dormant. In spring several tubers can be repotted together using fresh compost.

rooms are regularly heated to a living temperature. If the room cools at night, however, make sure growing plants are removed from chilly window ledges and placed where temperatures do not fall below their minimum requirements.

Containers: Although plant containers now come in a wide range of shapes and sizes, bulbs are best grown in those of standard pot shape. These being deeper than wide they provide a suitable depth for their delving roots. Whether plastic or clay is selected is largely a matter of personal preference. However, many bulbous plants must have a freely draining rooting medium which does not remain wet for too long. In winter time at least, when the temperatures stay on the low side, clay pots make this easier to achieve.

Composts: How well a plant thrives in a container largely depends on the rooting medium. Bulbs do not need rich soil but it must be well drained and contain all the essential plant food. Because the roots are confined to a comparatively small area, garden soil is seldom sufficient unless provided with extra fertilizers and organic matter. Unless one is growing large quantities of pot plants, however, it is not really worthwhile making up one's own compost.

Several types of potting compost are sold at garden centres and nurseries. There are two basic sorts, loam- or soil-based and all-peat or loamless. Loam is a subtle blend of clay, fine sand, humus and minerals. It is now in short supply. Partially sterilized to kill weed seeds, soil pests and diseases and then mixed with peat and a balanced plant food, it forms an ideal rooting medium for container plants. The widely used loam-based composts are of this sort, made in bulk of seven parts loam, three of coarse sand and two of moss peat, to each bushel of which is added a base fertilizer, and powdered chalk. Unfortunately the rich loam stipulated when these composts were developed is no longer easily available and most composts under this name are inferior to their potential. There is more control over the newer all-peat composts which hardly vary from batch to batch. Happily, most bulbous plants will thrive in them especially if mixed with coarse sand, two to four parts of compost to one of sand (by bulk) being recommended, depending on how sharply drained a rooting medium is needed.

Potting: With a few exceptions, such as *Nerine* and *Hippeastrum*, bulbs are completely buried when placed in containers. Smaller bulbs, *Lachenalia* for example, are most effective in groups of not less than five; larger ones, especially *Hippeastrum*, can be grown singly. To give an idea of the size of containers to use, about six *Lachenalia* bulbs will go nicely into a 13cm (5in) pot, but one full-sized *Hippeastrum* will need a 15cm (6in) vessel. Set the smaller bulbs so that their tops are about one third of the way down from the rim of the pot. Cover, firm the soil, water with a rosed can and place in the appropriate temperature.

Nerine undulata

Repotting: Most of the smaller bulbs, corms and tubers, *Brodiaea*, *Freesia*, *Gladiolus*, *Lachenalia*, *Tigridia*, etc., are best repotted annually. The pots should be tipped out, the large bulbs of flowering size selected for potting again and the offsets, bulblets or cormlets either discarded or grown on in separate containers. Clean pots and fresh compost should be used each time. Bulbs with permanent roots, *Crinum*, *Eucharis*, *Hippeastrum*, *Vallota*, etc., are dealt with somewhat differently. After tipping out the plants, as much as possible of the old soil should be teased away or shaken off, small offsets removed and the bulbs of flowering size returned to a container of the same size and filled around with fresh potting soil. If a larger bulb or clump is required then the whole root ball is put in a larger container allowing it at least 2.5cm (1in) all round for new compost. Technically, this moving into a larger vessel is known as potting-on.

Top-dressing: Several of the larger bulbs with permanent roots seem to resent frequent disturbance and are best left in the same container for several years until the bulbs become congested and produce fewer flowers. After the first one or two years top-dressing is beneficial. Just as new growth starts, remove the top layer of old compost with a small handfork or old kitchen fork. Do not worry about stripping any fine roots near the surface but stop when the thicker main roots show. Remove up to a quarter of the total depth of compost. Replace it immediately with fresh potting soil, lightly firm and water.

Feeding: To maintain healthy bulbs of flowering size a certain amount of supplementary feeding is necessary. This is most effectively done by using one of the general liquid feeds diluted to the makers' instructions. Among the various formulations available, that sold for tomatoes are recommended. Start feeding just as the leaves reach full size and continue at ten to fourteen day intervals until the leaves begin to yellow.

Resting: Most of the bulbous plants described below have a dormant period, when the leaves yellow, wither and disappear. Others are evergreen, such as *Vallota*, but they need to be kept on the dry side at the end of their growing season. For those that are fully dormant, watering should be less frequent after the growing season and, once the leaves start to yellow, phased out altogether. By the time the leaves are half-yellow watering should cease. Knowledge of the growth phases natural to these bulbs will help to decide when to dry them off. The winter-growing or Mediterranean types, such as *Freesia* and *Lachenalia*, shoot in autumn, grow and flower during the winter and early spring, die back in late spring and early summer and remain dormant in high summer. The summer-growing or savannah sorts shoot in spring, grow and bloom in summer and early autumn, die off in late autumn and are dormant in winter. Whichever season sees the bulbs dormant, store them in their pots of soil where they cannot get accidentally wetted. Keep the summer growers cool but well

Division of the rootstock provides a ready means of propagating *Canna*. This procedure should be carried out in the early spring before potting.

Alstromeria pelegrina

above freezing, and repot in early spring. Keep the winter-growers as warm as the summer allows and repot in late summer.

Watering: Most bulbous plants will not tolerate waterlogged soil conditions. To avoid this always wait until the surface of the potting soil feels dryish each time before watering again. For plants in clay pots scratch into the surface of the compost to a depth of about 6mm ($\frac{1}{4}$in); if it feels dryish all the way then give it water. For plastic pots scratch down to 10–12mm ($\frac{2}{5}$–$\frac{1}{2}$in) before deciding to water. When watering is carried out do it thoroughly, filling up the space between the rim of the container and the surface of the compost.

Propagation

The majority of bulbs multiply naturally and it is only necessary to remove or separate the young ones and grow them on to maturity.

Offsets: These are daughter corms, bulbs or tubers which form beside the main one. When repotting, they can easily be detached. The larger ones may flower the next season, the smaller ones need growing on for one or two seasons.

Bulblets and cormlets: Around the base plate of some bulbs and at the junction of the root and main corm, very small offsets occur – often, as in *Freesia* and *Gladiolus*, in clusters. These should be treated as for offsets but take longer to reach maturity.

Bulbils and cormels: These are aerial versions of bulblets and cormlets and usually arise on the flowering stem. Certain species of *Begonia*, *Watsonia* and *Achimenes* produce them, but they are not an important means of propagation among tender bulbs.

Seed: Most bulbous plants produce seeds which germinate freely and provide a ready means of increase. Because offsets and bulbils are so much easier and quicker to raise however, few gardeners bother with sowing seeds. The time lapse from sowing to maturity can be as little as one year, as in *Alstroemeria*, *Begonia* and *Gloxinia*, or two years, as in *Habranthus*, *Littonia*, *Watsonia* etc., but three years is about the average. Seed is best sown in potting compost to give it a good start in life. Use 7.5–10cm (3–4in) pots. Sow thinly, if possible, spacing them individually with forceps 5–10mm ($\frac{1}{5}$–$\frac{2}{5}$in) apart. Cover shallowly with 3–6mm ($\frac{1}{8}$–$\frac{1}{4}$in) of compost, water with a rosed can and place in a temperature of not less than 18°C (64°F). Cover with plastic sheeting or glass and screen from direct sunlight. When germination occurs, acclimatize the plants to direct light. Some bulbous plants do no more than produce one grassy seed leaf the first growing season. These are best left in the same pot for the first two seasons, feeding regularly during the second one. Others produce several leaves, and when the second or third one is present the plants are best carefully pricked out into larger containers. Alternatively, if the seedlings stay small they can be left in the seed pot until the start of the second year.

Pests and diseases

On the whole, bulbous plants are not afflicted with many pests and diseases. Symptoms and the causes and cures of the worst kinds are described below. When applying the cures make sure they are used to the makers' instructions; too great a concentration could damage the plant, too weak would almost certainly fail to eliminate the pest.

Pests: A yellowish freckling leading to yellowing and premature leaf-fall means red spider mite damage. These are minute, yellowish, red-spotted or wholly red creatures which suck sap and spin almost transparent fine threads. Spray with formothion or pirimiphos methyl and syringe daily with clean water to discourage breeding. Alternatively, try biological control using the red spider mite parasite *Phytoseiulus persimilis.*

Red, sometimes distorted, streaks on the leaves and buds, mainly on hippeastrums, denote bulb scale-mite damage. Severe infestation results in death or crippling of flower buds. Such bulbs are best destroyed.

A yellow or whitish streaking of the leaves of *Nerine* usually means infection by either narcissus yellows or white-stripe virus. Reduction in vigour and deformation of leaves and flower buds results. There is no cure and the bulbs should be destroyed.

If the leaves and flowers are curled and deformed and the bulbs feel soft this is likely to be due to eelworm infection. Destroy both the bulbs and the contained soil.

Several sorts of green to yellowish or pinkish green aphids (greenfly) may attack the young leaves and flower buds, sucking the sap and reducing vigour. Spray with malathion, diazinon, formothion or another insecticide.

Glasshouse whitefly and its even smaller greenish to whitish scale-like nymphs suck the sap and make the plants sticky with honeydew which in turn is colonized by the unsightly blackish sooty mould. Spray with bioresmethrin, permethrin or pyrethrum. Alternatively try biological control with the whitefly parasite *Encarsia formosa.*

Small, woolly, white insects which occur round the leaf bases and bulb necks are mealy bugs, allies of the aphids and protected by waxy filaments. They suck sap and produce a sticky honeydew. Apply spray strength malathion, nicotine or methylated spirit.

Guide to purchasing

In garden centres and similar establishments it is usually possible to select bulbs from trays. Choose the largest and plumpest specimens which feel firm when pressed. Avoid any bulb which feels soft or softish especially around the neck. Avoid also those with brown marks or scars which could denote the disease.

Many species of lily are easily propagated by the removal of the outer scales of the bulbs. Only firm healthy bulbs should be used.

Once detached, the scales should be planted into pots of compost and placed in a propagator or other warm, moist situation. Some growers use a polythene bag instead of a pot.

47

Recommended genera

ALSTROEMERIA (named after Baron Claus Alstroemer, 1736–94, botanist and student of Linnaeus)
This is a genus of about fifty species of tuberous-rooted perennials from South America. They are clump-forming, with erect, unbranched stems clad in narrow, upside-down leaves and topped by a cluster of six-tepalled, widely funnel-shaped blooms.

Among the best for pot culture are: *A. pelegrina* (including *A. gayana* of Philippi), with stems to 30cm (1ft) or more and 6cm (2½in) wide rose-purple and crimson flowers, the upper two tepals marked white or yellow, from spring to early summer (this species tends to grow in autumn and winter and is best kept dry in summer); *A. pulchella*, which varies from 60–90cm (2–3ft) in height, bearing crimson, darker spotted flowers tipped with green in summer; *A. violacea* is like a mauve-purple, dark-marked *A. pelegrina*, usually to 60cm (2ft) in height, and 'Walter Fleming' is a finer, sterile hybrid derived from it.

Pot or repot in early spring or when dormant, providing a winter minimum temperature of around 5°C (41°F), or 9°–10°C (48°–50°F) for those which grow in winter, and full light. Propagate by seed.

Amaryllis see *Hippeastrum*.

Anomatheca see *Lapeirousia*.

ARISAEMA (from the Greek *aris* or *aron*, an arum, and *haima*, blood, referring to its blood relationship to *Arum*)
This is a genus of about 150 species of tuberous or rhizomatous perennials from Asia, North America, Mexico and East Africa. Each tuber produces one or two large leaves divided into leaflets, and an arum-like spathe surrounding a spike (spadix) bearing tiny petalless flowers. They are more bizarre than beautiful.

The showiest species is *A. candidissimum* which has bold trifoliate leaves and sweetly scented spathes in summer. The latter are 10cm (4in) long, white, striped green without and pinkish-flushed within, and are at their best as the leaves unfurl. *A. sikokianum* is also trifoliate, bearing uniquely waisted, brownish-purple, green and white spathes to 20cm (8in) long in spring.

Pot or repot when dormant during the winter or spring months. Store frost-free. When in leaf, screen from direct sunlight. Propagate by offsets or seed.

BABIANA (from the Afrikaans *babiaan*, baboon, which reputedly eats the corms)
This is a genus of sixty species of cormous plants from Socotra, tropical and southern Africa. They have pleated, lanceolate leaves and six-tepalled, funnel- to

tubular-shaped flowers in short racemes in spring.

Recommended are the named and unnamed forms of *B. × hybrida* with 4–5cm (1½–2in) wide blooms in shades of white, yellow, red and purple. *B. stricta*, one parent of *B. × hybrida*, reaches 20–30cm (8–12in) in height and has flowers with the three inner tepals blue and the three other ones white. *B.s.* var. *rubrocyanea* bears blue flowers with crimson centres.

Pot the corms in late autumn and keep barely moist at a minimum night temperature of 7°C (45°F). When growing keep in full light and water more freely. Propagate by offsets or seed.

BEGONIA (named after Michel Bégon, 1638–1710, a French patron of botany)
This is a genus of about 900 species, several of which are tuberous-rooted. In general, begonias are characterized by their lop-sided or ear-shaped leaves and sexually dimorphic flowers. The flowers have two, four or five petals, the usually larger females being distinguished from the males by their three-winged ovaries.

Best known and among the showiest is *B. × tuberhybrida* and its many cultivars in shades of yellow, orange, red, pink and white, the male flowers semi- to fully double. Two main groups are recognized, Camellia-flowered and Pendula. The latter has arching

Arisaema candidissima

to pendulous, branching stems and semi-double male flowers. The camellia-flowered type is erect and very robust with sparse branching and massive, fully double, almost roselike blooms. There are named cultivars and seed strains. *B. sutherlandii* is more dainty, having slender, arching, branching stems, small leaves and a profusion of light orange single flowers. It makes an excellent plant for a hanging basket.

Pot the tubers in early to late spring, maintaining a minimum temperature of not less than 13°C (55°F). Shade them from the hottest sun, and when the leaves yellow in the autumn keep the plants dry and at a temperature of not less than 7°C (45°F). Propagate by seed, stem or leaf cuttings.

BESSERA (named after Dr W. S. J. G. von Besser, 1784–1842, a professor of botany at Brody)
This genus of one bulbous species comes from south-western and south-central Mexico. *B. elegans* produces several lax, linear leaves and slender erect stems 40–60cm (16–24in) tall, bearing umbels 4cm (1½in) long, with red and white nodding bell flowers in late summer.

Pot the bulbs in spring and maintain a night minimum temperature of 7°C (45°F). Provide full light and water freely when in full growth. Store dry and frost-free over winter. Propagate by offsets and seed.

(Left) *Babiana stricta*
(Below) *Begonia* × *tuberhybrida* 'Non-Stop'

BRODIAEA (named after James Brodie, 1744–1824, a Scottish botanist)

This is a genus of forty species of cormous plants in the same family as onions and garlic, which comes from western North and South America. On the basis of small floral characters, botanists have now divided it into several smaller genera, such as *Dichelostemma* and *Hookera*, but for convenience all are dealt with here. They produce linear leaves and naked slender stems topped by umbels of six-tepalled starry or tubular flowers in a variety of colours in early summer.

The showiest species is *B. ida-maia* (*B. coccinea*, or *Dichelostemma ida-maia*), the firecracker of California. It has stems 40–90cm (16–36in) tall and 2.5–4cm (1–1½in) long, and green-tipped bright red tubular blooms. *B. congesta* (*B. pulchella*, or *Dichelostemma congesta*) reaches 40cm (16in) in height and has light blue-violet flowers which are 12mm (½in) long and bell-shaped. *B. coronaria* (*B. grandiflora*, or *Hookera coronaria*) is usually under 30cm (1ft) tall with 2cm (¾in) long, lilac to violet, trumpet-shaped flowers. *B. hyacinthina* (*Hesperocordum*, *Triteleia* and *Hookera hyacinthina*, *Brodiaea lactea*) varies from 30–60cm (1–2ft) in height and bears starry white flowers 2.5cm (1in) wide, each tepal having a green mid-vein. For *B. ixioides* see *B. lutea*.

B. laxa (*Hookera* and *Triteleia laxa*) is known as grass nut and Ithuriel's spear. It grows to 40cm (16in) or more with trumpet-shaped purple-blue flowers 2–2.5cm (¾–1in) long. *B. lutea* (*Triteleia*, *Hookera* and *Brodiaea ixioides*) reaches 30cm (1ft) or more in height and bears starry yellow flowers 2cm (¾in) wide, each tepal having a deep purple mid-vein. *B. volubilis* (*Dichelostemma*, *Hookera* and *Stropholirion volubilis*) is unique in having a 60–150cm (2–5ft) long twining flowering stem. The bell-shaped, 2cm (¾in) wide flowers are pink.

Pot the corms in autumn, providing a winter minimum temperature of 5°C (41°F) and grow in full light. Tall growing sorts will need the support of slender sticks or canes. Propagation is by offsets or seed.

CANNA (from the Greek *kanna*, a reed, some species having tall reed-like stems)

This genus of fifty-five species comes from tropical and subtropical America. They are clump-forming perennials with tuber-like rhizomes and erect unbranched stems clad with lanceolate to oblong-ovate leaves. The somewhat orchid-like flowers are carried in terminal racemes and open in summer and autumn. Each bloom has a tubular base, three petals and one to five petaloid stamens, usually coloured like the petals, one of which forms a lip.

The group of hybrid cultivars technically known as *C. × generalis* make the best pot or tub plants for the conservatory or home. Recommended are: 'Bonfire', which is a deep orange, and reaches 90cm (3ft);

'Dazzler', which has rich red flowers, bronze-purple leaves, and grows to 90–120cm (3–4ft); 'Di Bartolo', with pink blooms, purple-flushed leaves, and reaching 90cm (3ft); 'Lucifer', which has scarlet flowers, yellow-edged leaves, and grows to 90–120cm (3–4ft). The best true species is *C. iridiflora*, with nodding rose flowers up to 13cm (5in) long and stems to 2m (6½ft) or more in height.

Propagation is by division at potting time. Pot or repot in early to mid-spring and provide a minimum temperature of 16°C (61°F). Place the plants in full light, though some shade is tolerated when the plants are in bloom. Water freely when in full growth but dry off in late autumn. Overwinter them in their pots at 7°–10°C (45°–50°F).

CHLIDANTHUS (from the Greek *chlide*, an expensive ornament or luxury, and *anthos*, a flower)

This genus of one species of bulbous plant, *C. fragrans*, is distributed from Mexico to Chile.

C. fragrans produces narrow strap-shaped leaves, and in summer small umbels of yellow flowers on 15–25cm (6–10in) stems. Each scented bloom has a 7cm (2¾in) long tubular base and six flared tepal lobes. Pot the bulbs in spring and provide a minimum night temperature of 7°C (45°F) and full light. Dry off in the autumn and store at 5°C (41°F). Propagation is by offsets.

× CRINDONNA, syn. × *Amarcrinum* – now the correct name (from *Crinum* and *Belladonna* – *Amaryllis belladonna* – the parents of this bigeneric hybrid) Culture

Chlidanthus fragrans

as for *Crinum*.

× *C. corsii* has flowers like those of *Amaryllis belladonna* and leaves similar to those of its other parent *Crinum moorei*. It blooms in the autumn.

CRINUM (from the Greek *krinon*, a lily)

This genus of 100 or more species of bulbous plants is widespread in the tropics and subtropics. Those in cultivation have large, long-necked bulbs, each one producing a sheaf of fleshy-textured, strap-shaped leaves which taper to a point. The trumpet-shaped blooms, which are carried in umbels on strong, erect, leafless stems, usually open in late summer and autumn but can appear at other times.

Tropical *C. asiaticum* varies in the size of its leaves and flowers. Usually it produces a flowering stem 90–120cm (3–4ft) in height and sizeable clusters of scented flowers 14–18cm ($5\frac{1}{2}$–7in) long. White is the basic colour but usually with a variable amount of pink or purple. Subtropical *C. bulbispermum* and *C. moorei* are similar. Both produce stems 60–90cm (2–3ft) tall and flowers about 15cm (6in) long, those of *C. bulbispermum* being pale pink with darker veins and fragrant. *C. moorei* usually has rosy pink flowers but white or white-flushed pink variants are known. Although classified as subtropical, both these species and their hybrid *C.* × *powellii* will stand some frost.

Pot or repot in spring, leaving the neck exposed. Once established, disturb as little as possible. Provide a minimum night temperature of 7°C (45°F) for the subtropical species, and 13°–16°C (55°–61°F) for tropical species. Bright light is essential but light shade is tolerated in summer. Propagate by offsets.

CYCLAMEN (from the Greek *kyklos*, circular, referring to the spiralling of the flower stalks as the seed capsules form)

This genus of about twenty species of cormous plants comes from Europe and the Mediterranean, reaching as far east as Iran. A few species are tender and make attractive plants for the cool conservatory or home. They produce tufts of long-stalked, rounded, sometimes lobed leaves, often with a silvery pattern, and pendent, five-petalled shuttlecock-shaped flowers from autumn to spring.

C. persicum is the best known species, with rounded to broadly ovate-cordate leaves variably patterned, or suffused with silvery white. The 3cm ($1\frac{1}{4}$in) slender fragrant blooms have twisted petals in shades of pink to purple and white. The florists' cultivars have a wider colour range and the plants are more robust, growing to 30cm (1ft) in height, with flowers twice as large and less elegant. There are double- and fringed-petalled cultivars, all mostly without scent. Other cultivars are hybrids between the species and the large florists' cultivars, such as the 'Puppet' strain.

Crinum bulbispermum

(Above) *Cyclamen persicum*
(Above right) *Eucharis amazonica*

C. libanoticum is hardier, sometimes having lobed leaves patterned dark green or greyish and yellowish-green. The 2.5cm (1in) long flowers are pale salmon-pink and open in late winter and spring.

Sow the seeds in early autumn or late winter for *C. persicum*, or spring for the other species, and keep at 13°–16°C (55°–61°F). Prick off seedlings singly into small pots when the second leaf shows. Keep cool and lightly shaded. *C. persicum* takes eight to twelve months to bloom. They can be brought into the home but must be kept cool and not overwatered.

CYRTANTHUS (from the Greek *kyrtos*, arched, and *anthos*, a flower)

This genus of about forty-five species of bulbs comes from tropical and southern Africa. Each bulb produces a tuft of narrow strap-shaped or linear leaves, and one or more erect stems topped by an umbel of tubular, down-curving flowers in spring or summer.

Among the most easily grown are *C. mackenii*, which grows 20–30cm (8–12in) tall and bears fragrant white, cream or pink flowers about 5cm (2in) long. *C. obrienii* is similar but has scentless bright red blooms. There are several species superior to these but they are rare in cultivation and must be diligently sought; these include *C. purpureus*, *C. contractus* and *C. galpinii*.

Pot or repot in autumn or late winter. Maintain a night minimum temperature around 7°C (45°F) and place in full light, though a little shade is tolerated in summer. Keep the plants dry or almost so during the winter.

EUCHARIS (from the Greek word for pleasing or charming)

This genus of ten species of evergreen bulbs comes from tropical South America. It is allied to *Hymenocallis* and bears similar six-tepalled flowers with a central cup or crown formed from stamen filaments.

E. amazonica (*E. grandiflora*), the Amazon lily, is the only freely available species. It has long-stalked, ovate to elliptic lustrous rich green leaves, the blades growing to 20cm (8in) long. Erect 30–60cm (1–2ft) tall stems are topped by three to six fragrant, white, narcissus-like blooms, each one 7.5cm (3in) wide. Summer is the usual flowering season, but if after each flush of new leaves has matured the plant is kept short of water for about six weeks, flowers may also appear in spring or autumn.

Pot or repot in spring, then disturb as little as necessary. Water freely when in growth and provide a minimum temperature of 16°C (61°F). Shade from direct sunlight in summer. Propagation is by offsets.

EUCOMIS (from the Greek *eu*, good and *kome*, hair, referring to the terminal tufts or bracts which have been fancifully likened to a head of hair)

This genus of fourteen species of bulbous plants comes

from tropical and southern Africa. Each bulb bears a rosette of fleshy, broadly strap-shaped leaves and, in the autumn, a robust, erect raceme of six-tepalled starry flowers topped by a tuft of narrow leafy bracts, like those of a pineapple, hence the vernacular name, pineapple lily. Although more or less hardy in sheltered sites outside, the species described make handsome and unusual pot or tub plants for the conservatory.

The largest and most statuesque is *E. pole-evansii*, with 90–180cm (3–6ft) high racemes of green-tinted, white flowers. *E. zambesiaca* is much smaller, and has pure white racemes up to 45cm (1½ft) in height. *E. autumnalis* is similar with greenish or white flowers and wavy leaves. *E. bicolor* has jade green blossoms edged with purple on racemes which grow to 45cm (1½ft) in height. *E. comosa* (*E. punctata*) produces yellow-green flowers, sometimes flushed purple, with a dark purple ovary, on purple-spotted stems which grow to 60cm (2ft) tall.

Pot in spring, ideally using a loam-based compost. Maintain a minimum temperature of 5°–7°C (41°–45°F). Light screening from the hottest sun is advisable. Keep barely moist and frost-free in winter.

FREESIA (named after F. H. T. Freese, a nineteenth-century German doctor and friend of the botanist who named the genus)

This genus of twenty species of cormous plants comes from South Africa. They have sword-shaped leaves and spikes of six-tepalled, crocus-like flowers in winter and spring.

F. × kewensis (*F. × hybrida*), a cross between *F. armstrongii* and *F. refracta*, is the only freesia in general cultivation. It grows 40–60cm (16–24in) or more in height and bears 5cm (2in) long fragrant flowers in shades of red, pink, mauve, yellow and white. There are several named cultivars and seed strains. If the latter are sown in late spring they will bloom the following late autumn to winter.

Pot the corms in late summer for winter flowering, and mid-autumn for a spring display. Maintain a minimum temperature of 7°–10°C (45°–50°F), nearer to the upper limit for winter blooming. Place in full light; a really sunny site is essential for the development of sturdy plants. Support with twiggy sticks if necessary. Dry off in summer and store in the pots in a warm place.

GLORIOSA (from the Latin *gloriosus*, glorious)

This is a genus of five species of tuberous plants from Africa and Asia. The slender flexible stems bear glossy oblong-lanceolate leaves which taper to a long point, each tipped by a small hooklike tendril. The flowers are reminiscent of those of a Turk's cap lily, but the six tepals at times are less reflexed, sometimes waved or

(Below left) *Eucomis autumnalis*
(Below) *Freesia × kewensis*

Gloriosa rothschildiana

crimped. They are borne on long stalks from the upper leaf-axils and are very showy.

Probably the best known species is G. *rothschildiana*, which usually grows to at least 2m (6½ft) in height from mature tubers. The leaves are up to 18cm (7in) long and the flowers have yellow-margined red tepals up to 7.5cm (3in) long. However, this is botanically regarded as a form of G. *superba*, the typical form of which has very narrow tepals with markedly waved and crimped margins.

Pot the tubers in spring and maintain a minimum temperature around 13°–16°C (55°–61°F). Provide light shade during the hottest summer spells. Use twiggy sticks, canes or netting for support. Keep the plants moist during the growing season but do not overwater. Dry them off in the autumn and store them in their pots at not less than 7°C (45°F). Propagate by offsets or seed.

HABRANTHUS (from the Greek *habros*, pretty or graceful, and *anthos*, a flower)
This genus of twenty bulbous species is allied to *Hippeastrum* and *Zephyranthes* and comes from subtropical and tropical America. They have strap-shaped leaves and erect naked stems bearing a solitary, six-tepalled, funnel-shaped flower.

H. *tubispathus* is rarely more than 15cm (6in) and produces yellow, coppery-red, striped or flushed flowers about 4cm (1½in) long. H. *brachyandrus* (*Hippeastrum brachyandrus*) grows to 30cm (1ft) in height with mauve-pink blooms up to 7.5cm (3in) long. Best

known is H. *robustus* (*Zephyranthes robusta*), which tends to produce its pink to rose-red 6cm (2½in) long flowers before the new leaves in autumn.

Pot in spring, then allow them to become crowded before repotting. Keep at a minimum temperature of 7°–10°C (45°–50°F) and in bright light. Propagate by offsets or seed.

HAEMANTHUS (from the Greek *haima*, blood, and *anthos*, a flower, referring to the fact that most species have red blooms)
This genus of about fifty species of bulbs comes from tropical and southern Africa, Arabia and Socotra. Some species have small flower-heads that resemble a shaving brush, subtended by persistent, sometimes coloured bracts. Others bear globular flower heads and are known as fireball lilies; some botanists place them in a separate genus, *Scadoxus*.

Unlike most other species, H. *albiflos* has white flowers in shaving-brush heads to 5cm (2in) wide. The evergreen leaves are tongue-shaped and fringed with white hairs. It is a surprisingly tolerant house plant. H. *katherinae* and H. *multiflorus* are true fireball lilies with spherical umbels of red flowers up to 15cm (6in) wide in

spring and summer. The deciduous leaves are oblong to lanceolate with distinct stalks. *H. coccineus* has massive strap-shaped leaves up to 60cm (2ft) in length and coral red shaving-brushes to 7.5cm (3in) in width in autumn before the new leaves appear.

Pot or repot in spring or when dormant, then leave them for several years before disturbing them again. Keep the tops of the bulbs above soil level and water very sparingly until new growth commences. Provide a minimum temperature of 10°C (50°F) and shade from the hottest summer sun. Propagation is by offsets or seed.

HIPPEASTRUM (from the Greek *hippos*, a horse and *hippeus*, a rider, referring to the buds and bractlike spathes which are thought to resemble the head of a horse)

This genus of seventy-five species of bulbs from Central and South America is popularly known as amaryllis. Each bulb produces a sheaf of strap-shaped arching leaves and an erect stem bearing one to several six-tepalled lilylike flowers.

Most popular of the tropical hippeastrums is the large-flowered race of hybrids listed under *H. × ackermannii*. These are derived from *H. aulicum*, *H.*

reticulatum, *H. striatum* and others and produce robust stems 45–60cm (1½–2ft) or more in height topped by two to four huge, thick-textured blooms in shades of red, pink, orange, white and striped bi-colours which appear mainly from late winter to late spring. *H. advenum*, *H. puniceum* and *H. pratense* are 'hardier', warm temperate species with smaller but more elegant flowers in shades of red. The first blooms in winter, the second in winter and spring, and the third in late spring.

Pot the bulbs when dormant and disturb them as little as possible. Maintain a night minimum temperature of 10°C (50°F), although 7°C (45°F) is acceptable for the warm temperate species. Screen from the hottest summer sun. Dry off the plants in later summer and keep them warm. Propagation is by offsets and seed. Seedlings can be grown on without a rest period and will flower in less than two years.

HOMERIA (from the Greek *homereo*, to meet, referring to the stamen filaments which are joined together to form a tube)

This is a genus of forty species of cormous plants from South Africa. Each corm throws up one to four stiff grassy leaves and a slender branched stem bearing

(Left) Hybrids of *Hippeastrum* flowering at Kew. (Above) *Homeria collina* 'Aurantiaca'

spindle-shaped green bracts. From the latter emerge one to several six-tepalled, bowl-shaped blooms in summer.

The only species likely to be encountered in cultivation is *H. collina* (*H. breyniana*), which has two to four leaves, stems about 45cm (1½ft) tall and 5cm (2in) wide flowers in shades of pink, yellow or cream. *H.c.* 'Aurantiaca' is orange-red.

Pot the corms annually in late autumn or early spring and maintain a minimum temperature of 7°C (45°F). Provide full light. Dry off when the leaves yellow in late summer. Propagate by offsets or seed.

HYMENOCALLIS (from the Greek *hymen*, a membrane, and *kallos*, beautiful, referring to the corona which is formed from membranous outgrowths of the stamens).

This genus of about thirty species of bulbs comes from the southern USA, Central and South America. They are allied to *Eucharis*, but the leaves are strap-shaped and the white or yellow flowers like spidery daffodils.

Best known is the hybrid *H. × festalis* (*Ismene × festalis*), which resembles one of its parents, *H. narcissiflora*, but is more vigorous and has longer stamens. *H. × macrostephana* also has *H. narcissiflora* as one parent. It grows 60cm (2ft) tall and has white fragrant blooms with coronas up to 7cm (2¾in) long in summer. *H. narcissiflora* also attains 60cm (2ft), bearing flowers with 5cm (2in) long coronas with stamens projecting well beyond.

Pot the bulbs in spring, leaving the necks just above the soil. Provide a minimum temperature of 7°–10°C (45°–50°F) and screen them from the hottest summer sun. Water freely when in full growth but keep on the dryish side in winter. Propagation is by offsets.

IXIA (the Greek word for bird lime, referring to the plants' sticky sap)

This is a genus of thirty to forty species of cormous plants from South Africa. Each corm produces a narrow fan of sword-shaped leaves and wiry-stemmed racemes of crocuslike flowers in late spring.

(Left) *Hymenocallis × festalis*
(Above) *Ixia* hybrids

The most freely available and decorative ixias are usually sold without a specific name or sometimes as hybrids. Derived from at least three species, they reach a minimum of 60cm (2ft) in height and produce 4–5cm (1½–2in) wide flowers in shades of purple, red, pink, orange, yellow and white. *I. viridiflora* is a little smaller in all its parts and produces blooms in a remarkable metallic blue-green with a contrasting purple-black eye.

Pot the corms in autumn and provide a winter minimum temperature of 7°C (45°F). Full light is essential, especially in winter. Dry off when the leaves yellow in summer. Propagate by offsets or seed.

LACHENALIA (named after Werner de la Chenal, 1736–1800, a professor of botany at Basle)

This genus of fifty species of bulbs comes from South Africa. Depending on the species, each bulb produces one to three strap-shaped, channelled leaves which may be spotted or mottled in a darker hue. The tubular bell-shaped six-tepalled blooms are carried in racemes above the foliage from late winter to spring.

Among the showiest and easiest species to grow is *L.*

aloides (*tricolor*), which has stems 15–25cm (6–10in) tall, bearing pendent 2.5cm (1in) long bells which are mainly yellow with orange-red bases and red-purple tips. *L.a.* 'Aurea' is orange-yellow throughout and 'Nelsonii' has green-tipped bright yellow blooms in longer racemes. *L. bulbifera* (*pendula*) is similar in its growth habit but has coral-red to vermilion flowers. *L. orchioides* produces dense racemes of 1cm (⅖in) long bells which face outwards or slightly upwards. It is variable in colouring but usually an iridescent blue-green and cream-tinted mauve. *L. reflexa* has reflexed leaves and short racemes of erect, green-tinted yellow blooms.

Pot the bulbs in early to mid-autumn and provide a minimum temperature of 7°–10°C (45°–50°F) and full light. Water with care, as over-wet conditions can promote root rot. Dry off when the leaves yellow in early summer. Propagate by offsets or seed.

LAPEIROUSIA (*Lapeyrousia*) (named after Baron Philippe Picot de la Peyrouse, 1744–1818, a Pyrenean botanist)
This genus of about fifty species of cormous plants comes from South Africa. They have narrow, sickle- or sword-shaped leaves and branched spikes of wide open six-tepalled flowers with slender tubular bases.

Leucocoryne ixioides

L. laxa (which is now more correctly known as *Anomatheca laxa*) is the only species generally available. Easily grown, 13–20cm (5–8in) tall, it bears 2.5cm (1in) long flowers of light carmine-crimson with darker basal spots in summer and early autumn, sometimes earlier or later depending on the temperature. *L.l.* 'Alba' has white blooms.

Pot in early spring and keep at a minimum of 7°C (45°F) and full light. Dry off in late autumn and store frost-free. Propagate by seed or offsets.

LEUCOCORYNE (from the Greek *leukos*, white, and *koryne*, a club, referring to the sterile stamens)
This is a genus of five or six species of bulbous plants from Chile. They have linear leaves and umbels of six-tepalled, upwards-facing wide open flowers in spring or early summer.

Sometimes known as glory of the sun, *L. ixioides* attains 30–40cm (12–16in) in height and produces umbels of six to ten starry flowers, each one 4cm (1½in) wide, milky-blue and with a sweet scent. *L. purpurea* differs in having more rounded blooms of lilac-purple with reddish centres.

Pot the bulbs in autumn and keep them in full light at a minimum temperature of 10°C (50°F). Dry them off when the leaves yellow and keep them warm. Propagation is by offsets or seed.

LILIUM (from the Latin vernacular name for the Madonna lily)

This genus of about eighty species of bulbs is distributed throughout the northern hemisphere. They have erect unbranched stems clad with mainly narrow leaves and topped by a raceme of comparatively large, six-tepalled flowers in the form of trumpets, stars, bowls or Turk's caps. In general they are hardy garden plants, but they respond well to pot culture and make splendid greenhouse or conservatory plants, blooming ahead of their normal season. In addition there are a few species which thrive best in a frost-free environment.

The best-known tender species is the Easter lily, *L. longiflorum*, which grows to 90cm (3ft) in height and bears pure white fragrant trumpets 13–18cm (5¼–7in) long in summer. *L. formosanum* (*L. philippinense* var. *formosanum*) is similar but has narrower leaves and flowers purple-flushed in bud.

Pot the bulbs in autumn or early winter, covering them with at least 10cm (4in) of compost to facilitate stem rooting. Place in a frame or greenhouse which is kept just frost-free. In late winter or early spring provide a minimum temperature of 5°–7°C (41°–45°F). Screen

Lilium longiflorum

from direct sunlight from late spring onwards. To speed the time of flowering increase the minimum temperature but do not exceed 13°C (55°F). Propagate by offsets or seed.

LITTONIA (named after Dr Samuel Litton, 1779–1847, a professor of botany at Dublin)

A genus of six or more species of tuberous climbing plants from Africa and Arabia. In growth habit they are exactly like *Gloriosa* but the six-tepalled flowers are bowl-shaped and nodding. Cultivation is as for *Gloriosa*.

L. modesta from South Africa, is the only species in general cultivation. It grows 1.5m (5ft) tall, sometimes more, with 4cm (1½in) wide bright orange blooms in summer and early autumn.

LYCORIS (from the Roman actress of that name, mistress of Mark Antony)

This genus of ten species of bulbs is distributed from the eastern Himalayas to Japan. They are similar to *Nerine*, having strap-shaped leaves and umbels of flowers formed of elegantly waved tepals and long, curving stamens, opening in late summer.

Easiest to flower is *L. squamigera*, which has stems 45–70cm (18–28in) tall and fragrant rosy-lilac flowers like a blend between *Nerine* and *Amaryllis*. *L. africana* (*L. aurea*) is little more than half as tall with yellow or yellow and orange flowers up to 7.5cm (3in) long (including stamens). *L. radiata* is similar but has bright red blooms, while *L.r.* 'Alba' (*L. alba*) is pure white.

Pot or repot in early spring or when dormant, and once established avoid disturbing the root system for several years. Maintain a night minimum temperature of 7°C (45°F) and place in full light. At the end of the growing season, when the leaves begin to yellow, dry off until growth starts again naturally. Unless the plants get plenty of sun and warmth in the growing season they will not bloom. Propagate by offsets.

MORAEA (for Robert More, an eighteenth-century British amateur botanist)

This genus of about 100 species of cormous perennials comes from tropical and southern Africa. They are very closely allied to *Iris* but the flowers lack tubular bases. They are best grown in a greenhouse or conservatory but can be brought indoors when in bloom.

Showiest of the cultivated species is *M. neopavonia* (*M. pavonia*), the so-called peacock iris. It has linear leaves, usually only one per corm, and a branched stem which grows to 60cm (2ft). The 6cm (2½in) wide flowers are bright orange-red, the falls bearing an iridescent bluish-black spot like the eye in the tail of a peacock. *M. spathulata* (*M. spathacea*) has one sword-shaped leaf and bright yellow fragrant blooms about 5cm (2in) across which appear in early summer.

Ornithogalum thyrsoides

Pot the corms in autumn and maintain a minimum temperature of 5°–7°C (41°–45°F). Provide a sunny position and water with care, especially in winter. Dry off when the leaves start to fade in summer.

NERINE (named after *Nereis*, the Greek water nymph. The first species to be described was brought ashore in Guernsey from a foundering ship.)
This is a genus of at least twenty species of bulbs from South Africa. They have strap-shaped leaves and erect, naked, unbranched stems topped by an umbel of flowers. Each bloom is composed of six, spreading, often wavy tepals with a lustrous texture. Late summer to early winter is the usual flowering period.

The most colourful and attractive species is *N. sarniensis*. Well grown it can reach 60cm (2ft) in height and bears umbels of up to eight flowers each with red or pink tepals up to 4cm (1½in) long. Many of the finest cultivar nerines have this as one parent. *N. flexuosa* has larger heads of smaller pink flowers; *N.f.* 'Alba' is white. *N. undulata* (*N. crispa* of gardens) has flowers with intriguingly crimped 2.5cm (1in) long tepals of delicate pink on stems 20–40cm (8–16in) in height.

Pot the bulbs immediately after flowering or before the new leaves develop. Flowering is best on undisturbed plants so do not repot or divide clumps more than every three or four years. Water freely when in full leaf, sparingly at other times and dry off when the leaves yellow. Keep at a minimum temperature of 5°–7°C (41°–45°F) in full light. Propagate by offsets or by sowing seeds, which are fleshy, as soon as they are ripe, otherwise they will soon lose their viability.

ORNITHOGALUM (from the Greek *ornis*, a bird, and *gala*, milk, reputedly referring to the excreta of doves) This genus of at least 100 species of bulbs comes from Africa, Europe and Asia. Each bulb produces one to several linear or strap-shaped leaves and a raceme of six-tepalled, mainly starry flowers usually on a theme of white and green. Many species are hardy garden plants but some of the finest are tender and make handsome pot plants.

Best known and among the finest is *O. thyrsoides*, the South African chincherinchee, with racemes of very long-lasting white flowers from a plant which attains 45cm (1½ft) or more in height. *O.t.* var. *aureum* is a little less robust with yellow or orange blooms. Also good is the fragrant *O. arabicum*, which has pearly white flowers with black-green pistils. *O. saundersiae* is similar but taller, well grown specimens can reach 1.2m (4ft) or more. It is sometimes called the giant chincherinchee.

Pot in early to late autumn or when dormant and maintain a minimum temperature of 5°–7°C (41°–45°F). Screen from the hottest summer sun. Propagate by offsets or seed.

POLIANTHES (from the Greek *polios*, whitish or grey, and *anthos*, a flower)

This is a genus of twelve species from Mexico. They are rhizomatous perennials with strap-shaped pointed leaves and erect racemes of narrowly funnel-shaped six-tepalled blooms.

(Left) *Polianthes tuberosa*
(Above) *Sandersonia aurantiaca*

The tuberose, *P. tuberosa*, is the only species commonly cultivated. It has racemes of richly fragrant, creamy white flowers 5cm (2in) or more long in summer and autumn. *P.t.* 'The Pearl' ('Plena') has double blooms. Plants raised from seed or division in temperate countries rarely bloom satisfactorily and it is best to purchase freshly imported rhizomes annually.

Pot in spring and provide a minimum temperature of 13°–16°C (55°–61°F). Place in full sun. Water freely when in full growth and dry off in late autumn.

SANDERSONIA (named after John Sanderson, a nineteenth-century secretary of the Horticultural Society of Natal and the original finder of this plant)

This is a genus of one species of tuberous perennials related to *Gloriosa* and *Littonia*. Cultivate as for *Gloriosa*.

S. aurantiaca has slender, flexible stems 30–90cm (1–3ft) in length. The lanceolate leaves taper to a point, the upper ones terminating in a small hooklike tendril. Each pendent flower is widely urn-shaped 2.5–4cm (1–1½in) long, rather like an orange Chinese lantern, opening in summer.

SAUROMATUM (from the Greek *sauros*, a lizard, referring to the mottled pattern within the spathe)

This genus of four to six species of tuberous plants comes from tropical Africa and Asia to west Malaysia. Each large rounded tuber produces a single long-stalked, pedately lobed leaf and an arumlike inflorescence composed of a narrow spathe and a long slender spadix.

Popularly known as the voodoo lily, or monarch of the east, *S. guttatum* is the only readily available species. The leaf exceeds 30cm (1ft) in width and is divided into three lobes, the side ones cut into narrower segments. In spring when it is leafless, a 30cm (1ft) spathe emerges, which is greenish on the back and yellowish inside with deep purple spots and blotches. It quickly rolls back and gives off a smell of bad meat, so this plant may not be popular indoors.

The voodoo lily is essentially a 'fun' plant as it will flower without soil. It is best grown for its boldly handsome foliage.

Pot in late winter or spring before leaf growth starts. Provide a minimum winter temperature of around 7°C (45°F). Water freely when the plants are in growth, then dry them off as the leaf yellows in the autumn. Propagate by offsets.

Scadoxus see *Haemanthus*.

Sauromatum guttatum

SPARAXIS (from the Greek *sparassein*, to tear, referring to the torn, papery bracts beneath the flowers) This is a genus of five species of cormous plants from South Africa. They have narrow fans of slender, sword-shaped leaves and wiry, branched, erect stems carrying six-tepalled, somewhat crocuslike flowers.

The so-called harlequin flower, *S. tricolor*, is the only species generally grown. It attains 30–45cm (1–1½ft) in height and in late spring bears 5cm (2in) wide flowers in shades of purple, red, yellow and white, usually with purple-black centres.

Pot in autumn providing a night temperature of 5°–7°C (41°–45°F) and full light. Water with care, especially in winter. Dry off in summer when the leaves begin to yellow. Propagate by cormlets.

See also *Streptanthera*.

SPREKELIA (named after Johann Heinrich von Sprekelsen, 1691–1764, a German lawyer and keen amateur plantsman)
This genus of one species of bulb from Mexico is related to *Hippeastrum* and *Amaryllis*. Cultivate as for *Hippeastrum*.

The Jacobean or Aztec lily, *S. formosissima*, has strap-shaped leaves which die away in autumn. Just before, or as the new foliage appears in spring or early summer, bright crimson, 10cm (4in) long flowers appear singly, on 20–30cm (8–12in) tall stems. Each bloom is inclined, the six tepals arranged to create an orchid-like shape.

STENOMESSON (from the Greek *stenos*, narrow, and *mesos*, middle; in some the tubular blooms are waisted)
This is a genus of about twenty species of bulbs from tropical America. They are allied to and somewhat resemble *Phaedranassa*, but the leaves are linear and the flowers narrowly funnel-shaped. Cultivate as for *Hippeastrum*.

S. incarnatum is well worth seeking, producing 10cm (4in) long flowers in umbels of up to six on robust, erect stems to 60cm (2ft) in height. Each bloom is red, striped or marked with green and opens in late summer to late autumn.

STREPTANTHERA (from the Greek *streptos*, twisted, and *anthera*, an anther)
This genus of two cormous species comes from South Africa. They are like dwarf versions of *Sparaxis*, in which genus they are now more correctly included. Cultivate as for *Sparaxis*.

S. cuprea produces stems 15–23cm (6–9in) high and 5cm (2in) wide flowers of coppery pink with a purple eye and black-purple basal zone or white with yellow and purple eyes (the latter previously known as *S. elegans*). They are carried in short spikes in spring or early summer. *S.c.* var. *coccinea* is light orange.

Tecophilaea cyanocrocus

TECOPHILAEA (named after Tecophila Billiotti, a botanical artist and daughter of Luigi Colla, 1766–1848, a professor of botany at Turin)

This genus contains one species, a cormous perennial from Chile sometimes called the Chilean crocus, *T. cyanocrocus*. It has that rare colour among bulbous plants in general – pure, deep gentian blue. Each corm produces a few linear leaves and somewhat crocus-like six-tepalled blooms about 4cm (1½in) across, each with a white eye, in spring.

T.c. var. *leichtlinii* is a paler blue with a larger white eye, and var. *violacea* is entirely blue-purple. The Chilean crocus is essentially a cool greenhouse plant but can be put in a sunny window while in bloom. It is almost certainly extinct in the wild and now exists only in cultivation.

Pot or repot in the autumn and provide a minimum temperature of around 5°C (41°F) and full light. Water with care at all times as an over-wet rooting medium can lead to corm and root rot. Dry off in summer and store warm in the greenhouse or home. Propagation is by offsets or seed.

TIGRIDIA (from the Greek *tigris*, a tiger, referring to the patterning on the tepals; early Spanish explorers in Central America confused the spotted jaguar with the striped tiger of Asia)

This genus of about twenty-seven species of bulbs comes from Mexico and Chile. They form fanlike tufts of narrow leaves and bear showy, somewhat iris-like flowers in summer.

The common tiger or peacock flower, *T. pavonia*, is the showiest species in cultivation, with intriguingly pleated leaves and stems 30–40cm (1–1ft4in) in height. Each 8–13cm (3¼–5in) wide flower has a bowl-shaped base, three large spreading outer tepals and three much smaller inner ones. Red is the main colour with a yellow centre and purple spotting, but colour mixtures are now available covering shades of red, orange, yellow and white.

Pot in the spring, maintain a minimum temperature of 7°–10°C (45°–50°F) and place in full light. Water freely when in full growth, sparingly at other times, and dry off in the autumn. Store in frost-free conditions. Propagate by offsets or seed.

TRITONIA (from the Greek *triton*, a weathercock, referring to the positioning of the stamens)
This genus of possibly fifty species of cormous plants comes from tropical and southern Africa. They are reminiscent of freesias and are allied to that genus, *Ixia* and *Sparaxis*. Cultivate as for *Freesia*.

Best known are the South African species, notably *T. crocata*. This species grows to 30–45cm (1–1½ft) in height and has bright tawny-yellow blooms which open to 5cm (2in) or more in width in late spring or early summer. *T.c.* var. *miniata* produces smaller, bright red flowers. Another form is orange, the spathulate tepals having an almost transparent margin.

VALLOTA (named after Pierre Vallot, 1594–1671, a French doctor and botanist)
This genus of one bulbous species comes from South Africa. Though allied to *Cyrtanthus*, and now usually treated as such by botanists, it more nearly resembles a small *Hippeastrum*. Sometimes called the Scarborough lily, *V. speciosa* (*V. purpurea*) has strap-shaped leaves which are present the year round. In late summer and autumn umbels of three to ten flowers are borne on stems 40–60cm (16–24in) in height. Each bloom is funnel-shaped, and is composed of six bright red tepals

Vallota speciosa

7–10cm (2¾–4in) long.

Pot or repot in spring but do it as little as necessary as root disturbance is resented. Maintain a minimum night temperature around 7°C (45°F) and provide full light, although some shade during the hottest summer period is acceptable. Water moderately throughout the year but less in winter. Propagate by offsets.

VELTHEIMIA (named after August Ferdinand von Veltheim, 1741–1801, a German patron of botany)
This genus of two species of bulbs comes from South Africa. Each bulb forms a rosette of substantial, widely strap-shaped leaves and a sturdy, erect, naked stem topped by a raceme of pendent tubular flowers reminiscent of a red-hot poker (*Kniphofia*).

Most commonly seen is *V. bracteata* (*V. undulata, V. viridiflora* and sometimes erroneously as *V. capensis*). It has wavy-margined, glossy rich green leaves and 30cm (1ft) tall racemes of 3–4cm (1¼–1½in) long flowers. They are light rosy-purple, speckled with yellow and appear in summer. *V.b.* 'Rosalba' produces white flowers flushed pink at the base. *V. capensis* (*V. glauca*) has glaucous leaves and 2.5cm (1in) long pale pink flowers tipped with green. Yellow- and red-flowered forms have been recorded. It is confused in cultivation with *V. bracteata* despite the obvious differences between them.

Pot in late summer or early autumn and provide a winter minimum temperature of around 7°C (45°F). Place in full light. *V. bracteata* is more or less evergreen and should be watered throughout the year though sparingly in winter. *V. capensis* dies back in early summer and should be kept dry until the autumn. Propagate by offsets or seed.

WATSONIA (named after Sir William Watson, 1715–87, a British doctor and scientist)
This genus of sixty to seventy species of cormous perennials comes from South Africa. They produce fanlike tufts of sword-shaped, six-lobed flowers. Being tall, they make fine plants for the conservatory.

Very attractive and easily obtainable is *W. pyramidata* (*W. rosea*), which can attain 1.5m (5ft) in height, although usually less. The 7.5–10cm (3–4in) long flowers may be deep pink or rose-red and open in summer. *W. beatricis* is 30cm (1ft) shorter and has orange-red blooms about 5cm (2in) long in late summer. *W. mariana* has flowers which vary in colour from rose-red to pink and white. This species was previously known as *W. ardernei*. They seldom grow taller than 1m (3ft 3in) and flower in early summer.

Pot or repot in early spring and provide a night minimum temperature of 7°C (45°F) and full light. Water freely when in full growth but keep the plants almost dry when dormant in winter. Propagate by offsets, or cormlets, or seed.

Zantedeschia aethiopica 'Green Goddess'

ZANTEDESCHIA (named after Francesco Zantedeschi, 1797–1873, an Italian botanist)
This is a genus of about six species of plant with tuber-like rhizomes from tropical to southern Africa. They produce long-stalked, saggitate to lanceolate leaves and tiny petalless flowers enclosed within a cornucopia-shaped coloured spathe.

Best known is the so-called arum or calla lily, *Z. aethiopica* (*Richardia africana*), a robust plant growing to 1m (3ft 3in) in height, though usually less. It has large, shining, rich green, saggitate leaves and pure white spathes 13–25cm (5–10in) long, sporadically through the year but mainly in spring and summer. *Z.a.* 'Green Goddess' has spathes lined and flushed with green, 'Minor' and 'Childsiana' are smaller growing. *Z. elliottiana* grows to 60cm (2ft) in height with dark green, ovate-cordate leaves bearing translucent white spots. The golden yellow spathes are up to 15cm (6in) in length and appear from late spring or early summer onwards depending on the temperature. *Z. rehmannii* rarely exceeds 40cm (16in) tall and has lanceolate leaves and red to purple or pinkish spathes 7–13cm ($2\frac{3}{4}$–$5\frac{1}{4}$in) long. It has been crossed with *Z. elliottiana* to create a multicoloured race of hybrids.

FURTHER INFORMATION

Bibliography

There are no books dealing exclusively with tender bulbs but the following provide further sources of reference and illustrations:

Beckett, K. A., *The R.H.S. Encyclopaedia of House Plants—including conservatory plants* (Century Hutchinson, 1987)

Chittenden, F. J., *The R.H.S. Dictionary of Gardening* (4 vols and a supplement, Royal Horticultural Society, 1951, 1969)

Everett, T. H., *The New York Botanical Gardens Illustrated Encyclopedia of Horticulture* (10 vols, Garland Publishing, 1980–1982)

Mathew, Brian, *Dwarf Bulbs* (Batsford, 1973)

—, *The Larger Bulbs* (Batsford, 1978)

Mason, Hilda, *Western Cape Sandveld Flowers* (C. Struik, 1972)

Rix, Martyn, *Growing Bulbs* (Croom Helm Ltd, 1983)

Synge, Patrick M., *Collins Guide to Bulbs* (Collins, rev. edn, 1961)

Pot in autumn and maintain a winter minimum temperature of 7°–10°C (45°–50°F). Place in full light in winter but shade from the hottest sun when in bloom. Water freely when in full leaf, moderately at other times. With the exception of *Z. aethiopica*, dry off when the leaves yellow in summer and store in their pots in warmth. Propagate by offsets or seed.

ZEPHYRANTHES (from the Greek *zephyros*, the west wind, and *anthos*, a flower, presumably referring to their western hemisphere origins)

This genus of about forty bulbous species comes from the warmer parts of the Americas. They much resemble and are closely related to *Habranthus* with their linear leaves and six-tepalled crocuslike blooms. Cultivate as for *Habranthus*.

The most popular species is *Z. grandiflora* with 6.5–10cm (2½–4in) long blooms ranging from pink to rose red on stems 20cm (8in) in height from late summer onwards.

PLANTS FOR SPECIAL PURPOSES

LIGHT REQUIREMENTS

Shady situation	Direct sunlight
Arisaema	Alstroemeria
Begonia sutherlandii	Babiana
Crinum asiaticum	Brodiaea
Cyclamen	Eucomis
Eucharis	Freesia
Hymenocallis	Haemanthus
Lilium	Lachenalia
Sauromatum	Leucocoryne
Veltheimia bracteata	Lycoris
Zantedeschia	Sparaxis
aethiopica	Tecophilaea
	Tritonia

EASE OF CULTIVATION

Suitable for beginners	Moderately easy
Begonia	Alstroemeria
Canna	Amaryllis
Eucomis	Arisaema
Freesia	Babiana
Habranthus	Brodiaea
Hippeastrum	Chlidanthus
Ixia	Crinum
Lapeirousia	Cyclamen
Ornithogalum	Eucharis
Sauromatum	Gloriosa
Sparaxis	Haemanthus
Tigridia	Homeria
Vallota	Hymenocallis
Zantedeschia	Lachenalia
Zephyranthes	Lilium
	Nerine
	Polianthes
	Sprekelia
	Veltheimia

GOOD FOLIAGE

Cyclamen	Sauromatum
Eucomis	Veltheimia
Haemanthus	Zantedeschia
Lachenalia aloides	

LARGE FLOWERS

Alstroemeria pelegrina
A. violacea
Amaryllis
Begonia × tuberhybrida
Crinum
Gloriosa
Haemanthus
Hippeastrum
Lilium
Sprekelia
Tigridia
Vallota
Zantedeschia

SCENTED FLOWERS

Arisaema candidissima
Chlidanthus
Cyclamen, some cvs
Eucharis
Freesia
Hymenocallis
Lilium longiflorum
Polianthes
Zantedeschia
aethiopica

LONG FLOWERING PERIOD

Alstroemeria
Begonia
Canna
Cyclamen
Eucharis
Eucomis
Freesia
Lachenalia
Lapeirousia
Lilium
Nerine
Ornithogalum
Polianthes

SPRING FLOWERING:

Allium	Leucocoryne
Alstroemeria	Lilium
Babiana	Sauromatum
Cyclamen	Sparaxis
Cyrtanthus	Sprekelia
Eucharis	Streptanthera
Freesia	Tecophilaea
Hippeastrum	Tritonia
Lachenalia	Zantedeschia

SUMMER FLOWERING:

Alstroemeria	Littonia
Arisaema	Lycoris
Begonia	Moraea
Brodiaea	Ornithogalum
Canna	Sandersonia
Chlidanthus	Sparaxis
Crinum	Sprekelia
Cyrtanthus	Stenomesson
Eucharis	Streptanthera
Gloriosa	Tigridia
Habranthus	Tritonia
Homeria	Vallota
Hymenocallis	Veltheimia
Lapeirousia	Watsonia
Lilium	Zantedeschia

AUTUMN FLOWERING:

Amaryllis	Lapeirousia
Canna	Nerine
× Crinodonna	Stenomesson
Crinum	Vallota
Cyclamen	Watsonia
Eucharis	Zantedeschia
Habranthus	aethiopica

WINTER FLOWERING:

Cyclamen	Lachenalia
Freesia	Nerine
Hippeastrum	Zantedeschia

CARNIVOROUS PLANTS

SINCE THE dawn of time green plants have been the basic food source of animals. The mobility of animals has allowed them to exploit plants wherever they grow, chewing and grinding their leaves, stems, roots, fruits and seeds, robbing their pollen and even sucking their sap. But carnivorous plants have modified their leaves, stems and sometimes roots to form elaborate traps, by which they are able to turn the tables on animals and utilize them as a food source.

The range of animals caught by carnivorous plants is obviously limited by the size of the plants and the traps. Flying and crawling insects are unquestionably the chief prey and may range in size from midges to cockroaches. Invertebrates other than insects are, however, frequently caught and, in greenhouses, the remains of woodlice and millepedes are often found in the pitchers of *Nepenthes* and *Sarracenia*. The efficiency of the traps is quite astonishing; the white-topped American pitcher plant *Sarracenia leucophylla*, for example, is so adept that in the wet meadows of the south coastal plains of Georgia, its native homeland, the 60cm (2ft) high pitchers may become full to the brim with insect remains. No less successful are the sundews, *Drosera anglica*. In Norfolk in August 1911 it was recorded that colonies of these plants along the east coast ensnared an estimated six million cabbage white butterflies arriving from their continental breeding grounds.

Mice, frogs, tadpoles, fish fry and even small birds have been reported as hapless victims, and therefore the term carnivorous, rather than insectivorous, is preferred for plants of this kind.

(Above) *Utricularia reniformis* (Opposite) *Sarracenia purpurea*

It must not be assumed, however, that carnivorous plants are dependent upon, or even require, insects at all for their successful cultivation, for they do not. In the home or the greenhouse they are able to grow perfectly well without them, when the growing conditions are satisfactory.

In nature, the distribution of carnivorous plants is worldwide; they are found on every continent and in a wide variety of environments including tropical rain forests, ponds, ditches, wet savannah and even semi-deserts and Arctic tundra. But it is chiefly in the acid boglands of the world that the carnivorous habit has evolved in certain plant families, thereby enabling them to supplement their diet from the bodies of the insects they catch. It appears to be nitrogen which is in short supply in the habitats where such plants are found, and nitrogen is undoubtedly the major element obtained from insect tissues, although phosphorus and other minerals and vitamins are possibly also utilized.

The discovery of the spectacular Venus' fly trap in the New World in 1765, and the astonishing evidence it presented that nature could mould plant leaves into vegetable gin-traps, capable of snapping shut on unsuspecting intruders, heralded much speculation about flesh-eating vegetation.

The early nineteenth century was a fertile period for newspaper accounts of the supposed discovery in far-off lands of man-eating plants. Artistic licence and the Victorian fascination with the macabre led to illustrations of bloodthirsty trees bedecked with the empty skulls of unfortunate explorers, and even the sacrificing of a maiden or two to tentacle-waving, clamlike plants. This was considered good newspaper copy and led ultimately and inevitably to the all-devouring triffids of science fiction.

By Darwin's time, however, knowledge had replaced the myths, and the ability of a variety of plants to attract, ensnare and digest a wide range of insects and similar small invertebrates was well established. Careful experiments by Darwin and others proved conclusively that such plants were able to benefit from the tissues of the animals they caught and, moreover, that they could respond to different forms of animal protein.

Special features of the plants

The evolution of carnivorous plants is complex and beyond the scope of this book. It is, however, appropriate to consider their characteristics, which are the capacity to attract, ensnare, digest and finally utilize the insects or other small animal prey found in their natural habitats. Whatever the form of the vegetable trap, a prerequisite for a carnivorous existence appears to be the presence of specialized glands for the secretion of digestive enzymes and the resorption of the products of digestion. Not all species secrete digestive enzymes, however, and some such as *Darlingtonia* and *Heliamphora* rely on the action of bacteria to break down their

Dionaea muscipula, the Venus fly trap, an example of an active trap, showing an enlargement of the trigger hairs which close the trap.

prey. Many plants are able to attract and ensnare insects, without being able to benefit from them. The viscid leaves and stems of *Silene* (catchfly) is a typical example. Petunias and the scented-leaved pelargoniums of southern Africa also afford examples of the seemingly endless variety of plants providing a sticky but less advantageous end to crawling and winged insects of many kinds.

Not the least fascinating aspect of the cultivation of carnivorous plants is the opportunity to observe the development and function of their ingenious traps and remarkably beautiful flowers.

The trapping mechanisms may be active or passive, depending upon whether or not the trap parts actually move to ensnare the insect. The most popular and obviously active is the Venus' fly trap, *Dionaea muscipula*. Charles Darwin was so impressed by the form and rapid movement of this vegetable gin-trap that he described it as 'the most wonderful plant in the world'. The 'waterwheel plant', *Aldrovanda vesiculosa*, has traps similar to *Dionaea* but very much smaller and produced below water at the tips of the whorled and divided leaves, where they catch minute forms of aquatic animal life.

Sundews or *Drosera* species, often referred to as 'flypaper traps', are also active trappers, though in a less spectacular fashion, unless observed by time-lapse photography, when the glue-tipped stalks covering the leaf are seen to envelop the luckless insect in a progressive tentacle-like embrace.

The many species of butterwort, *Pinguicula*, exhibit an inward rolling of the leaf margins when excited by the struggles of insects entrapped on the surface of the mucilage-covered leaves, so these too must be considered active traps.

Of all the active trappers, however, the bladderworts, *Utricularia*, are truly remarkable in possessing the most rapid plant movements known. The traps, which are borne on parts that are usually below water, mud or wet moss, consist of small distended bladders with a hinged door guarding the entrance. Water fleas brush against trigger hairs attached to the door, which disturbs the seal of the door, causing it to open, the fleas are then swept into the bladders by the inward rush of water. In contrast to most carnivorous plants, there is no evidence that aquatic animals are attracted to the traps in any way, but rather that they blunder into the trigger hairs, giving structures of this kind the name 'blunder traps'.

Carnivorous plants with passive trap devices are far more common and include the so-called pitfall traps such as the *Nepenthes*, or pitcher plants. The pitchers may indeed be large enough to accommodate the bodies of small rodents and birds, although they are not the usual fare of such traps. The several species of trumpet pitchers or *Sarracenia* are also passive pitfall traps. They differ widely in size, form and coloration, but all consist of single leaves modified into elaborate and often beautiful hornlike shapes. The squat and curious Australian pitcher plant,

The trap of a *Sarracenia* cut down the middle. Inside the pitcher is an accumulation of dead, partially digested flies.

Cephalotus, and the elegant cobra plant, *Darlingtonia*, of the north-west USA, are again passive pitfall traps to which insects are enticed by colour and nectar-like secretions.

Cultural requirements

Despite the great variation of natural habitats in which carnivorous plants are found, it is perfectly possible to produce satisfactory growing conditions for many of them in the home and greenhouse, provided that certain basic requirements are met. Light, temperature and humidity are the three main factors controlling the growth of these plants in enclosed environments and, fortunately, they can be adjusted (within limits) to satisfy most carnivorous plant requirements.

Conditions in the home: Placing plants in situations where they benefit from a main light source (usually a window) will ensure they have the amount of light necessary for good growth. North, east, south and west aspects can all be used to good advantage, though direct sun through a south-facing (or north-facing in the southern hemisphere) window should be utilized with caution. It is quite acceptable to most carnivorous plants during the winter, but scorching and rapid drying out may be a problem during the summer months, when a move to east- or west-facing windows would be more acceptable. The amount of light reaching plants falls off rapidly as they are moved away from a window and, if they are to be grown far back in the room, supplementary artificial lighting will be required to prevent premature yellowing and etiolation. Illuminated growth cabinets and terrariums in a range of attractive designs are now easily obtainable in which the light source is provided by fluorescent tubes of suitable wattage.

Room temperatures may not be so easily adjustable, but placing the plants near a radiator can provide sufficient warmth. Proximity to windows on cold nights may result in temperature-related problems which can easily be avoided by temporarily moving the plants away from the windows, should frost threaten. In homes without central heating systems, growth cabinets with thermostat-controlled heating may well be the answer.

Atmospheric humidity is often all-important to the growth of carnivorous plants. In the home, this can be provided by placing pot-grown plants on trays of sand or gravel which is kept permanently moist. Deeper plastic or polythene-lined containers filled with moist peat, bark chips or moss may also be used. Plants grouped together in this way will also help to produce a more humid micro-climate. Needless to say, growth cabinets or even glass fish tanks are ideal for providing a close environment, and thereby increasing atmospheric humidity. When illuminated, they can also be very attractive features in the home. Regular spraying of the leaves with soft (rain) water is a traditional way of providing the moist growing conditions required by many plants.

Nepenthes alata 'Luzon'

This can be achieved with inexpensive plastic sprayers, which produce a fine mist-like spray, or by pump-action sprayers.

Conditions in the greenhouse: It is, of course, much easier to produce good growing conditions in a greenhouse than in the home. In the first place, all-round natural light is available to the plants, and this is particularly important during the winter months. Should shading from the summer sun be required, as with *Nepenthes* for example, it can be provided by wood-lath or woven green nylon blinds on a roller system fixed to the outside of the glass. Such systems may be operated manually or automatically when triggered by a photocell which switches on an electric motor. Green plastic sun blinds are also available which operate on the inside of the glass, but these are not always as satisfactory. To obtain maximum benefit from the winter sun, the siting of the greenhouse is particularly important and care should be taken to ensure that it is not shaded by trees or nearby structures.

Cooling the greenhouse atmosphere in summer is also easily controlled, by manual or automatic ventilators or even by electric extractor fans triggered by an adjustable thermostat.

The all-important atmospheric humidity can be provided by plastic pneumatic pump sprayers or by automatic misting jets positioned above the plants. Time-switches, photocells or hydrostats (electronic leaves) may be used to switch on the misting

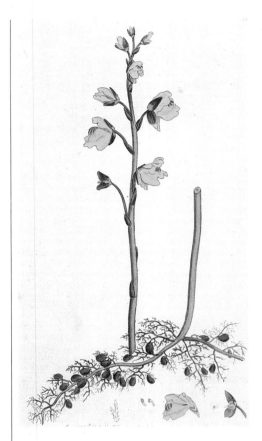

Utricularia vulgaris

jets as required. For most carnivorous plants, soft or non-alkaline water is essential, and with misting systems operated from the mains water supply, it will be necessary to check that the pH of the water has a reading of seven or below.

For carnivorous plants from temperate regions a minimum winter temperature of about 6°C (43°F) will be satisfactory. Winter heating can be provided by a variety of heaters ranging from portable paraffin kinds to gas-burning and electric fan types. Though more expensive in terms of running costs, electric heaters are fumeless, require little attention and have the advantage of being automatically operated by thermostats.

Tropical carnivorous plants such as *Nepenthes* and some *Utricularia* species require warmth throughout the winter months, and a minimum temperature of about 15°C (59°F) will be needed. In summer, heating may be necessary only at night and during cold damp spells. Measures to control heat loss from the greenhouse are well worth considering; these could be windbreaks, glazing with twin-wall polycarbonate and, within the greenhouse, thermal screens, polythene film and 'Bubbleair' inner linings.

Basic cultivation

Containers: There is little to choose between traditional clay or plastic flower pots; both kinds are quite suitable for the majority of terrestrial carnivorous plants which, generally speaking, have very modest root systems anyway. Because of the permanently moist conditions under which carnivorous plants are grown, however, clay pots do tend to become colonized with green algae whereas plastic pots do not. *Nepenthes* are generally best grown in slatted hardwood baskets, although clay orchid pots with holes around the sides are quite suitable, as are the slotted plastic baskets used for the cultivation of waterlilies. Half-pots are popular for the smaller rosette-forming sundews and shallow plastic seed trays may be used quite successfully for colonies of Venus' fly trap. Communal planting containers can be made from 12cm (4¾in) deep wooden boxes lined with polythene film or, alternatively, large rigid plastic trays approximately 10–12cm (4–4¾in) deep which may be purchased from garden centres and are traditionally used for the display of houseplants. Terrariums usually have a plastic tray base, which may be filled with a suitable compost in which the plants are arranged naturally and allowed a free root run.

Composts: The traditional loam-based and loamless composts used for most ornamental pot plants are, in general, not suitable for carnivorous plants, and it is important to ensure that the ingredients for their preparation are of a suitable kind. Peat, sand and moss are the chief ingredients from which the composts are made, but other materials are leaf mould, perlite, bark chips, loam fibre and charcoal. Peat should be of the granulated sphagnum kind; peats of sedge origin are rarely satisfactory because they are often somewhat alkaline. Sphagnum peat, which is normally purchased compressed into bales of varying sizes, will require breaking down and wetting before use. It is essential that the water used for this purpose, and indeed for all carnivorous plant uses, is non-alkaline; mains water may be quite unsatisfactory and must, therefore, always be tested to ascertain its degree of hardness. Rain water, distilled or de-ionized water is suitable, but not water obtained from a domestic water softener because of the possibility of the presence of toxic salts.

Suitable sands must be relatively large-grained, sharp and free from chalk and shell residues. Builders' sands are rarely suitable because of the fineness of the grains and the possible presence of impurities such as clay, silt, shell, etc.

The moss used for these plants is traditionally sphagnum moss, preferably fresh and green with a fair proportion of growing tips. The shoots should be laid together with the growing tips in the same direction; these may be broken off with approximately 2cm ($\frac{3}{4}$in) of stem and used, in certain cases, as a living surface layer once potting is completed. Though not essential, leaf mould is a most useful addition to many carnivorous plant composts but, again, it is important to ensure that it is of the right kind. Leaf mould prepared from oak leaves growing on neutral or acid soils is generally regarded as the best product. Avoid mould prepared from trees on alkaline soils, particularly beech. The leaves should be reasonably well decayed and, before use, it is advisable to pass the material through a 1cm ($\frac{2}{5}$in) sieve, removing any acorns or foreign matter.

Perlite is also a useful addition to certain composts, including those prepared for sundews, though make sure that it is a good horticultural grade and not of building or insulation quality. Medium-grade bark chips of the type used by orchid growers (as a substitute for osmunda fibre) is a new and useful material for incorporation into the composts for *Nepenthes*, which always requires an open and freely drained medium. It can also be used to bulk up the mix for planting beds in a terrarium or greenhouse. Loam fibre, the fibrous residue left from sieving loam for other purposes, is also a useful material for *Nepenthes*, which is traditionally grown as an epiphyte in teak orchid baskets suspended from the roof of the greenhouse. Charcoal has also long been valued as an ingredient of composts. It is reputed to be useful in preventing composts from becoming sour, and it undoubtedly helps to maintain their essential open nature.

Potting: As the days lengthen in early spring it is a good time to plant or repot. *Sarracenia* and *Darlingtonia* begin growth early in the year and must be handled before their drumstick-like flower buds are more than a few centimetres (an inch or two) high. The composts should be thoroughly mixed and moistened. Remove established plants carefully from their existing pots by supporting

Pinguicula grandiflora

Drosophyllum lusitanicum

the plant with two fingers placed on the compost either side of the crown, inverting the pot and tapping the rim sharply against the edge of a wooden bench or table to dislodge the rootball. Tease away the old compost, taking care not to damage any young roots. Finally, trim off any dead or decaying leaves or sections of rhizome with a sharp knife. Repot by placing a sufficient quantity of compost around the roots, which should be evenly spread out, and gently return the plant to a suitably sized pot. Finally, place the plants on a level surface, water thoroughly with a fine-rosed can and return to the appropriate position in the home or greenhouse.

Traditional crocking and drainage material is unnecessary for carnivorous plants, which generally require far wetter conditions than the majority of potted plants. Throughout potting operations never allow the plants to dry out; sprinkle or spray them with soft water immediately before and after potting. Potting-on (to larger containers, baskets etc.) is usually accomplished with a minimum of root disturbance but, as *Nepenthes* dislike being disturbed, they should be repotted only when absolutely necessary and frequent attention paid to syringing once the operation has been completed. *Drosophyllum* also resents being disturbed; seedlings are potted-on by enlarging the hole at the base of the pot and encouraging the tap-root system to grow through the hole into a pot of a larger size. In this way large woody-stemmed specimens, several years old and colonizing several pots, may be produced.

Certain carnivorous plants possess definite cycles of growth and rest which correspond to the wet and dry, or cold and warm seasons of their native habitats. With the onset of the dormant season, water is gradually withheld and the plants kept on the dry side until spring. Northern-hemisphere rosette *Drosera* species produce tight, winter-resting buds, as do the Australian pygmy sundews, with the onset of the dry season.

With the exception of the tuberous *Drosera* species and *Drosophyllum*, it is acceptable and most convenient to water pot-grown plants by capillarity, that is by immersing the base of the pot in water. Indeed, a suitably sized plastic tray with 3–6cm ($1\frac{1}{4}$–$2\frac{1}{2}$in) of water may be used with the pots stood permanently in the water. This arrangement will provide additional humidity around the plants and, by raising or lowering the pots on gravel or pieces of slate, the amount of water reaching the plant can be adjusted. With overhead watering it is usual to use a can with a fine rose. At each watering care should be taken to saturate the compost thoroughly. Living sphagnum moss, when mixed with the compost or used as a top-dressing, is a useful indicator of the moisture content of the compost; when dry it assumes a whitish green appearance, when wet it is a much brighter green.

Feeding: As a general rule carnivorous plants do not respond to feeding with fertilizers of any kind because they have adapted to low-nutrient conditions and may obtain their nutrients from the food they trap. However, *Nepenthes* does benefit from very dilute liquid feed which contains nitrogen and this may be given at ten- to fourteen-day intervals during the growing season.

In a greenhouse or living-room it is quite likely that insects will be caught, particularly during the warm summer months, so it should not be necessary to feed the plants deliberately. However, from a general-interest point of view, active carnivorous plants do respond to small amounts of any kind of animal protein such as milk, tiny pieces of cheese or meat. But this must not be overdone, otherwise the plant tissues will rot and the plants may die. Occasionally, large insects such as bluebottles are caught and, in the case of *Dionaea*, this results in the trap remaining closed until the softer parts of the insect have been digested. Traps which have caught a substantial insect or have been given a small piece of meat become sluggish and will hardly operate effectively again. Those which have been persuaded to close by simply disturbing the trigger hairs will reopen again within twenty-four hours, though repeated deception will eventually reduce the responsiveness of the trap.

Dionaea (Venus' fly trap) attracts its prey by colour and nectar. Tiny hairs inside the modified leaf trigger the trap mechanism when disturbed by an insect.

A fly trapped on a *Drosera* (sundew) leaf.

Propagation

There are various means of propagation, depending on the species; they range from stem, leaf and root cuttings, to division of the crowns and roots, to sowing seeds. A few species are self-propagating from gemmae, or small ancillary buds.

Stem propagation is suitable for *Aldrovanda* and *Nepenthes*. For the former, cut actively growing stems into 2cm ($\frac{3}{4}$in) lengths and plant them in finely sieved potting compost. With *Nepenthes* make sure that the shoots have at least two well-formed leaves and cut the stems with a basal cut below a leaf joint. Place the cuttings through the hole of an upturned 8cm ($3\frac{1}{4}$in) diameter clay pot filled with green sphagnum moss and keep it under close humid conditions. They should take six to eight weeks to root.

For some genera leaf cuttings can be prepared from whole leaves cut in spring and early summer, and placed in containers filled with living sphagnum moss rubbed through a fine sieve. This technique is suitable for *Cephalotus*, some species of *Drosera*, *Pinguicula* and *Dionaea*. With the last two remove the leaves complete with basal sheaths and maintain close atmospheric conditions while the cuttings are rooting. A small propagator is ideal. *Pinguicula* is also self-propagating by means of gemmae.

Root cuttings of 2cm ($\frac{3}{4}$in) can be taken from *Byblis gigantea*, *Cephalotus* and some species of *Drosera*. Take cuttings in late spring and cover them lightly with finely sieved compost.

Following a successful season's growth, *Dionaea*, *Pinguicula*, *Cephalotus*, *Heliamphora* and some *Drosera* species multiply their crowns, and these may be carefully separated and potted-off as individuals. Some plants, such as *Sarracenia*, require dividing; this is done by teasing or cutting apart the rhizomes, ensuring that a good, healthy, growing point and young roots are present with each division. *Drosera binata* and its variants possess bootlace-like root systems with crowns of young leaves. Any section of root is capable of forming new crowns, and by dividing up the roots into pieces 3–4cm ($1\frac{1}{4}$–$1\frac{1}{2}$in) long, large colonies can be quickly established. With *Darlingtonia* the young plants are divided from the parent plant complete with a portion of rhizome, taking care not to disturb the parent plant.

Seeds can be sown for *Byblis*, *Drosera*, *Drosophyllum*, *Nepenthes* and *Sarracenia*, in late spring. Using individual pots a small quantity of seed should be sown thinly on a compost of one part moss peat or leaf mould, one part light sandy loam and two parts sharp sand. Traditional clay pots are best, placing a small quantity of green sphagnum in the base of the pot before filling with compost. While most of the resulting seedlings can be grown on conventionally, those of *Drosophyllum* should be thinned, leaving three undisturbed seedlings to grow on. After one year's growth the drainage hole at the base of the pot should be enlarged, and the pot and its contents placed in a larger pot of the same compost. This technique allows the roots to penetrate into the larger pot without damage or disturbance. In this way plants may be kept growing for many years.

Pests and diseases

The only pests likely to be encountered are aphids (greenfly) and scale insects. Occasionally clusters of greenfly are found early in the growing season on the young leaves and growing points of *Sarracenia* and *Dionaea*. As soon as they are observed, they should be sprayed with a general insecticide formulated for use on indoor plants. If you keep tropical or other fish close to the plants, do not spray the plants with formulations containing derris; although an excellent insecticide, it is one of the most effective fish poisons known. Colonies of scale insects, which are sometimes troublesome on the pitchers of *Sarracenia*, *Heliamphora* and *Darlingtonia*, can be controlled with a general insecticide or by painting with a mixture of methylated spirit and water. Leaves or pitchers with severe infestations should be removed and burned.

Tarsonemid mites are occasionally troublesome in *Pinguicula*. The tiny creatures (invisible to the naked eye) cause severe distortion of the leaves. The insecticide dicofol can be used.

Fortunately, few diseases attack carnivorous plants, although grey mould (*Botrytis*) is sometimes troublesome where temperatures are low and dead tissue has been allowed to remain on the plants. Benlate or benomyl is a general fungicide which, applied as a spray, enters the plant tissues and is translocated to all parts of the plant. Hygiene is most important, and any leaves or rhizomes exhibiting brown or soft rot must be removed with a clean, sharp knife and the exposed surfaces of the cuts treated with benomyl. During cold weather, reducing the atmospheric moisture should help to prevent mould and bacterial rot.

Several genera of carnivorous plants, including *Drosera*, can be propagated by root cuttings. The cuttings will then be covered with a thin layer of potting compost.

Guide to purchasing

Several nurseries specialize in the cultivation and sale of carnivorous plants and addresses may be obtained from the Secretary of a local Carnivorous Plant Society or from the International Carnivorous Plant Society (see page 87).

Membership of a society is strongly recommended, not only for the opportunity to attend organized lectures and visits but also to exchange information and plant material with fellow members.

Occasionally in the spring months, plants of *Dionaea* are offered in garden centres and supermarkets. These, however, almost always comprise dormant buds only, often without roots and enclosed in little more than a container of sphagnum moss. Such plants may be difficult to establish and they will, in any case, require immediate transfer to a more suitable compost.

Recommended genera

ALDROVANDA (named after the Italian botanist Ulisse Aldrovandi, who died in 1605)
This genus, known as the waterwheel plant, has a single species, *A. vesiculosa*, which is a rootless aquatic plant with a wide natural distribution throughout central Europe, India, Japan and Australia. Nowhere is it particularly common.

The submerged stem, 12–15cm ($4\frac{3}{4}$–6in) long, produces whorls of six to eight leaves arranged like the spokes of a wheel, hence the common name. The traps, which resemble and operate like miniature Venus' fly traps, are about 2mm ($\frac{1}{12}$in) in length and produced at the very end of each leaf. They are adapted to ensnare and digest small aquatic animals such as *Daphnia* and rotifers. In nature the plant prefers shallow acid water and is usually found in association with reeds and other marginal aquatics.

For cultivation in the home or greenhouse small glass fish tanks or polythene containers with a capacity of about 2–3 litres ($3\frac{1}{2}$–5 pints) will be required. To prepare suitable acid water, cover half a teacup of sphagnum peat with a little rain water and bring it to the boil. Add this to approximately 4 litres (7 pints) of rain water and, when cool, dispense it into the growing tanks to approximately two-thirds their depth. Once the solution has settled and is partially clear, the plant may be introduced and left to float freely. Avoid placing the tank in direct sunlight which the plant dislikes and which will encourage the growth of green algae. A cover of domestic cling-film will also help to prevent contamination with algae. A temperature of 18°C (64°F) is required for continuous growth, otherwise the tips of the stems produce turions (tight resting-buds) until warmer temperatures prevail.

BROCCHINIA (named after Giovanni Brocchi, one-time director of the Brescia Botanic Garden in Italy)
This genus of twelve species is a member of the pineapple family BROMELIACEAE; it has only one species so far described as carnivorous. *B. reducta*, which grows on the sandy wet savannahs of Guyana and Venezuela. The waxy golden leaves are funnel-shaped and clasp each other at the base, forming a watertight vase or urn. Insects attracted by colour and scents find the waxy inner walls of the vase a precarious foothold and invariably finish up in the water where they are broken down by bacteria. The resulting nutrient soup is absorbed through special glands at the base of the inner leaves. A compost of equal parts of peat and perlite with a dash of leaf mould suits this plant, which has only recently found its way into cultivation. For temperature and light requirements see *Heliamphora*.

BYBLIS (named after the beautiful daughter of Apollo's son Miletus)
This is a genus of two species of passive flypaper plants, known as the rainbow plant, and endemic to Western and northern Australia.

B. gigantea is shrub-like in habit, up to 50cm (20in) tall and with narrow, tapering leaves, clothed with mucilage-tipped tentacle-like glands. In sunlight the whole plant glistens with a rainbow effect. In the wild it is adapted to seasonal rainfall and is dormant during the dry summer season, producing new shoots and leaves with the onset of the winter rains. *B. liniflora* is a much smaller and more delicate plant although the leaves can be surprisingly long.

In nature, both species are often subjected to bush fires which hastens seed germination. A useful pre-sowing treatment is to scatter the seeds over a single sheet of newspaper which you then set alight. The seeds may then be sown on the surface of a compost consisting of two parts sand or perlite to one part of sieved sphagnum peat. Kept moist and in a temperature of 21°C (70°F) germination should take place in three to four weeks. Transplanting the seedlings to flowering-size pots, 12–15cm ($4\frac{3}{4}$–6in), is a delicate operation and should be carried out with great care once the seedlings are large enough to handle safely. A compost of equal parts perlite, sand and sphagnum peat with the addition of one part sieved leaf mould will be satisfactory. Stand the pots in shallow saucers of water, to ensure that the compost is reasonably moist. Good light conditions are essential for healthy growth and flowering.

CEPHALOTUS (from the Greek *kephale*, a head, presumably referring to the helmet shape of the pitcher)
This genus has one species, *C. follicularis*, which is endemic to the peat and sand swamps near King George's Sound in south-western Australia, where its main insect prey consists of ants, flies and beetles. It is commonly known as the Australian pitcher plant. It is a remarkable passive pitcher plant, producing leaves of two distinct kinds – one pitcher-like and carnivorous and the other a normal flat-bladed foliage leaf. Both arise from the same growing point, eventually forming a tight rosette about 9cm ($3\frac{1}{2}$in) across. It is fairly easy to cultivate providing attention is paid to compost, temperature and light requirements. A good growing medium consists of equal parts of chopped sphagnum moss, moss peat, sieved leaf mould and perlite or sand. Repot in the spring; established plants with more than one crown may be divided at the same time.

Once potting has been completed place living tips of sphagnum moss on the top of the compost; with careful attention to watering these will colonize the surface,

(Opposite) *Cephalotus follicularis*

provide a good base for the pitchers and will serve as an indicator of watering requirements.

Cephalotus is a cool greenhouse plant with a winter resting period when the plants should be removed from their saucer-base water supply and kept somewhat drier, though always under good light conditions. During the summer months some light shading from direct sunlight will be required. Temperatures in the range of 13°–16°C (55°–61°F) suit it best.

DARLINGTONIA (named after Dr William Darlington, physician and amateur botanist of Philadelphia) The genus contains a single species, *D. californica*, and is commonly known as the cobra lily.

Perhaps the most attractive passive carnivorous plant, it inhabits the peat and moss bogs of the coastal plains and foothills of the Rocky Mountains in Oregon and California. Its common name is an indication of the curious yet elegant form of the trapping leaves which

(Below) *Darlingtonia californica*
(Opposite left) *Dionaea muscipula*
(Opposite right) *Drosera capensis*

may reach a height of one metre (approximately one yard). Strangely, the traps do not secrete digestive enzymes in the manner of the closely related *Sarracenia*, but it is thought that the bodies of entrapped insects are broken down entirely by the action of bacteria.

A compost of one part moss peat to three parts living sphagnum moss is a suitable growing medium. Following spring potting (in which the rhizome's position close to the surface should be retained), a fairly moist atmosphere will be required for a few weeks to allow the plant to become established. During the summer a sunny situation suits it best and will encourage flowering, but it is also a wise precaution to shade the pot from sunlight in order to keep the roots cool. Like *Sarracenia* and *Cephalotus*, the pots may be stood in shallow saucers of water, although they also respond to a morning and evening overhead sprinkling with cool rain water with the aim of flushing out the existing water. *Darlingtonia* forms stolons which are capable of producing young plants at great distances from the parent plant: plants have been observed multiplying in this way a metre (about a yard) or more from the main plant in an outdoor sphagnum bog in South Wales.

DIONAEA (from the Greek, one of the names of Venus)

This genus, commonly known as the Venus' fly trap, has one species, *D. muscipula*, and is perhaps the best known carnivorous plant. It is found naturally in localized situations in the wet savannahs of North and northern South Carolina. In the wild it has possibly the most restricted range of any carnivorous plant – a radius of no more than 112km (70 miles).

The trap consists of a modified leaf divided into two spine-edged lobes, united by a vegetable hinge. It has a remarkable resemblance to a gin-trap and operates speedily by means of trigger hairs positioned on the inner surface of the lobes. Two impulses on the same or different hairs are required to operate the trap, which reduces the risk of wind-blown debris or rain springing the trap unnecessarily. Insects are attracted to the traps by colour and by nectar secreted from glands between and beneath the marginal spines. Invariably, in their search for nectar, they brush against the trigger hairs. Astonishingly, the closure of the trap is brought about by the rapid growth in size of the outer cells forming the hinge. In healthy plants the trap may close in less than one-fifth of a second, but long before this, the marginal spines interlock, entombing the intruder. Death of the insect undoubtedly occurs from the considerable pressure exerted by the progressive closure of the lobes, which is followed by the secretion of digestive enzymes to break down the soft tissues of the insect.

Full sun is an essential requirement for the good growth of *Dionaea*; it also encourages the development of the red coloration on the inner lobes of the traps. Ideally, potting or annual repotting should be carried out in spring when the plants are starting to grow. A suitable compost is made up of equal parts sphagnum moss peat, sieved leaf mould, and sharp non-alkaline sand. As with most terrestrial carnivorous plants, the pots may be placed in shallow saucers of water which will help to maintain a humid atmosphere around the plants and reduce the risk of drying out during hot sunny weather.

DROSERA (from the Greek *droseros*, dewy, referring to the glistening, mucilage-tipped glands present on the upper surfaces of the leaves, hence the common name of sundew)

With possibly over one hundred species this is one of the largest genera of carnivorous plants. They are mostly native to temperate climates and acid boglands on all the continents. In form and habit they differ widely and, for convenience, may be roughly classified as pygmy, rosette, forked-leaved, tuberous, stem-forming and rain-forest kinds. The pygmy species come mostly from Australia, Tasmania and New Zealand. They are characterized by diminutive crowns of leaves which may be no more than 6mm ($\frac{1}{4}$in) across, as in *D. occidentalis*. By contrast their flowers are often very large and colourful; in *D. platystigma* they are pale orange in colour and often 2.5cm (1in) or more in diameter. Most are comparatively easy to grow, although a few species, such as *D. leucoblasta* (*D. miniata*), have a reputation for being difficult to overwinter. The pygmies multiply naturally by means of gemmae or resting buds which form in the centre of the crowns during the winter months. They should be teased out of the crowns in early spring with a fine paint brush on to a compost of equal parts moss peat, leaf mould and sharp sand and kept moist from below with a saucer of rain water.

Rosette-forming sundews include the hardy British and European species, *D. anglica*, *D. rotundifolia* and *D. intermedia*, which are less suited to indoor cultivation. The tuberous kinds are mainly South African and Australian in origin and are adapted to dry, sandy habitats of seasonal rainfall. *D. cistiflora* is a well known example, with perhaps the largest flower of the genus in shades of white, pink and red. Its cycles of growth and rest relate to wet and dry seasons, and it is important in the cultivation of this species to provide a drying-out period in summer.

The forked-leaved sundew, *D. binata*, a species from south-eastern Australia, Tasmania and New Zealand, is easily cultivated. Its leaves may grow up to 50cm (20in) in length, the catching surfaces of which are covered with glistening glue-tipped tentacles. The crown buds supported by long bootlace-like roots can be started into growth in early spring by potting into a mixture of equal parts moss peat, chopped green sphagnum moss, leaf mould and sharp sand or perlite. *D. binata* and its handsome stag's-horn cultivar 'Dichotoma' will grow equally well in baskets, suspended in the greenhouse or against a window.

Stem-forming sundews have their small rounded leaves disposed at regular intervals on wiry branching stems; *D. gigantea* from Australia has tuberous roots and stems capable of reaching 75cm (2$\frac{1}{2}$ft) in height. Like others of its kind it requires a dormant or resting period when water should be withheld. Tropical rain-forest sundews require warm temperatures, a humid atmosphere and shading from the sun. *D. adelae* and *D. schizandra* are examples and they are probably best suited to warm greenhouse or terrarium cultivation.

DROSOPHYLLUM (from the Greek *droseros*, dewy)
This genus consists of a single species, *D. lusitanicum*, known as the dewy pine or Portuguese sundew, a remarkable semi-desert plant inhabiting the rocky coastal regions of Spain, Portugal and Morocco. Unlike most other carnivorous plants it is a xerophyte or drought-tolerant species, with a persistent woody stem and long moisture-searching roots which may penetrate deep into the cracks and crevices of rocks. In cultivation, a sandy, freely drained soil in full sun suits it best and no attempt should be made to transplant seedlings, which may result in the breaking of the tap roots.

In habit it is shrublike with the stem supporting a spidery tangle of long narrow leaves. On the under-surface it is clothed with stalked red-tipped glands which secrete a glistening, sticky, scented mucilage, capable of ensnaring the largest insects.

GENLISEA (presumably named after the Comtesse de Genlis, a French courtesan popular at the court of Louis XIV)
This is a genus of about fifteen species from the tropics and subtropics of Africa and Central and South America. Above ground the plants give little indication of their carnivorous habit but below ground (or, more correctly, below water-saturated moss or mud) are two-pronged and spiralled structures; slits allow the entrance of minute aquatic animals which are conducted along galleries of reflexed hairs into a swollen digestive chamber.

As plants of *Genlisea* have arrived in cultivation only recently, little is known about their growing requirements. It seems likely, however, that they would require similar conditions to the tropical and subtropical species of terrestrial *Utricularia*.

HELIAMPHORA (from the Greek *helos*, marsh, and *amphora*, a pitcher, hence the common name of marsh pitcher)
On the rainswept Guyana highlands of South America are found the six species of this genus. The table-top mountains on which they grow are for the most part vertical-sided, independent of each other and set in a lowland sea of tropical rain forest. The species are at the same time remarkable in their distinctiveness and similarity, having evolved in isolation from each other from a common ancestor. In form they appear to be the most primitive of the pitcher plants, consisting of little more than a single leaf rolled into the form of an open, flared-top vegetable scoop. The margins of the leaf are united at the base to form the water-filled pitfall trap into which the insect prey are lured.

Only three species have found their way into cultivation, *H. nutans*, *H. heterodoxa* and *H. minor*. The most graceful and free-flowering of the trio is *H. nutans*

Heliamphora nutans

with its apple-green leaves and soft pink pendent flowers. It is a welcome winter-flowering addition to any indoor plant collection. *H. minor* is a diminutive version no more than 6–8cm (2½–3¼in) in height, whereas *H. heterodoxa* grows to around 25cm (10in) in height. The reputation they enjoy for being difficult to grow is, in the light of a greater understanding of their cultural requirements, completely unwarranted.

They may be classed as cool-house plants and are able to tolerate winter temperatures as low as 8°C (46°F) without harm. With the heat of the sun, daytime temperatures may soar, but it makes little difference provided that the plants receive regular overhead watering or, more correctly, sprinkling with cool rain water. This cultural requirement cannot be overdone and five or six times a day will provide only a fraction of the precipitation the plants receive in their natural environment. Repotting is best carried out early in spring. The compost which has proved most satisfactory consists of equal parts moss peat, living sphagnum moss and leaf mould. Maximum sunlight is a requirement during the winter months although a little shade from summer sun is desirable.

NEPENTHES (from the Greek, a name used in Homeric times for a plant with grief-relieving properties; commonly known as the tropical pitcher plant)

This is a genus of about seventy species of tropical and subtropical woody-stemmed perennials distributed throughout Madagascar, Asia, Malaysia and even northern Australia. Some grow in savannah and scrubland but they are more usually found on the margins of forests. Many are vigorous climbers, which means that the pitcher traps can position themselves in the upper leaf-canopy of the forest, whereas others are low growing and shrublike. The pitchers are produced from an extension of the mid-rib of the leaf, which may also be tendril-like and assist the plant in climbing to considerable heights – over 30m (100ft). In size, shape and colour they exhibit great variety and are some of the strangest and most remarkable of plant structures.

In cultivation, they are plants with a requirement for high atmospheric moisture and are therefore most suited to cultivation in the greenhouse where frequent spraying and summer-shading is possible, or in a larger terrarium with its closed humid environment. Their temperature requirements divide them into two distinct groups – the highland species, which occur in habitats above 1000m (3300ft), and the lowland species which occur in situations below this elevation. To the lowland group belong N. ampullaria, the strange, horned N. bicalcarata, N. mirabilis and the well known N. rafflesiana. For good growth they require a temperature range of 21°–25°C (70°–77°F). Night temperatures may be allowed to fall a little below this providing the drop is not prolonged nor too frequent. The highland species are not so demanding and a range of 15°–20°C (59°–68°F) is

Nepenthes ventricosa

usually acceptable; here again, night temperatures may be allowed to fall a little without serious harm. Among the more popular species of this group are N. alata, N. gracillima, N. fusca and N. ventricosa. Most of the cultivated plants are hybrids of the lowland species, i.e. N. × coccinea, and almost without exception these many differently named clones are very vigorous, produce large pitchers and are easier to grow.

Nepenthes are usually grown as epiphytes in hanging baskets of teak or plastic. With established plants, some early spring pruning will be required which will keep the plants within bounds and encourage the development of young leaves and pitchers.

PINGUICULA (from the Latin *pinguis*, fat, referring to the appearance of the greasy leaf surfaces, hence the common name of butterwort)

This genus of about fifty species of small perennial herbs contains some of the most attractive flower and leaf combinations of all the carnivorous plants. They are, with only a few exceptions, plants of the wetlands of the northern hemisphere. The leaves, arranged in a flat starlike rosette, are often golden-yellow in colour and glisten with a surface cover of greasy mucilage, to which insects are attracted and ensnared. All the species of *Pinguicula* are regarded as active trappers, exhibiting a slight inward rolling of the leaf margins in the regions where an insect has been caught.

The spurred flowers may be large and almost viola-like, as in the rose pink *P. moranensis*, or resembling small, violet-coloured tropaeolums as in *P. grandiflora*. A most unusual colour in *Pinguicula* is the yellow-flowered *P. lutea* from northern Florida and the adjacent states. *P. gypsicola* from Mexico is a purple-flowered species with a remarkable winter rosette of short leaves, giving the whole plant the appearance of a *Sempervivum* or houseleek.

The British *P. vulgaris* and other temperate-climate species have a dormant phase during the winter months when the whole plant assumes a resting-bud condition. Some species reproduce vegetatively by means of small axillary buds or *gemmae* which form at the onset of the dormant period and are a convenient means of increasing the stock.

In cultivation, most species and varieties of *Pinguicula* may be regarded as cool-house plants. They require good light conditions, though light shading from strong summer sun is desirable. A suitable general compost for most species is made up of equal parts of moss peat and leaf mould with a half part of sharp sand. A loam-based compost in place of the sand content is preferred by some growers though this is by no means essential.

SARRACENIA (named after the French botanist and physician Dr Michel Sarrasin)

Sarracenia flava

This is a genus of eight species, commonly known as trumpet pitchers, which are native to the temperate boglands of the east coast of North America. They are the backbone of any worthwhile collection of temperate carnivorous plants. The modified leaves, in an astonishing variety of forms and colours, arise from a thick basal rhizome which travels progressively along the surface of wet meadows and bogs.

The rhizomes, complete with the pitchers of the previous year, should be prepared for repotting in midwinter by trimming away decaying pitchers or back portions of the rhizome with a sharp knife. Pot firmly into a compost of equal parts moss peat, leaf mould, chopped green sphagnum moss and half a part of sharp sand or perlite. Water in thoroughly from a can with a fine rose and place the pots in a saucer or tray of soft water. All the species and varieties will grow well in the cool greenhouse and they are among the best candidates for cultivation on window sills.

The widely distributed *S. purpurea* is represented by two distinct geographical forms, ssp. *venosa* which occurs as far south as Florida, and ssp. *purpurea* which is found from New Jersey to northern Canada. The latter, which prefers cooler temperatures (it survives winter temperatures of $-23°C$ $(-10°F)$), is suitable for unheated greenhouses. Both subspecies are purple-flowered and are regarded as comparatively easy plants to grow. *S. flava* produces magnificent golden yellow trumpets 60cm (2ft) or more in height, with glorious yellow pendent flowers. The pitchers of *S. leucophylla*, the white trumpet, are tall and slender with a white top, prominently veined in red; the flowers are burgundy red. *S. minor* is the so-called hooded trumpet, a smaller-growing species with the top of the pitcher completely arched over. Opaque windows distributed around the hood encourage insects to enter the pitcher before their downfall.

S. psittacina is the parrot pitcher of the southern states bordering the Gulf Coast. The pitchers, which grow horizontally, are swollen and pouchlike at the terminal end. They are pale green with a network of red veins. The entrance to the pitcher is inverted and positioned under the arched hood, and this leads to the inner chamber lined with reflexed hairs. In shape and habit of growth it is quite unlike any other species.

There are many natural and man-made hybrids between the eight species of *Sarracenia*. *S.* × 'Daniel Rudd' has slender greenish-yellow pitchers and red flowers, whereas *S.* × *mitchelliana*, an obvious hybrid of *S. purpurea* and *S. leucophylla*, has inherited the best characteristics of its parents.

UTRICULARIA (from the Latin *utriculus*, a small bottle, referring to the insect-trapping bladders borne on the underground or underwater parts)

This is a genus, commonly known as bladderwort, with over 250 species distributed throughout the world. They may be submerged aquatics, where only the flowering stem appears above the water surface, or mud-dwelling, or even epiphytes, growing in rain forests on moss-covered branches and rotting logs. The subterranean leaves and runners (for these plants have no true roots), develop inflated bladders which trap aquatic insects, crustaceans and other small forms of animal life. They are drawn through an ingenious trapdoor by an inrush of water caused by differential pressures. The colourful toadflax-like flowers are borne on long, slender stems and, in the epiphytic species, may be large and very attractive.

The terrestrial kinds, which may be grown on a compost of equal parts moss peat, leaf mould and sand or perlite, should be kept permanently moist with the pots standing in saucers or trays of water. They are suitable subjects for the window sill or greenhouse, though light shading from strong sun is advisable. *U. subulata* is a delightful miniature with fairy wands of clear yellow flowers. *U. sandersonii* bears a profusion of pale lavender flowers above light green leaves, whereas *U. menziesii* has bright red pouched flowers reminiscent of an alpine calceolaria. Aquatic species include *U. vulgaris*, the greater bladderwort, a British native which has bright yellow flowers and finely divided submerged leaves clustered with tiny bladders. Like many temperate species it has a dormant winter condition, when it appears as tight buds (turions) which sink to the bottom of the container. *U. volubilis* is an Australian species with twining flower stems and purple flowers. For the size and beauty of its lavender-coloured flowers few species can compare with *U. humboldtii*, a strange plant from the rain forests of Guyana, which colonizes the water-filled cavities formed by the leaf-bases of certain bromeliads. *U. reniformis*, with large kidney-shaped leaves and racemes of lavender flowers, is popular and easy to grow. *U. longifolia* is a similar species with tall panicles of mauve flowers with a golden patch on the basal petal. *U. alpina* is a tuber-forming species from the West Indies and South America, which has large white to pale lilac flowers with a distinctive yellow palate.

Glass or opaque plastic containers holding perhaps $1\frac{1}{2}$ litres (about 3 pints) of soft, peaty water are suitable for the aquatic kinds and the peat/water preparation recommended for *Aldrovanda* (see page 78) would be quite suitable. Green algae is often a problem with aquatic cultures and it is important to sterilize all

Utricularia longifolia

PLANTS FOR SPECIAL PURPOSES

MINIMUM TEMPERATURE REQUIRED	LIGHT REQUIREMENTS

Cool (5–10°C [41–50°F])

Darlingtonia californica (requires protection from only the hardest frosts)

Dionaea muscipula (at low temperatures dormant winter buds are formed)

Drosera (all temperate species, which includes many rosette kinds and winter dormant species such as *D. binata*)

Pinguicula (all temperate species, though many form winter resting buds)

Sarracenia (all species and varieties where a minimum temperature of 5°C (41°F) can be maintained. *S. purpurea* ssp. *purpurea* is quite hardy and suitable for the coldest situations.)

Utricularia (most temperate species, though many aquatic kinds form turions or dormant winter buds)

Shady situation

Nepenthes (all species and varieties are classic shade plants, requiring a good atmospheric humidity and screening from the sun at all times)

Utricularia (all rain forest and epiphytic species)

Direct sunlight

Dionaea muscipula (requires good light conditions during the growing season to develop red pigmentation inside the traps)

Drosera

Drosophyllum lusitanicum (adapted to semi-desert conditions and requires maximum light at all times)

Sarracenia (all species and varieties respond to good light conditions, particularly those with red or yellow pigmentation)

EASE OF CULTIVATION

Suitable for beginners

Dionaea muscipula	*Sarracenia flava*
Drosera aliciae	*S. leucophylla*
D. binata and cvs	*S. purpurea* ssp. *purpurea*
D. capensis	*S. purpurea* ssp. *venosa*
D. spathulata	*Utricularia longifolia*
Pinguicula grandiflora	*U. reniformis*
P. moranensis	*U. vulgaris*
P. vulgaris	

ATTRACTIVE FLOWERS

Drosera (some)	*Pinguicula*
Drosophyllum	*Sarracenia*
Heliamphora nutans	*Utricularia*

GOOD FOLIAGE

Darlingtonia	*Nepenthes*
Drosera	*Sarracenia*
Drosophyllum	*Utricularia reniformis*

Moderately easy	Fairly difficult		
Byblis	*Aldrovanda*	*Heliamphora*	*Sarracenia*
Cephalotus		*Nepenthes*	*psittacina*
Drosophyllum			

containers immediately before use with boiling water.

Epiphytic species require an open orchid-type compost. Equal parts of peat moss, bark chips and chopped green sphagnum moss, with the addition of a little granulated charcoal or perlite, is suitable.

Utricularia multifida and *U. tenella* are annual species formerly included in the genus *Polypompholyx*. In *U. multifida* the delicate pink flowers are borne on slender stems 20cm (8in) or so in length, the lower trilobed petal-lip resembling an apron or skirt, hence the common name, pink petticoats. *U. tenella* is the other species which differs in its smaller size and fewer flowers. Both species are raised from spring-sown seed distributed thinly on the surface of a compost of two parts moss peat, one part leaf mould and one part sharp sand. Do not transplant the seedlings but rather allow them to grow on and flower in their germination pots. The pots should be stood in a shallow saucer of rain water and never watered from above.

FURTHER INFORMATION

Bibliography

Cheers, G., *Carnivorous plants* (Angus and Robertson, 1983)

Overbeck, C., *Carnivorous plants* (Lerner Publications, 1982)

Schnell, Donald E., *Carnivorous plants of the United States* (Winston-Salem, 1976)

Slack, A., *Carnivorous plants* (Ebury Press, 1979)

—, *Insect Eating Plants and How to Grow Them* (Alphabooks, 1986)

Societies

The Carnivorous Plant Society
24 Osborne Road
Brentwood
Essex
England

The International Carnivorous Plant Society
Fullerton Arboretum
California State University
Fullerton, Calif 92634
USA

BROMELIADS

ALTHOUGH BROMELIADS have been known horticulturally for more than a century and a half, it is only within the last thirty years or so that they have become popular as house plants in the British Isles. It does not seem that long ago that very few bromeliads were ever seen included in nurserymen's lists or even in florists' displays and it was rare to see more than two or three species offered for sale anywhere. Nowadays, however, there is hardly a high street anywhere in the country which does not have a supermarket or chain-store with at least half a dozen or more different types on offer over the year. The reason for this popularity is that it has been found that, given the right conditions for growth, many types can be grown quite as easily in the house as they were originally, in conservatories and greenhouses. Also, with the introduction of a wider variety of these plants, their diversity of form and attractive foliage, fruits and flowers, can now be appreciated, and they are proving to be excellent subjects for home decoration.

In many ways their attraction almost rivals that of orchids in popularity for display purposes. Whereas the orchid is attractive only while it is flowering, bromeliads, in many instances, show a wide range of leaf colour changes in the run up to flowering. When in flower, many show brilliantly coloured bracts which are evident well before the flowers open and once the flowers have passed their prime, the bracts of many species retain their beauty until the fruits mature. Even the fruits themselves can be unusual and colourful, in shades of blue, yellow, orange to red and even white when ripe. This period

(Above) *Fascicularia bicolor*   (Opposite) *Tillandsia ionantha*

of colour can last for several months, and is a quality no orchid can claim.

Bromeliads belong to a very large family of plants, the BROMELIACEAE. It gets its name from the genus *Bromelia* which honours the Swedish botanist, Olaf Bromelius. It comprises some 2000 or more species, of which the common pineapple is the most widely known. The history of the bromeliad is almost as colourful as the individual members of the family. It dates back to the discovery by Christopher Columbus, in the late fifteenth century, of the cultivation of the pineapple in the island of Guadeloupe. Almost from that date the pineapple has been cultivated throughout the tropics and there cannot be a single country with the right climatic conditions in which it is not grown. It is also notable as the only member of the family which is of any great economic value.

With the exception of one species of *Pitcairnia*, which is native to West Africa, the family is restricted to the tropics and sub-tropics of the New World, where it occurs from the southern United States to southern Chile and Argentina, including the West Indies. The species cover a vast range of altitudes, from sea level on the Pacific and Atlantic coasts, up to heights of over 3900m (12,500ft) in the Peruvian Andes.

Habitats and adaptations

The habitats in which they are known to occur are almost as varied as their geographical distribution. The majority of bromeliads are epiphytic, growing on the limbs and trunks of trees and shrubs, but many others are terrestrial or grow anchored to rocks (lithophytic). Epiphytic species may also be found growing terrestrially if they have fallen from their host tree. Those species which grow naturally as epiphytes occur in areas varying from the steamy rain forests of northern South America, or the somewhat cooler and drier forests farther south, to the drier desert areas where occasionally some species may be epiphytic on certain species of cacti.

They have what appears to be a perfectly normal root system, but these organs are used solely as a means of anchorage to the host and are not used in any large way for feeding. The majority of epiphytes have rosettes of broad leaves with closely fitting bases which form watertight seals between them. This enables water to collect, forming small reservoirs or tanks into which plant debris, insects and small animals fall, die and eventually disintegrate. It is the nourishment provided by the water and debris which is absorbed by special glands at the bases of the leaves, on which the plants solely survive. Examples of these 'tank' bromeliads, as they are known, occur widely in such genera as *Billbergia*, *Aechmea*, *Nidularium* and *Neoregelia*. But not all epiphytes and saxicolous species obtain their nourishment in this manner.

Other epiphytes, such as many of the narrow silver-leaved species of *Tillandsia*, obtain their water from moisture-absorbing scales which cover their leaf surfaces. These scales absorb moisture and its mineral content from the air and pass it into the leaves; at the same time they serve to protect the plant from excessive heat, drought and strong winds which would otherwise increase transpiration and subsequent water loss. This adaptation is found in many of the coastal species and those growing at high altitudes.

The popular name for this type of bromeliad is air plant, as it appears to survive on nothing but air and moisture. A good example of this is *Tillandsia recurvata*, a species frequently found growing on telephone wires especially in Central America. Another species which behaves in the same way is *T. usneoides*, or Spanish moss. This has filamentous stems and leaves and may be seen hanging in great festoons from the forest canopies from the southern United States to Argentina. Both these examples are densely covered with scales and, in the main, have no contact with any source of food and water other than the air.

The many species which grow normally as terrestrials also occur in very different types of habitats, from the leaf litter deep in the wet and dry forests, to deserts or other open spaces, such as coastal shorelines within the salt-spray zone and very wet freshwater areas, such as marshes and swamps.

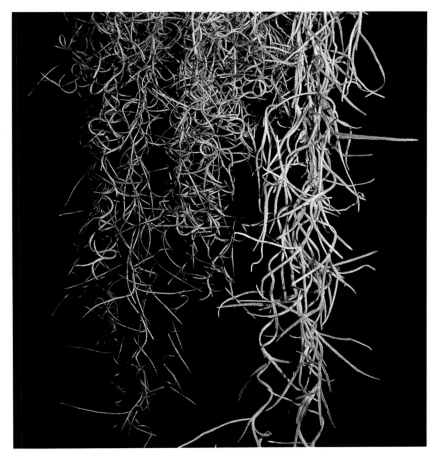

Tillandsia usneoides

Diversity of size is also another interesting feature within the family. Bromeliads may be as small as 5cm (2in) and mosslike, as in *Tillandsia bryoides*, or as large as the Andean *Puya raimondii*, which has leaves up to 2.5m (8ft) long and a spikelike inflorescence up to 5m (16ft) tall.

Cultural requirements

One of the main reasons for bromeliads fast becoming favourite houseplants is that they are very easy to grow and tolerate the climatic conditions in the modern home. Once established, their requirements are few and they can tolerate conditions far removed from those of their natural environment. They will thrive if their natural conditions, adequate sunlight and a humid atmosphere, are duplicated or nearly so, but are quite tolerant of artificial light and a somewhat lower humidity. Of course, the home can offer much that they desire, such as natural light from the windows in most rooms and high humidity in kitchens and bathrooms.

Light: Light is probably the most important factor in growing bromeliads, as it is this which brings about the wide range of leaf colours and markings which are the most attractive feature of some species. Their flexibility is such that even the sun-lovers will survive in shady situations and those that favour shade can survive in bright light, but of course it is preferable to try and meet their optimum conditions for successful growth. It is not too difficult to decide on the right conditions for your plant if no further information is available. In general, those species in which water is retained in the rosettes are usually forest species which rarely grow in full sunlight and will tolerate shadier places in the home; these are usually species which have softer, green leaves with little obvious scaling. Those which have thicker, more spiny, scaly leaves usually prefer as much sunlight as possible. It must be remembered too, that in their natural tropical environment most plants are used to about twelve hours of daylight, and although they will tolerate far less in the home it is always advantageous to be able to supplement this with artificial light.

Temperatures: In the wild, bromeliads are able to withstand a range of temperatures, with some Equatorial species living in temperatures which reach 32°C (90°F) or above around midday, while others in the high Andes suffer night temperatures down to freezing. Fortunately the temperature in the modern house is perfectly adequate where, with central heating, it may fluctuate between 7°C (45°F) at night to 21°C (70°F) or above during the day. Again it must be remembered that those species which are grown in a greenhouse or conservatory must not be subjected to prolonged spells of cold. During the worst period, they should be protected by covering against possible frost and, where appropriate, have the water removed from their reservoirs to prevent freezing.

Watering: The water requirements of bromeliads are also varied, though all of them prefer a basically humid environment. The soft, green-leaved species prefer plenty of liquid and may be watered freely every day and not less than three times a week. Always remember to keep the water reservoirs filled. Those with stiffer, scaly leaves need to be watered only twice or three times weekly. The former should be mist-sprayed daily to create the right humidity, or even have their pots set in pans with a layer of pebbles in the bottom, which is then kept watered to just below the tops of the pebbles. Of course, if the plants are kept in the kitchen or bathroom where the humidity is higher, such attention to watering may be relaxed. As with other house plants, more watering is needed during the period of maximum growth in the summer months than in the winter.

Basic cultivation

Bromeliad cultivation in general is not at all difficult. If a few basic facts are remembered, all types of bromeliads, be they epiphytic, terrestrial or lithophytic, can be grown equally successfully in the home.

Containers: All of them can be grown in pots but the various merits of the container must be considered. Clay or plastic pots or pans may be used but they should always have drainage holes at the base. Clay pots are heavier, provide good aeration but dry out rapidly, whereas plastic pots are more restrictive of aeration, dry more slowly and are easily overbalanced as the soil dries out. As to

Aechmea recurvata

pot size, except for the very large species, most bromeliads will fit into 7.5–12cm (3–4¾in) pots. It is better to underpot as most of them thrive on being root-bound and only need further potting when they become top-heavy. Some such as aechmeas and billbergias prefer to be crowded in the pot and do not need to be thinned out until the container becomes really overcrowded.

Apart from pots, the forest species with trailing inflorescences, such as certain cryptanthus and *Aechmea filicaulis*, may quite successfully be accommodated in hanging baskets. These forest epiphytes and those terrestrials that prefer moist soils, such as neoregelias, nidulariums and similar genera, do well in a basic compost mixture of equal parts of peat and perlite or its equivalent. Just place the plants in the container, add the mixture and press firmly down around the plant roots, remembering not to plant too deeply as moisture around the crown frequently results in rotting. If the plant needs support until a good root-system develops it may be staked using bamboo or wooden splints and twine. Do not use wire or galvanized supports unless they are plastic covered as these may cause burning. With experience of the plant's requirements, additional materials such as granite chippings, sand, gravel, bark chips or leaf-mould may be added to help drainage and stability.

For most of the dry-growing epiphytic tillandsias, some vrieseas and guzmanias, and others which prefer a well-drained medium, it is best to pot them into fern fibre over about one-third of a pot of broken crocks. Press the plants well down and stake if necessary. Those species which are of a more xerophytic habit (used to hotter and drier climates) need dry periods between watering. They do well in a mixture of one part of peat or leaf-mould, one part of coarse gravel and two parts of sharp sand.

There are other methods of planting bromeliads for display purposes: for example, mount the small silvery-leaved tillandsias on to ornamental rocks, shells, driftwood or the like as table decorations; or suspend them on pieces of cork bark as wall decorations.

Propagation

Vegetative increase: Propagation is also generally easy, but, as in all other types of gardening, accidents and losses can occur. Nearly all bromeliads, once they have flowered, eventually fade and die, but in most cases not without first producing one or two, or even a sizeable crop of offshoots or offsets. These usually arise at the base of the plant or occasionally between the lower leaves. Once formed, they grow quite rapidly and soon take on the general appearance of the parent plant and can easily be removed when they are about one-third the size of the parent. This removal is best made in the spring by gently easing the offshoot away from the parent plant (which is quite easy if woody tissue is already present)

Most bromeliads produce offsets, usually after the major rosette has flowered. These offsets can be used to create additional plants if they are cut off close to their point of attachment with the mother plant, inserted into cutting compost and kept in warm, humid conditions. If they are attached by a long 'runner' or stem this may be trimmed off before insertion.

until it can be snapped off. Alternatively, as in the case of neoregelias and nidulariums, the still soft and green offsets can be gently removed with a sharp knife, taking a small heel of parent stem with it. In either case these offsets may be planted immediately into a medium similar to that of the parent plant or left for a day or two to dry before potting. A rooting hormone and fungicide powder may be applied to the cut surface if desired. It is important to remember that the removal of offsets helps to stimulate the parent plant to produce more, as they no longer deprive it of sap or strength.

Seeds: There are bromeliads, however, such as certain vrieseas, which do not produce offsets, and the only possible way of propagation is by raising them from seed. Fortunately, most bromeliads produce fruit easily and the ripe seed, although it is viable for only a short time, may be sown in shallow pans on to a mixture of one part sand and two parts sphagnum moss. Press the seeds firmly down without burying them, water well and place the container either in a plastic bag or, more preferably, into a heated propagator. After a week or two, with the temperature at about 25°C (77°F), they will germinate. Leave the seedlings, still in the propagator, in bright light until four or five leaves have developed and then gradually acclimatize them to room temperature for a week or two, by lengthening the periods of ventilation. Once six to eight leaves have developed, the young plants can then be planted out in a similar medium as used for the mature plants.

Pests and diseases

Fortunately, pests and diseases are seldom a problem on bromeliads and, other than slugs and snails on those grown in the greenhouse or conservatory, the only pests which can be any problem, are scale insects and red spider mite. To control scale, dip the whole plant into a solution prepared according to the manufacturer's instructions, drain the reservoir several times and allow the solution to remain on the plant overnight. After this, wash out the reservoir several times and refill with fresh water. The scale which persists on the leaves after the death of the insects can be removed with the fingernail or a blunt knife. Red spider mite can initially be treated by washing the leaves with a warm, mild soap solution and followed for one week by heavy daily mist spraying, concentrating on the undersides of the leaves. This may be followed by three treatments at five-day intervals of spraying with malathion or an insecticide recommended by the supplier as suitable for bromeliads. Mealy bugs also occasionally appear on bromeliads but very rarely so, and if they do, they can be removed either by swabbing off the cottony tufts from the leaves with a solution of equal parts of alcohol and water or by treating the plants with malathion as recommended above for scale insects.

'Air plants' such as *Tillandsia schiedeana* can be raised from seed, though not by the familiar methods used for most other types of plant. The seeds, which are each attached to a fluffy parachute of hairs known as the pappus, should be collected from the dry fruit capsules as they start to discharge (above). Conifer twigs, preferably juniper or thuja, are made into bundles held together by wire. The seeds are then sown on to the surface of the bundle and sprayed with a fine misting of water, which causes them to adhere to the foliage of the conifers. The bundle can then be attached to a hook and hung in a propagator or other moist, shady situation.

Recommended genera

ABROMEITIELLA (named after J. Abromeit, a German botanist)
This small genus of only two species occurs at altitudes from 1500 to 2500m (4700–8000ft) in the Andes of north-western Argentina and southern Bolivia. Strangely *Abromeitiella* is not widely included in horticultural works on bromeliads, although it may be seen advertised occasionally in plantmen's lists of succulent plants. It can be found in many collections of succulents and alpine plants and becomes an outstanding plant once it is established. It is terrestrial in habit and forms large cushions or mats of small, individual, densely leaved rosettes.

In *A. brevifolia*, the leaves are just over 2cm ($\frac{3}{4}$in) long, triangular in outline, somewhat succulent and with a short, spiny margin. It has no flower stalk, but one to three flowers, each about 3cm ($1\frac{1}{4}$in) long, arise from the centre of the rosette and are a strong yellow-green in colour. The second species, *A. lorentziana*, is similar in its

habit and appearance but has distinctly longer leaves up to about 15cm (6in) long. They are not difficult to cultivate and require only a lot of light and little water; they may be kept quite cool in the winter. Propagation too is no problem since unlike most other bromeliads, they do not die after flowering but, instead, divide naturally from the upper leaf-axils.

AECHMEA (from the Greek *aichme*, a point, referring to the spiny tips of the sepals in many species)
This genus contains some 170 species, most of which are epiphytic. They range over almost all regions where bromeliads occur, from Mexico to Argentina, and are found in a wide range of habitats from the forest canopy to the forest floor. The largest number are native to the cloud and rain forests of Brazil. They may also be found at sea-level on the coastal shoreline and up to exposed areas on mountains at altitudes of about 2000m (6500ft).

In their sterile, flowerless state, before the inflorescence becomes evident, some species may easily be

Aechmea fulgens

mistaken for billbergias. In both *Aechmea* and *Billbergia* the leaves are generally broad and straplike and in all species are spiny on the margins. In most species of *Aechmea* the spines are very prominent and obvious whereas in a few species only closer examination shows their presence. In the latter case the spines may be both very small and either spaced at wide intervals on the margin or present only on the margin of the sheathing base. The overall appearance of their leaves is very diverse – they can be thick and leathery, soft and flexible, glossy or dull, and heavily scaled. Their colour is also varied; they may show a different colour on each surface and can range from light or dark green, reddish- or purplish-brown to maroon. They may be banded, striped or mottled with white, brown or purple. Either state in different species may be brought about by pigmentation, in the glossy-leaved species; or by differently coloured scales, in the non-glossy members. In some species the leaves are arranged in an open, spreading rosette whereas in others they may form a tall, tubular reservoir. These characteristics also apply to most species of *Billbergia*.

It is only when we consider the inflorescence that the differences between the genera become apparent. Many species produce very colourful flowers with the inflorescence surrounded by large, brightly coloured bracts. The individual flowers come in a wide range of colours and it is not only the petals which carry the most brilliant colours. In many cases the sepals are brightly coloured and frequently in colours contrasting with the petals. One of the distinguishing generic characters is the presence in most species of a minute to large spine at the tip of the sepals. The range of flower coloration varies from white, through various shades of yellow and orange to red, plus blue to purple and even green. In contrast with most other house plants, their attraction does not stop with flowering, for the fruits are berries which at maturity can be blue, orange, yellow or white.

There are a number of aechmeas on the market but only those which are suitable for the home or greenhouse and can be conveniently grown in pots are mentioned here. One of the best known and probably the most popular is *Aechmea fasciata* (*A. rhodocyanea*), with a cylindrical or funnel-like rosette of grey-brown leaves marked with horizontal silvery bands. The white, woolly stalk bears a pyramidal inflorescence of dense pinkish-red bracts which give rise to blue or purple flowers. These flowers become red as they age and the plant remains colourful for many months.

A. chantinii is another popular, scaly-leaved species but differs greatly from *A. fasciata* in many ways. The banding of the leaves is similar but the inflorescence is many-branched, with the short branches having large, bright red bracts at their bases. Each branch bears a broad, swordlike spike of orange flowers which arise

from within pinkish-green bracts. These two species can be grown quite easily despite their size, which is usually about 60cm (2ft) tall.

A. fulgens is a much smaller species, reaching only about half that height. It is a green-leaved plant with leaves which often have a slight banding on the upper surface, and it forms a more open rosette. The inflorescence is also different, being a totally red panicle with the sepals and ovary appearing as shiny red 'berries' from which bright blue petals develop. There are two varieties of this species found in cultivation, the typical var. *fulgens* as described here and var. *discolor* in which the upper surfaces of the leaves are dark green, contrasting with a purple underside and lightly covered with white scales. Very close in appearance is *A. miniata* var. *discolor* which differs in having a more compact inflorescence and glossier leaves without the general dusting of white scales.

An even smaller plant is *A. recurvata* which is found as the typical variety with narrow leaves about 1–2cm ($\frac{2}{5}$–$\frac{3}{4}$in) wide which become greenish-red to red at the centre of the rosette and reflex just above the sheath. The red-bracted inflorescence of purple or pinkish-red flowers extends above the level of the sheath. Var. *ortgiesii* has the inflorescence sunken in the centre of the rosette of harsh spiny leaves whereas var. *benrathii* is similar but has almost entire and apparently non-spiny leaves.

Other species worthy of mention include *A. mexicana*, which is one of the larger cultivated sorts, notable for its large panicle of hundreds of pale pink flowers from which develop pearl-white berries which last for several months, and *A. mertensii*, with its bright red inflorescence stalk, large orange bracts and yellow flowers, giving rise to white berries which gradually turn bright blue when mature. Although not yet commonly seen in cultivation, *A. filicaulis* is notable because of its unusual inflorescence. This open-rosetted plant from the Venezuelan cloud forest has a long, threadlike, pendent and branched flowering stem which may reach over 2m (6$\frac{1}{2}$ft) in length. Its short branches bear large, white flowers with bright red bracts which are followed by attractive blue berries.

ANANAS (from the Brazilian Indian word for pineapple)
This is a genus of eight terrestrial species from the humid forests and drier and more arid areas of Brazil, Venezuela, Peru and Paraguay.

In this genus, the very spiny leaves, which are hardly enlarged at the base, form a dense, open rosette which does not hold water. The conelike inflorescence of violet to purple-blue or red flowers is borne terminally on the stout inflorescence stalk and is crowned with a tuft of sterile, leaflike bracts. When ripening, the ovaries

(Above) *Ananas bracteatus*
(Opposite) *Billbergia pyramidalis*

combine with each other, the bracts and the axis, to form a fleshy, compound fruit, or syncarp.

Only two species are commonly found in cultivation, including the commercially grown edible pineapple, and both of these occur in several varieties. In its typical state, *Ananas comosus* (syn. *A. sativus*), the common pineapple whose origin has never been certainly determined, is a large plant with leaves which can reach 1m (3ft 3in) or more in length, with an inflorescence stalk up to 45cm (1½ft) tall. The leaves are barely more than 1.5cm (⅝in) wide and bright green. The attractive cultivar 'Variegatus' is more often seen cultivated in the home and has leaves which are longitudinally striped with green, cream, and pink, and, if grown in a strong light, the whole plant develops a pink coloration, including the small, edible pineapple. In its commercially cultivated form, this species contains many cultivars, the most interesting of which is 'Smooth Cayenne', with almost spineless leaves.

A. bracteatus is a plant of similar size to the former, but differs in having bright pink flower bracts which protrude from the mature fruit, giving it a distinctly leafy appearance. *A. bracteatus* 'Tricolor', with leaves with longitudinal cream stripes, is also grown. Pineapples develop offsets around the base of the fruit as well as at the base of the plant. It is the latter which are usually used to propagate the domestic pineapple.

See also USEFUL PLANTS.

BILLBERGIA (named after the Swedish botanist, Gustave Billberg, who died in 1844)
This genus contains fifty species of epiphytes which are mostly native to Brazil, but also occur from Mexico, through Central America and down the western seaboard as far as Peru, and on the eastern coast to Argentina.

As mentioned under *Aechmea* these two genera, in their sterile states, can often be difficult to differentiate, both having spiny leaves, many of which form tubular rosettes. However, there are one or two characteristics which more easily distinguish sterile billbergias. Generally they have fewer leaves than aechmeas (five to eight being the usual range), are more often much taller and tubular and also more often cross-banded in a silvery grey with paler cream mottling or blotching. Whereas most inflorescences in aechmeas are stout and erect, in many billbergias they are recurved or nodding and in the latter the sepals are usually spine-free. Most species have a large, bright pink or red inflorescence and stalk bracts and very unusual flowers. These may have petals which can be green, as in *B. porteana*, yellow to glossy golden-yellow in *B. zebrina*, purple in *B. brasiliensis* or blue, red or white in *B. pyramidalis*. Some species such as *B. nutans* have combinations of these.

Probably the commonest billbergia to be seen in home cultivation is *B. nutans*, a small plant with narrow recurving leaves rarely exceeding 30cm (1ft) in length. It has a slender, pendent inflorescence with pink bracts and pale green-petalled flowers which are edged with dark blue. *B. nutans* var. *schimperiana* has broader, non-spiny leaves and petals which are dark blue at the apex as well as on the margins. Almost as commonly met with is *B. amoena* which may be seen in one of its many varieties. The typical var. *amoena* is a green-leaved, tubular plant with pale green, blue-tipped petals not unlike the last. Var. *rubra* has broader leaves which are red with pale yellow spots; var. *penduliflora* has orange-red bracts and a more markedly pendent inflorescence, whereas in var. *minor* the whole plant is much smaller and has an almost erect inflorescence.

Another species which is currently available is *B. pyramidalis*, which has long, minutely toothed leaves, often banded beneath in a rather open rosette. The pyramidal inflorescence which tops the stout, mealy white stalk, is surrounded by bright red bracts, and has flowers with bright red sepals and bright red petals which are blue towards the apex. A totally red-flowered variety, var. *concolor*, is also known from cultivation. All of the three species mentioned immediately above have petals which, as they open, gently recurve, but in certain other species the petals curl backwards almost to the base in a tight spiral; these include *B. brasiliensis*, *B. porteana*, *B. venezuelana* and *B. zebrina*.

With their striking inflorescences, billbergias are among the most attractive of the bromeliads, but regrettably the flowers are short-lived and usually do not last for more than two weeks. They have the advantage that they are the easiest to propagate, however, producing many suckers or offsets which can be removed and cultivated in the usual way. They also readily produce ripe fruit and are very easy to grow from seed. The rosettes must be kept filled with water and they must be sprayed daily throughout the year. During the growing period, it will help to water with a little liquid fertilizer either by leaf-spray or directly to the potting medium.

CRYPTANTHUS (from the Greek *cryptos*, meaning hidden, and *anthos*, a flower)

This is a genus of some twenty-two species, all native to eastern Brazil and with many varieties, most of which can be found in cultivation. All cryptanthus are terrestrial and occur in a very wide range of habitats from the coast to the forests, in shade or bright sunlight

Cryptanthus acaulis

and in both moist and dry conditions.

Unlike many other bromeliads, these plants, popularly known as earth-stars, have their relatively small, broad leaves arranged in a wide, open rosette and in most species, lying almost flat on the ground. Because of this habit, they do not form water-holding reservoirs. In almost all cases the leaves have spiny margins and, again unlike most other members of the family, do not produce showy flowers. All the species have rather insignificant white flowers produced low in the centre of the rosette, but this lack of floral attraction is more than compensated for by the unusual and attractive foliage. The leaves of the different species vary between 5cm and 30cm (2–12in) in length and usually have undulating, wavy margins. They are often covered or banded with silver scales and their colour varies widely from pale or dark green, to brown, or dark or purplish-red and often in combinations of these colours.

One of the most common is *C. acaulis* which is a small plant, probably the smallest in the genus and about 10–12cm (4–4¾in) in diameter. It has shiny, apple green leaves, and because of its size is very popular as a bottle-garden plant. Even more attractive are *C. acaulis* var. *argenteus*, which has silvery scales on the upper surface of the leaves, and var. *ruber*, which has dark brownish-red scaly leaves. A somewhat larger plant, with rosettes about 20–25cm (8–10in) across, is *C. zonatus*. This has thinnish green leaves cross-banded with wide, irregular, silver bands and silvery white undersides. Var. *fuscus* is generally similar but differs in having slightly smaller leaves which are reddish-brown, but also with similar silver banding. *C. bivittatus* has a rosette about 15–20cm (6–8in) across, with green leaves striped longitudinally, either greenish-cream in var. *bivittatus*, or reddish in var. *atropurpureus*.

All of these are excellent for display along with other bromeliads, as well as being attractive in their own right. They are also easy to propagate, producing offsets freely and not only at the base of the plant but, unlike most other bromeliads, also between the leaves. These are very easily removed quite early in their development and grown on in the usual way.

FASCICULARIA (from the Latin *fasciculus*, a bundle, referring to the clustered flowers)
This is a genus of five species which are all terrestrial and native to Chile. Only two species are cultivated and both are the only bromeliads which can survive permanently out of doors in temperate climates, mainly in the milder and more protected areas. Clearly, they are also good candidates for cultivation in the cold greenhouse, but unfortunately in many cases their size precludes them from being cultivated even there. Their leaves, which are long, narrow and heavily spined, can reach about 1m (3ft 3in) in length, forming a large rosette and no reservoir. In time, many rosettes crowd together to form large hummocks.

The cultivated species are very similar to each other in overall appearance, with *F. bicolor* being the smaller. It has grey-green leaves about 50cm (20in) long which form a dense and open rosette. The flowers, of which about thirty to forty comprise the deeply sunken inflorescence, are pale blue and surrounded by creamish bracts. The other species, *F. pitcairniifolia*, has pale green leaves which can reach 1m (3ft 3in) long, and has many more slightly darker blue flowers. In both species the bases of the leaves surrounding the inflorescence turn red at flowering time.

Fascicularia pitcairniifolia

GUZMANIA (named after the eighteenth-century Spanish naturalist, Anastasio Guzman)
This is a genus of over 125 species, closely related to *Tillandsia* and *Vriesea*. They occur from southern Florida, through the West Indies and Central America to western Brazil, but they are found mainly in the rain forests of Andean Colombia and Ecuador. The species are predominantly epiphytic, although some of the larger ones have developed as terrestrials and all inhabit shady, humid forests from sea-level up to altitudes of about 3000m (10000ft).

They are open-rosette in habit with the rosettes composed of many spineless, glossy leaves which frequently have fine, longitudinal lines of purple to purplish-brown at the base of the blade and sheath. The inflorescences are always erect and borne at the end of usually stout stalks, and have short-lived flowers composed of yellow or white petals. These flowers are usually set within large, brilliantly coloured bracts of yellow, orange to red, and the whole inflorescence is

(Opposite) *Guzmania musaica*
(Below) *Guzmania monostachia*

long-lasting. The forms of inflorescence within the genus are varied and can be of simple, cylindrical spikes as in *G. monostachia* (syn. *monostachya*); a compound inflorescence of some ten to fourteen small, three-flowered spikes, widely spaced along the main stalk, as in *G. donnell-smithii*, or forming many-flowered 'heads' of small branches as in *G. musaica* and *G. zahnii*.

For the size of the genus, only a comparative few are currently found in cultivation and, with one exception, they are all grown for their attractive inflorescences. That exception is *G. musaica*, a species so named because of its beautiful, horizontal, mosaic-like leaf markings of dark green against a pale green background and reddish to violet undersides to the leaves. In addition to the foliage, this species has an attractive inflorescence of a compact, globular head of yellow flowers, set in shiny brilliant red bracts which top a similarly coloured inflorescence stalk. When not flowering, and by its leaves alone, this plant can easily be confused with the closely allied *G. lindenii*.

G. lingulata is probably the guzmania most frequently seen and occurs in several varieties. It is a smallish to medium-sized plant with a very open rosette spreading up to 50cm (20in) across. The typical *G. lingulata* var. *lingulata* has an inflorescence stalk which can reach 30cm (12in) in height and is capped by a starlike rosette of somewhat triangular, brilliant red bracts around the clustered yellow-white flowers.

The equally large var. *splendens* (syn. *G. peacockii*) has reddish leaves and a purplish-red inflorescence spike, but the most attractive is var. *cardinalis*. This is the largest of the varieties and the most spectacular by reason of its more shiny brilliant red inflorescence bracts. The smallest, var. *minor* (syn. *G. minor*), is a much more delicate plant of a more upright habit, with thin, yellowish leaves and a short stalk bearing a raised cup of yellow or red bracts and whitish-yellow flowers.

G. zahnii is also a largish plant with a rosette of up to twenty-four leaves. These are an attractive reddish to green with longitudinal stripes of dark red, all of which become a coppery red when exposed to bright light for long periods. The compact, branched inflorescence composed of bright yellow floral bracts, sepals and petals, surrounded by large, bright red bracts, tops a similarly red inflorescence stalk.

The only other species occasionally seen is *G. monostachia*, and in this the inflorescence is a compact, narrow spike about 10–12cm (4–4¾in) long of white flowers, each enclosed in striking triangular bracts of pale green, heavily marked with blackish-purple longitudinal lines. The inflorescence is topped by a sterile, flowerless area of shiny, brilliant red bracts.

Guzmanias need a well-drained, porous potting medium and grow best in temperatures between 19°–27°C (66°–80°F) throughout the year; they will not

tolerate temperatures below 10°C (50°F). They prefer moderate to shady light conditions, with some, such as *G. zahnii*, producing better coloration after periods in bright light. The potting medium must be kept lightly moist, the reservoirs regularly filled with water and the foliage mist-sprayed daily.

NEOREGELIA (named after Eduard E. von Regel, a nineteenth-century German botanist who was superintendent of the Imperial Botanic Garden in St Petersburg, Russia)

This genus of about seventy species comes mostly from the rain forests of eastern Brazil, with a few found in eastern Colombia and Peru. They are mainly epiphytic with very few occurring naturally as terrestrials. With their spiny-margined leaves and generally open-rosette habit, their classification over the years has been very complex, and this has not been made any easier because of their similarity to the closely allied genus *Nidularium*. There are, however, certain differences which can help to distinguish them. For example, although the species of both genera have spiny leaves, in *Nidularium* the blades are narrow and sword-shaped with the apices tapering to narrow, sharp points. In *Neoregelia* they are wide and straplike with broad, rounded tips which end in a very short spine that is frequently bent backwards. In *Neoregelia* the inflorescence is usually simple, with the individual flowers being stalked and forming a raceme,

Neoregelia ampullacea

or cluster, which in turn is usually sunk deep in the rosette. This means that the flowers are less showy than those of many other bromeliads, so the attraction of the genus is really in the foliage. The inflorescence of *Nidularium*, however, is compound and made up of small groups of sessile (stalkless) flowers which usually top the inflorescence stalk. In contrast to *Neoregelia*, the flower stalk rises above the centre of the rosette and is quite evident. When mature, the tips of the petals of *Neoregelia* spread almost horizontally, whereas in *Nidularium* they remain almost erect. It must be emphasized, though, that these are only pointers in differentiating the genera, and they are not infallible.

There is one exception to the open-rosette habit among cultivated bromeliads, *N. ampullacea*. This species is probably the smallest in the genus, rarely exceeding 15cm (6in) in height, with the leaves erect and forming a small flasklike rosette. The leaves, which are about 1.5cm (⅗in) wide, are dark green and irregularly blotched or banded with purplish-brown. Deep in the rosette are borne several small, blue-petalled flowers with white bases. This plant is stoloniferous (able to develop roots and therefore new plants from shoots lying along the ground) and, being so small, makes a very good subject for cultivation in a large pan or hanging basket.

Another favourite is the much larger *N. carolinae*, probably the best known member of the genus. It has a very open rosette, about 60cm (2ft) across, of shiny green leaves which, around flowering time, turn brilliant shades of red at the base along with the similarly coloured inflorescence bract. The pale lilac flowers last only a short while, but the brilliant colour of the leaves and bracts persists for several months. Even more attractive is var. *tricolor*, which has leaves longitudinally banded in various widths of creamy white which take on a pinkish tinge if grown in full sunlight. Another species of similar size to the last is *N. spectabilis* which has dark green leaves, white banded on the lilac-green underside, each one tipped with a dark blood-red spot. Around flowering time, the bases of the leaves turn red, while the bracts surrounding the inflorescence of blue flowers become purple-brown.

Different again is *N. concentrica* which is possibly the largest cultivated member of the genus. This has leaves which reach about 40cm (16in) or more in length and are very flat and about 10cm (4in) wide. They vary from pale to dark green on the upper surface, with irregular blotches and spots of blackish-purple; the undersides are covered with a coat of silvery grey scales. At flowering

time, the bases of the leaves take on an unusual lilac colour and surround the broad, many-flowered, flat inflorescence of pale blue flowers.

All these species form reservoirs which must be kept filled with water at all times. Apart from *N. ampullacea*, they can be propagated from offsets.

NIDULARIUM (from the Latin *nidus*, a nest, referring to the formation of the leaves around the inflorescence) This is a genus of more than twenty species, all but one of which are known only from Brazil. The exception, *N. delonii*, comes from south-western Colombia. In the wild they occur both as epiphytes and terrestrials, living mostly in the dark, humid, lower-altitude forests. Like the closely related *Neoregelia*, they are open-rosetted in habit with soft, glossy, spiny leaves which form reservoirs at the bases. Unlike most neoregelias, however, in many instances the inflorescence is not so deeply sunk into the centre of the rosette but is raised above it. As the flowers, which range in colour from red to blue or white, are not the showiest in the family, the attraction of the species is in their leaf coloration. The leaves vary from plain green to dark purple but may be striped or spotted. In *Neoregelia* the bases of the leaf blades assume a different and contrasting colour around flowering time, but in *Nidularium* the inner leaves of the

Nidularium innocentii

Nidularium Innocentii NOE.

rosette are much smaller and take on this change of colour over their whole length. These inner leaves may be coloured red, bright pink to maroon, or, as in *N. billbergioides* var. *citrinum*, the inflorescence is surrounded by bright yellow bracts.

There are several species popularly grown in cultivation, the smallest of which is *N. burchellii*, whose rather dull leaves with purple-red undersides form a rosette a little more than 20cm (8in) across. Its inflorescence of white flowers turns a beautiful orange colour and is known to last for several months. Another favourite is the attractive *N. fugens* with a 40cm (16in) diameter rosette of soft, bright green leaves, with dark green spots or blotches. In this species, the inner leaves of the rosette become brilliant pinkish-red and eventually turn pale lilac-blue to lavender.

Probably the most attractive of all the species in cultivation is *N. innocentii*, a species which has its inflorescence sunk deeply in the rosette and the white flowers set off by brilliant red inner leaves. There are several varieties in this species, all of which show marked variations in the leaf colour patterns. The typical var. *innocentii* has dark green to magenta leaves; var. *lineatum*, pale green leaves covered with fine longitudinal white lines; var. *paxianum* has a single broad white line running the full length of the blade. There are several other

Quesnelia quesneliana, a compact flowered species, close to *Q. testudo*, from coastal south-west Brazil.

varieties of this species and all form rosettes which are about 40–60cm (16–24in) across.

Nidulariums need a temperature in the range of $13°–30°C$ ($55°–86°F$) throughout the year, but of all the bromeliads they are able to tolerate the lowest light conditions, which makes them excellent plants for house decoration. Always remember to keep the reservoirs filled with water. Keep the potting medium just moist and mist-spray daily to maintain the humidity.

QUESNELIA (named after M. Quesnel, a one-time French consul in Cayenne)
This genus of about fourteen species is endemic to Brazil, where it occurs as terrestrials on the coastal sands almost to the water's edge, and as forest epiphytes and lithophytes in both the humid and drier forests up to altitudes around 1500m (5000ft). Their habit varies from open to upright, tubular, urnlike rosettes, with inflorescences ranging from compact, candlelike spikes to loosely flowered open racemes, very similar in appearance to those of billbergias. Although they are not as decorative as many other bromeliads, nevertheless they are good house plants, demonstrating characteris-

tics not found in other genera.

So far only four species are cultivated and even these not yet commonly so. The largest, *Q. testudo*, has a semi-open rosette consisting of leaves up to about 45cm (1½ft) long, which are green above with fine white banding on the undersides. The inflorescence is a compact cylinder from 10–20cm (4–8in) long which is very striking as it is borne upright on a thick, white stalk reaching above the leaves. The white or violet flowers are surrounded by rose-red bracts. The whole inflorescence is likened to a turtle's head, hence its Latin name *testudo*. *Q. quesneliana* is a compact-flowered species, closely related to *Q. testudo*, from south-west Brazil.

Another interesting species is *Q. liboniana* which at first appears to be a billbergia, with its tubular rosette and small, slender-stalked, arching, racemose inflorescence of loosely spaced, dark purple flowers, set off by large orange bracts. Different again is *Q. marmorata*, an upright urnlike plant with leaves which fan out instead of arising spirally as in other bromeliads. These leaves are a pale blue-green, densely mottled with maroon spots. The erect inflorescence, which droops somewhat towards the top, consists of a stalk covered with pink bracts, topped by large rose-pink floral bracts

and blue-petalled flowers. *Q. seideliana* is the last of those in general cultivation and reaches about 40cm (16in) tall, with a tufted rosette of green, spiny leaves covered with white scales. The slender, white, woolly inflorescence stalk bears a small 3cm (1¼in) densely flowered inflorescence of white-sepalled, bright blue flowers.

Temperature, water and light requirements for quesnelias are similar to those of nidulariums. As very few offsets are formed, it is advisable to allow these to become almost full-sized before separating them.

TILLANDSIA (named after the seventeenth-century Swedish botanist and physician, Elias Til-Landz)

This is by far the largest genus in the family and currently contains well over 450 species, with more still being discovered and described as new. It occurs over the whole range of the family, with about one-third found in the southern USA. The rest are spread throughout Central America and the West Indies and the whole of South America, although most of the species are found mainly within the tropics. They are found in a wide range of habitats, from humid rain and

Tillandsia lindenii

Tillandsia tenuifolia

cloud forests, to the cooler montane forests, where they nearly all grow epiphytically or are lithophytic and found on cliffs and rocks or even telegraph poles and wires. They are also found as terrestrials, especially in the drier areas where some thrive in almost waterless deserts.

The species are very variable both in size and appearance. One of the smallest is the mosslike *T. bryoides*, which rarely grows bigger than 5cm (2in) tall, whereas species such as *T. rauhii* and *T. fendleri* may reach 3m (10ft) in height. Some species, and these are mainly from the more humid forest areas, have soft, straplike, green leaves which are not apparently heavily scaled and form open rosettes. These rosettes often retain water in their centres and the plants look very much like

vrieseas, a genus in which many species are almost indistinguishable from tillandsias. In fact the two genera are only botanically separated, by reason of the presence of small scales at the base of the petals inside the flower tube of *Vriesea*, while *Tillandsia* has none. The majority of tillandsias, however, belong to the group which have leaves covered, to varying degrees, with silver, brownish or golden scales and which in form are grass-like or roughly triangular in cross-section, but rarely, if ever, straplike. These species come from the hotter, drier areas and grow either on rocks or cliffs or even terrestrially, and, if as epiphytes, then usually high up in the treetops. None of these have water-retaining reservoirs and rely solely for their moisture from the atmosphere, be it rain, fog or dew, which is absorbed through their covering of scales. Very rarely do these plants develop a normal root system, as they do not normally use roots to obtain their nourishment and moisture, but solely as a means of support and attachment to their hosts.

The inflorescences of tillandsias are very varied and can either be of solitary flowers appearing in the axils of the leaves, as in *T. usneoides*, or more usually in various types of spikes or racemes born at the ends of an inflorescence stalk. Some of these inflorescences can be very striking and attractive and composed of brightly coloured bracts in shades of yellow, red, lilac or purple. The individual flowers are usually shades of blue or violet, but in a number of species, the flowers are coloured red, pink, yellow, green or white.

Considering the large size of the genus, it is surprising that comparatively few species have so far reached cultivation. Two species, however, have been cultivated for a long time and are still the most popular. *T. cyanea* is a smallish plant with erect, narrow, greyish-green leaves, with somewhat reddish-brown stripes towards the base, and about 30cm (1ft) long. Some forty or fifty leaves form a rather close rosette about 30cm (1ft) across, from the centre of which arises the inflorescence. This is a large, flattened, elliptical spike composed of closely overlapping pinkish or green opposite bracts. The stalk, which is up to about 9cm ($3\frac{1}{2}$in) long, is not usually evident as it is surrounded by the leaf bases, giving the impression that the 15cm (6in) long, 6cm ($2\frac{1}{2}$in) wide spike is stalkless. The flowers, which appear singly from between the bracts, are violet-blue in colour and 3–5cm ($1\frac{1}{4}$–2in) across. This plant is often confused with the second most popular, *T. lindenii*, which differs in having a much longer inflorescence stalk of up to 30cm (1ft) long, bearing a similar but somewhat longer spike. In this species, the flowers are deep blue with a white centre. Recently a third species with a similar habit and inflorescence has been introduced to the market, *T. anceps*, but this is easily distinguished when in flower, as the petals are much smaller, narrower and pale lilac-blue.

With the introduction of tillandsias mounted on shells, driftwood and various *objets d'art*, several species not hitherto cultivated in this country are becoming popular. One of these is the delicate *T. recurvata*, a denizen of telephone poles and wires in much of the Americas. It is a small, fine-leaved plant which has the habit of curling round its host, with each plant appearing like a ball. The leaves, which are about 2–10cm ($\frac{3}{4}$–4in) long and covered with grey scales, twist and curve backwards along the stem. Very thin, wiry inflorescence stalks up to about 15cm (6in) long develop from near the ends of the stems, each bearing a spike of from one to five small, closely arranged, pale blue or violet flowers. Although not the most beautiful of tillandsias, it is one of the easiest to grow and its only requirements are bright light and a regular light spraying.

Probably the easiest of all to grow is Spanish Moss, *T. usneoides*. This long, trailing, wiry-stemmed plant grows happily almost anywhere. With its grey-green, threadlike stem and small, fine leaves about 2.5–5cm (1–2in) long, it forms an excellent plant to attach to, or drape over, rails in a bright position in the bathroom or kitchen. In the wild it produces solitary, small, yellow-green flowers with spreading petals, but unfortunately these are rarely seen in cultivation or are overlooked. Another very small but more attractive plant is *T. stricta*, which is found in two forms, one covered with silvery grey scales and the other almost green-leaved. In both, the short stalk is arched and bears a drooping inflorescence about 5cm (2in) long, composed of spreading, bright pink bracts surrounding blue to violet petals.

There are three other species which are frequently confused with the last, but two of them, instead of being almost stemless and regularly open-rosetted in habit, have distinct stems up to 30cm (1ft) long, with the leaves curved to one side: *T. tenuifolia* is distinguished by its 2cm ($\frac{3}{4}$in) long pink, blue or white flowers, whereas *T. araujei* has much longer white flowers, more loosely arranged in the inflorescence than in *T. stricta*. Both *T. tenuifolia* and *T. araujei* have very narrow flower bracts closely pressed to the sepals. The fourth species in this complex is *T. aeranthos*, which more closely approaches *T. stricta* in appearance, with flower bracts midway between *T. stricta* and the other two, but it differs from all three in having fewer and deep blue-purple flowers.

Two other species are occasionally seen, *T. bulbosa* and *T. baileyi*: they differ from most other tillandsias by being unusually bulbous at the base. *T. bulbosa* is a smallish plant with bright green leaves 15cm (6in) long, the blades of which are about 1cm ($\frac{2}{5}$in) wide and rolled inwards, while the bases are 2.5–3cm (1–$1\frac{1}{4}$in) wide and densely covered with pale grey scales. About twelve to fifteen leaves with closely fitting bases form a hollow, inflated, ovoid and bulb-like rosette. The flower stalk is very short, upright and red, supporting one to several short red or green spikes of violet-blue flowers. Not to be confused with the latter is *T. baileyi*, which is somewhat larger and has numerous, similarly shaped leaves, but they are densely covered with silvery grey scales and clearly marked with longitudinal, deep brown stripes. The dull red inflorescence stalk reaches 40cm (16in) in length and bears a branched inflorescence of purple or blue flowers.

Proof of the expanding interest in this genus is made obvious by the example of yet another introduction to the popular market, even as this is being written. The latest is the exceptionally attractive *T. ionantha*, a small plant barely 10cm (4in) tall, with tightly tufted rosettes of short, erect or spreading silvery grey leaves which, before flowering, turn pale pink to bright red. The

Vriesea splendens

comparatively large deep violet flowers are borne at the top of a very short stalk, deep in the centre of the rosette.

Other examples which have yet to become generally popular and available show even more different forms within the genus, such as *T. juncea* and *T. tricolor* (syn. *T. xiphostachys*), with fine, grass-like leaves; *T. flabellata* with its short inflorescence stalk bearing several radiating spikes of purple flowers; *T. flexuosa* with green leaves densely cross-banded in silvery grey; and *T. caput-medusae*, with its contorted grey leaves and branched inflorescence. These, and many others, such as the yellow-flowered *T. ixioides* and green-flowered *T. plumosa* (syn. *T. atroviridipetala*), should be sought after, as they are exciting additions to any indoor collection.

Contrary to popular belief, tillandsias are easy to grow if treated correctly. As the majority of them live in the tops of trees and are exposed to bright sunlight and wind, these are their main requirements in the home. A

FURTHER INFORMATION

Bibliography

Padilla, V., *Bromeliads* (Crown Publishers, 1973)

Rauh, W., *Bromeliads for Home, Garden and Greenhouse* (Blandford Press, 1979)

Wilson, L., *Bromeliads for Modern Living* (Merchants Publishing Co., 1977)

Societies

British Bromeliad Society
Mr R. J. Lucibell
Department of Plant Biology
Queen Mary College
London E1 4NS
England

Bromeliad Society Inc.
Lindar Harbert
Membership Secretary
2488 E. 49th
Tulsa, Okla 74015
USA

position giving them maximum bright light and free circulation of air without being draughty is the most desirable. They prefer temperatures in the range of $10°$–$32°$C ($50°$–$90°$F) all the year round and need to be mist-sprayed frequently in the summer and allowed to dry out quickly after spraying. For those in pots, the medium needs to be watered once or twice each week and a moist atmosphere is preferable at night (which makes them good candidates for cultivation in bright kitchens and bathrooms). If grown from seed, it should be noted that it takes up to eight years for most species to flower.

VRIESEA (named after Professor Willem de Vriese, 1806–1862, of Amsterdam and Leyden)
This genus of about 250 species occurs in Mexico, Central America and South America with the greatest number coming from Brazil. They are mostly epiphytic and inhabit rain forests up to altitudes of about 3000m (10,000ft) although a number grow naturally as terrestrials on cliffs and bare mountainsides.

In general, vrieseas are medium-sized plants which have broad, straplike, soft green leaves without spines and water-holding reservoirs at the base. They are open-rosetted in habit. The green leaves vary in shade and may be anything from light to blackish-green, often spotted, blotched, banded or covered with irregular markings. The inflorescences are mainly of flattened, simple or branched spikes, covered with brilliantly coloured red or yellow bracts.

Most commonly seen in cultivation is *V. splendens*, a fine, medium-sized plant with broad, deep green, purple-banded leaves reaching 30–45cm (1–1½ft) in length, with a long swordlike inflorescence of overlapping brilliant red bracts and yellow flowers. Similar is *V. splendens* var. *longibracteata* which differs in having plain green leaves and often a totally yellow-green inflorescence. Grown together, these two make a fine showing with their colours complementing each other. Another well-known example is *V. psittacina* which is a much smaller plant with thin, pale green leaves. The slender, bright red inflorescence stalk bears up to about twelve widely spaced flowers, each composed of floral bracts, which are red at the base, yellow above and green at the tips, and enclose green-spotted, yellow-petalled flowers. Not nearly as colourful as the previous two, by reason of its inflorescence, is *V. hieroglyphica*. A large plant with a rosette up to 1m (3ft 3in) across, it is a very regal plant and worthy of the long-standing name of king of the bromeliads. Each rosette is made up of some forty or so broad leaves, pale green and marked on both surfaces with irregular cross-bands in dark green or purplish-black. In comparison, the tall, green spike of dull yellow flowers is quite insignificant.

Very few distinct vriesea species are seen in cultivation, but innumerable hybrids have been made and are offered widely for sale. Many of these crossings have been made using one or other of the first two species mentioned above as one of the parents.

Vrieseas generally require a little more care in cultivation than many other bromeliads, but still adapt to being grown in the home. They need to be warm all the year round with a temperature between $18°$–$27°$C ($64°$–80F) and they thrive where they have a humid atmosphere most of the time. Water should be kept in the reservoirs, the medium kept moist and the plants mist-sprayed daily.

PLANTS FOR SPECIAL PURPOSES

MINIMUM TEMPERATURE REQUIRED			LIGHT REQUIREMENTS	
Cool (5–$10°$C [41–$50°$F])	**Moderate to warm** (10–$19°$C [50–$66°$F])		**Shady situation**	**Direct sunlight**
Abromeitiella brevifolia, A. lorentziana Aechmea recurvata, A. mexicana Fascicularia bicolor, F. pitcairniifolia Neoregelia (stiff-leaved species)	Aechmea Ananas Billbergia Cryptanthus Guzmania	Neoregelia Nidularium Quesnelia Vriesea	Cryptanthus Guzmania Nidularium Vriesea	Aechmea Ananas Billbergia Quesnelia Tillandsia

COLOURFUL FLOWERS, FLORAL BRACTS OR FRUITS	GOOD FOLIAGE	LONG FLOWERING PERIOD	EASE OF CULTIVATION	
			Suitable for beginners	**Moderately easy**
Aechmea Billbergia Fascicularia Guzmania Nidularium	Aechmea Ananas (some cvs) Billbergia Cryptanthus Guzmania Neoregelia Nidularium Vriesea	Aechmea Billbergia Fascicularia Nidularium Vriesea	Aechmea Ananas Billbergia Cryptanthus Fascicularia Neoregelia	Abromeitiella Guzmania Nidularium Quesnelia Tillandsia Vriesea

TENDER FLOWERING CLIMBERS

IN THE greenhouse or conservatory, sun-room or porch, climbing plants can both transform the scene and modify the environment by covering the roof in greenery and making valuable displays at eye level. Climbers with nodding and pendent flowers have a particular charm when grown in this way and more especially when they contribute perfume to areas used for relaxation and dining. Many climbers flower for longer and more frequently than other plants. On a more functional level, they can be trained to disguise pillars or other roof supports and also to provide shade when needed. In the home they effectively clothe screens and room partitions.

A climber is any plant which has greatly elongated its stems to reach for the light, ensuring its survival in competition with other vegetation. Looking at the range of the world's flora, by far the majority of climbers are tropical or sub-tropical in origin. Many become huge in size as they grow lushly in the warmth and humidity of forests and scramble from the forest understorey towards the sunnier forest canopy, where they flower. A few of these are obtainable commercially and form superb plants for a large, warm conservatory. Their origin is a clue to why so many climbers become bare at the base and need plants displayed in front of them. It also shows why climbers need training and thinning – or all the flower is carried way above our view.

However, there are temperate climbers of a smaller stature commensurate with the vegetation in which they compete for light, and which are more suitable for cultivation in a room or on a window sill, or in a small

(Above) *Passiflora sanguinolenta*   (Opposite) *Ipomoea horsfalliae* var. *briggsii*

greenhouse. A key to the demand for space of the climbers covered here is given on page 135. Rather more temperate species are included than is representative of their world distribution because fewer people have the warmth and space to grow the true tropicals. Some will flower in one season from seed and are best treated as annuals, although botanically they are perennials.

Cultural requirements

Conditions in the home: Since by their very nature climbers compete for sunlight, it is not surprising that nearly all need good light to flower well or at all. The more common climbers tolerant of low light, which are grown for their foliage alone (such as the philodendrons, *Rhoicissus* and *Cissus*), are omitted here. Conservatories, sun-rooms and south-facing window sills (north-facing in the southern hemisphere) are the best sites for most.

Conditions in the greenhouse: It is far easier to grow most climbers in the greenhouse because of the unrestricted light. In addition, they can be planted out in the border or in beds to give them the unlimited root run and nutrition they need. Anyone who has seen a honeysuckle struggling outside a porch in a tub will know the truth of this statement. If a conservatory or lean-to greenhouse is available, preferably south-facing (north-facing in the southern hemisphere), so much the better.

Basic cultivation

Containers: Most climbers are deep-rooting and need containers which are deep in proportion to their width. These are not always easy to find. Plastic pots dry out less quickly than clays and are generally best for vigorous plants.

Compost: Since climbers grow rapidly it is a good idea to use a rich loam-based compost. Try the products of different suppliers because the quality of loam is important and varies considerably from sample to sample. Loam-based composts provide steadier nutrition than peat-based ones and are heavier, a useful point with plants which grow tall and become top-heavy. One or two climbers need acid soil or poor soil. This is noted under the species.

Repotting and top dressing: Repot as growth demands. When this becomes difficult due to the unwieldy top-growth, remove the top 4cm (1½in) of soil and top-dress with new compost, firming lightly and watering in.

Feeding: Climbers in pots need a good liquid feeding programme weekly when in growth. Follow the manufacturer's recommendations on dilution.

Resting: There are a number of climbers which need a dry period in winter to allow them to rest and initiate flower buds for the following season of growth. See the list on page 135. As autumn approaches reduce watering until it is only given once a month to

The use of tendrils is a method employed by climbers to make their ascent. Passion flowers are a good example of this type.

stop the compost from becoming really dry. Plants treated in this way may well become drought-deciduous for this period. Clear away the leaves to stop fungal problems developing.

Training: Climbers have developed various adaptations to make their ascent and a knowledge of the major methods is useful in their training. Some kinds merely lean or arch their growth over others; these are called scandent in habit and several are excellent when trained flat on to a wall for support. Others twine their stems in a circular fashion clockwise or, more usually, anticlockwise. Others develop tendrils which grasp any support provided. Some improve on this by developing suction pads on the ends of tendrils. Another group cling by thorns or recurved hooks or whiplike extensions of the leaf mid-rib but, not surprisingly, few of these are popular house plants. Some sorts develop adventitious roots so that they literally adhere to a wall and save the work of tying in. The various methods by which vines climb fascinated the great evolutionary scientist Charles Darwin, and useful descriptions are found in his *The Movements and Habits of Climbing Plants.*

Unless the climber is a self-clinger it should be trained from the beginning on to a tripod of canes or on to a small-mesh trellis if free-standing. To cover a room divider, the training should be started early. Use plant rings which will expand as growth progresses, without restricting the plant. Never use wire to tie in. String ties need to be inspected and loosened as the plant grows.

Growing in beds: This is by far the easiest way to grow climbers satisfactorily although they will need more training. Ensure that your beds have good drainage and fill them with a mixture of three parts sterilized loam, one part coarse grit, one part moss peat and one part forest bark by volume. These basic constituents are easily available bagged at garden centres. Since much greater vigour can be expected from bed culture, ensure that there is a good structure for supporting the growth before planting. Stretch horizontal wires between vine eyes on a wall, or vertically between collars mounted on the top and bottom of pillars or other roof supports. If the vine is not self-clinging, a trellis can be mounted on the wall, leaving space behind it for tying in. Make sure the trellis matches the vigour of the chosen species as there are many flimsy kinds on the market.

Preferably plant in the spring, having raked in a good handful of general balanced fertilizer per metre run of bed. Start training a good framework of growth immediately and tie in well. Do not let the beds dry out during the period of growth, but gradually reduce watering in the autumn for those species needing a winter rest – almost no water will be needed until spring with bed culture.

Pruning: Most climbers tend to outgrow the space available and pruning is inevitable. It is, however, a time-consuming task that is made easier if you have trained a good initial framework for the perennial species. Thereafter, prune annually during the winter resting period for those which need a rest, and after flowering for

Bougainvilleas climb by means of thorns in combination with their flexuous stems.

Aristolochia sp. illustrating the twining habit common among climbing plants.

all the others. Cut out old and dead wood and reduce the younger stems to the number for which there is space. Do not cut back the leading growth of genera such as *Solandra* which bear flowers at their branch tips. Species which bear flowers on old growth, however, such as *Clerodendrum schweinfurthii*, are best spurred back in winter to a framework of older stems. Very vigorous vines can be reduced in vigour by pruning the roots. Do this at the same time as you reduce the top growth. Old, overgrown and tatty specimens in beds are best propagated and the parent removed, the bed resoiled and a young plant set out as a replacement.

Propagation

Seed: It is difficult to obtain plants of some climbers from nurserymen – shrubs seem to be a much easier market. You can, however, obtain many climbers from specialist importers as seed. Trust the supplier to deliver seed soon after harvesting as the seed of many tropical species has a limited viability. Sow immediately and follow the supplier's instructions about the germination temperature required. Heat is usually needed and this can be supplied using one of the inexpensive electric propagators with a heating element beneath it. Climbers grown as annuals are sown in the spring to flower in summer and autumn and should then be discarded. It is generally advisable to soak the seed of all genera in the pea family (Leguminosae), and also all *Ipomoea* and *Passiflora* species, in warm water for twenty-four hours, to soften the seed coat and to get rid of germination inhibitors. Remember that seedlings require maximum light after germination.

Cuttings: In spring, existing climbers will usually root in a propagator from soft shoot tip cuttings, severed immediately below a node. Chances of success can be improved by using a liquid hormone rooting dip. Legumes are difficult to root and are best grown from seed. Some genera, including *Stephanotis*, come best from a more mature cutting consisting of a short section of stem containing a pair of leaves and their axillary buds. A few, such as *Beaumontia*, will generate new plants from root cuttings.

Layering: Many climbers layer themselves naturally into the bed, or root into wall crevices, providing new plants. Remove and establish these in pots in spring. Alternatively, and more reliably, peg one-year-old stems into small pots of sandy soil. If the part of the stem to be buried is nicked or sliced halfway and the wound treated with a rooting powder, success is usually assured. Spring is the best time.

Pests and diseases

Climbers are not particularly prone to pests and diseases, perhaps because they grow so vigorously. Species in the legume family, however, are apt to attract red spider mite, especially in a conservatory or glasshouse environment with bright light and low humidity. If spotted areas on the leaves and fine webs appear, immediately start a weekly spraying programme using liquid derris or a systemic acaricide. Alternatively, introduce the predatory mite *Phytoseiulus persimilis*.

Whitefly is also occasionally troublesome. Spray with products based on natural or synthetic pyrethrins every four days or introduce the parasitic wasp *Encarsia formosa*.

Mealy bug is not a common problem with climbers but if small woolly white insects are found on stems or roots, drench the pot or bed soil with a systemic insecticide such as dimethoate diluted exactly to the manufacturer's recommendations. The same remedy is useful for attacks of scale insects which look like tiny limpets on the leaves and stems, and also for the common or garden aphids which generally gather on any young, succulent growth.

It is a good idea to deal with pests at an early stage when they are more containable and also to prevent the production of honeydew, which is the excretion of waste sugar from their sap-sucking activities. This will otherwise encourage sooty mould which disfigures climbers and is very difficult to remove. Always clear away dropped flowers and leaves and prunings to avoid the build-up of fungal diseases, and ventilate the room or greenhouse well on warm days.

Guide to purchasing

Where plants are available in garden centres choose those showing some obvious signs of vigour and rich leaf colour. Avoid plants dropping their leaves which is a sign of drought or temperature shock. Plants with woody stems and weedy pots will be old stock which may well be starved. Avoid plants loose in their pots, which shows that they have not rooted well since their last potting in the nursery.

In general, climbers are offered trained in one of five ways. Most commonly they are clipped with open rings on to a single cane. A more vigorous plant with several stems may merit a tripod of canes or even a small triangular frame to help with initial training. *Tetrastigma* may be offered growing up a moss pole. Bougainvilleas, passifloras and stephanotis are usually sold in flower as a single stem about 1.2m (4ft) in height, trained several times around a wire hoop for compactness. These can be carefully unravelled after flowering if they are to be planted out but they should then be cut back to induce branching. With many climbers you actually pay for the height of woody stem achieved. It may be cheaper to buy a younger, green-stemmed plant which will grow quickly from a spring planting. These are often sold in small pots in plastic mesh bags to protect the soft growth, and this is probably the way ahead for the marketing of many climbing plants.

Propagation of *Lapageria rosea* by air layering.

Allemanda cathartica

Recommended genera

ALLEMANDA (named after Dr F. Allemand, an eighteenth-century Swiss botanist, but commonly spelt *Allamanda*)

This genus contains fifteen species, of which the most commonly available is *A. cathartica*. This is found in both moist and seasonally dry areas of Central America and north-eastern South America. Here it produces terminal clusters of five-petalled, golden flowers up to 8cm (3¼in) across, which pervade the air with the fragrance of rich vanilla custard. Known as the golden trumpet flowers, these are some of the most free-flowering of all tropical scandent shrubs, flowering from late spring until the autumn in temperate regions. They are not true climbers, coming more into the category of leaners or scramblers. The leaves are lance-shaped and attractively whorled on the stem, though paired on older growths. In the large-flowered cultivar 'Hendersonii' the flower colour is deeper, the buds brownish and the opened flowers veined brown. It is altogether more vigorous than the true species. There is

a rare double-flowered form, var. *williamsii*. Less space-demanding is *A. neriifolia*, with leaves reminiscent of the oleander, which produces flowers up to 4cm (1½in) across.

All allemandas need rich, moist soil and good light. They usually sucker freely from the base in the summer months, and this growth is best trained in to replace old flowered wood, which should be pruned out in the winter.

ANTIGONON (from the Greek *anti*, in place of, and *polygonon*, knotweed, referring to the close relationship between these two species)

This is a genus of eight tropical American species. *Antigonon leptopus* is a pretty relative of the common-or-garden Russian vine and comes from Mexico. It is common in northern South America, where it is called the coral vine, and in the Hawaiian Islands, the Honolulu creeper. It is naturalized in Florida.

A. leptopus has distinctively heart-shaped leaves and rose-coloured flowers which are borne in profuse racemes, ending in hooked tendrils by which the plant climbs. It is rarely out of flower in the tropics, but is more difficult under glass where it needs warmth and unrestricted light. It is easily raised from seed (although the shade of flower colour will vary) and it will soon form root tubers. Bees love it. It looks charming when grown with *Thunbergia laurifolia*.

ARISTOLOCHIA (from the Greek *aristos*, best, and *locheia*, parturition, referring to its medicinal use) Members of this huge temperate and tropical genus of some 350 species are commonly known as birthworts. They are rhizomatous perennials which have some of the most sculptural flowers of all the tropical climbers and tend to appeal to lovers of carnivorous plants. None of them actually devours insects, but most have flowers which are adapted to temporarily trapping flies to ensure cross-pollination. The odour of rotting meat which many emit is too convincing to allow them entry into most conservatories, although children find them fascinating. Some of the finest are also the smelliest, namely *A. brasiliensis*, the rooster flower, *A. grandiflora*, the pelican flower, and the hybrid *A.* × *kewensis*. Rather easier to live with is *A. elegans*, the calico flower, with a well-named elegant flower up to 7cm (2¾in) across, cream and purple and brown-veined, followed by ridged seed-pods which open like a Chinese lantern. *A. gigantea* is the giant of the genus with huge, hooded

(Right) *Aristolochia grandiflora*
(Below) *Antigonon leptopus*

purple-brown flowers up to 20cm (8in) long and with no smell. Both these species come from Brazil. From Paraguay comes *A. salpinx* with tiny but charming flowers, which is well worth acquiring.

Aristolochias are best planted out rather than grown in pots. They are moisture-lovers when in growth but prefer a dry period in winter to rest. Most of the flowers are produced on the young wood, so new growth should be encouraged by pruning back to old growth during the winter. The main stems often produce attractive corky outgrowths.

Other interesting species are *A. cymbifera*, which has boat-shaped flowers, and *A. tricaudata* and *A. ridicula* which both have tailed flowers. Most species start flowering when they are young and bloom recurrently during growth. Propagate by seed.

BEAUMONTIA (named after Lady Diana Beaumont, died 1831, of Bretton Hall, Yorkshire) Only one of the fifteen species in this genus is cultivated. *B. grandiflora* is fragrant and white-flowered. It occurs naturally in forests in the eastern Himalaya, Burma and Yunnan where it festoons the lush forests with leathery leaves up to 23cm (9in) long. These develop from attractive rusty-brown buds. The blooms are trumpet-shaped and up to 15cm (6in) long in groups of six to eight. This species needs a cool dry resting period, when it should be pruned to curb its vigorous growth. If fed and watered copiously while in growth it should flower well. Raise from seed. There is a particularly fine cultivar called 'Lady Woolverton'.

BILLARDIERA (named after Jacques Julien de la Billardière, 1755–1834)

Nine species comprise this Australasian genus of which two or more are worth growing. *B. longiflora* comes from south-eastern Australia and Tasmania. Slender stems produce lance-shaped leaves to 5cm (2in) long and bear bottle-shaped yellow or cream bells 2–4cm ($\frac{3}{4}$–$1\frac{1}{2}$ in) long flushed purple inside. These go on to bear inedible blue berries 2.5cm (1in) long which give the plant its common name of purple apple-berry. This is an unusual climber for a cool greenhouse where space is restricted, and it can be grown well from seed. *B. erubescens* is a Western Australian relative, also seed-raised, with glossy dark green leaves and bright red waxy bells.

BOMAREA (named after Jacques Christophe Valmont de Bomare, 1731–1807, a French patron of science)

This is a sizeable genus of around 120–150 species of rhizomatous or tuberous-rooted perennials. They are mostly slender twiners usually reaching 1–3m ($3\frac{1}{4}$–10ft) in pot culture, and all come from the higher and cooler, moist regions of tropical America. All bear lilylike, stem-clasping leaves. Their pendent terminal clusters of bell-like flowers are orange, red, yellow or pink, some spotted or flecked with green, a reminder of their close relationship with *Alstroemeria*. A few species are available, the red- and yellow-flowered *B. multiflora* among them, and also some hybrids. This genus hybridizes freely and the species themselves are very variable. The plants will flower on a window sill if supported on a cane and given good moisture when in growth. They are usually dormant in winter when they should be kept drier.

BOUGAINVILLEA (named after the French admiral Louis Antoine de Bougainville, 1729–1811, a famous explorer and scientist)

A genus of eighteen species, bougainvilleas are woody climbers originating from subtropical areas of South America and extensively hybridized and naturalized in the gardens of the tropics and subtropics. Their showy bracts are probably responsible for introducing more colour into tropical gardens than any other genus. They climb by hooks in the axils of the leaves and bear

Bomarea × cantabrigiensis

Bougainvillea spectabilis hybrida

Double-flowered and double-bracted cultivars have been developed by bud sports from *B.* × *buttiana*. These include 'Manila Magic Red' and the golden 'Doubloon' which are reputed to hold their bract colour very well.

In temperate areas bougainvilleas are often sold in flower, trained on a single cane or around an arched hoop, and thereafter disappoint by not flowering again. The secret of success is to plant them out in a south-facing conservatory border (north-facing in the southern hemisphere) where their wood can be well-ripened and to allow them a dry period in the winter, when they will drop their leaves.

CANARINA (named after the Canary Islands, home of the first described species)

From a small genus of three species the best known is *C. canariensis*, an unusual endemic plant of the Canary Islands related to the bellflowers (*Campanula*). It grows from a tuberous rootstock and produces semi-succulent, scandent stems bearing triangular, lobed leaves, slightly reflexed and of a lovely glaucous hue. It has no climbing adaptation and needs staking to reach its 1.2m (4ft) height. This plant is normally dormant in early summer, when it should be kept dry, and grows rapidly in late summer to flower in the autumn and winter. The pendent bells are reddish-orange with deeper red veins and are strikingly large at 4–6cm (1½–2½in) long. They flare attractively at the mouth. This is a light-demanding

Canarina canariensis

terminal inflorescences of tiny white flowers surrounded by the showy, papery bracts. They have ovate to elliptic leaves.

The oldest species are the purple-bracted *B. spectabilis* and *B. glabra*, known from the 1820s and 1850s respectively. *B. peruviana* was introduced into Trinidad in 1920 and is a parent (with *B. glabra*) of the crimson cultivar 'Mrs Butt' (correctly a cultivar of *B.* × *buttiana* but sometimes now sold as 'Crimson Lake'). Later hybridization has centred on the West Indies with S. C. Harland in St Vincent, but has spread to Calcutta, Queensland, and to Kenya and Natal. Later colours have originated as bud sports ('Mrs McLean', carmine-red, and 'Mary Palmer', variously white to purplish) or through further cross-pollination.

There are now at least sixty named hybrids. Some of the finest are: 'Barbara Karst' (magenta); 'Killie Campbell' (bright red); 'Golden Glow' (pale orange); 'Scarlet Queen' (crimson); 'Louis Wathen' (carmine-red); 'Rosa Catalena' (an old hybrid with rose-scarlet bracts); 'Poulton's Special' (fuchsia purple); 'Brilliant' (ruby-red); 'Margaret Bacon' (rose); 'James Walker' (magenta) and 'Jennifer Fernie' (white). *B. glabra* 'Variegata' has green and white variegated leaves.

plant, best in a cool conservatory or greenhouse, but it is possible to get it to flower on a sunny window sill. Raise it from seed or from cuttings of basal shoots.

CLERODENDRUM (from the Greek *kleros*, chance, and *dendron*, a tree, said to refer to the variable medicinal properties)

This genus of some 400 mainly tropical and subtropical species includes shrubs and trees. There are two commonly cultivated climbing clerodendrums native to tropical West Africa. *Clerodendrum thomsonae* is named the bleeding heart vine after its flowers which consist of a cream calyx surrounding a blood-red corolla. The inflorescences are both terminal and axillary and flower profusely throughout the summer and autumn. The dying calyces become flushed with rosy-purple and reveal blue fruits which are attractive in themselves. This is a spectacular twining vine which can reach 7m (23ft), but is usually less. It was introduced into Europe in 1861 and is sometimes sold in the pot-plant trade. It is easily raised from cuttings.

C. splendens has more rounded leaves and is usually less vigorous in cultivation, twining only to 3m (10ft) in height. The flowers of this species are borne terminally. They are brilliant red throughout and the exserted stamens, common to the family Verbenaceae, reach 2.5cm (1in) in length. The calyces turn purplish-red when the corollas have dropped. *C. schweinfurthii* is a scandent shrub which is best trained against a wall, performing the same function as a climber and reaching as high as 3m (10ft). This species has pale green, softly hairy leaves and large heads of white flowers borne only on the old wood in early summer. It is best spur-pruned in winter or the flowers will be lost.

CLIANTHUS (from the Greek *kleos*, glory, and *anthos*, a flower)

Only one of the known species is widely and easily grown, *C. puniceus*, the parrot's bill or lobster claw plant from New Zealand, which is one of the three members of this Australasian genus. It is an arching, scandent shrub in the pea family which makes an excellent display trained as a wall shrub in a frost-free greenhouse. It will cover an area of 2m (6½ft) square with its soft pinnate leaves and pendent clusters of scarlet flowers, up to eight in a bunch. Each flower has a hooked keel petal which has given rise to the common names. There is a pink form and also a white one which comes true from seed. The seed should be soaked for twenty-four hours in warm water before sowing. This plant does best in full sun in well-drained and poorish soil, but tolerates some shade.

CLITORIA (from the Latin *clitoris*, referring to the structure of the flower)

C. ternatea, the butterfly pea or mussel-shell pea, was

Clerodendrum thomsonae

Clianthus puniceus

Clitoria ternatea

Cobaea scandens 'Variegata'

named by Linnaeus and introduced from the Island of Ternate in the East Indies in 1739. It is a member of a genus of some forty tropical and subtropical species, and is a perennial climber with soft, pinnate leaves bearing five to nine leaflets. It twines to about 3m (10ft) in height and bears its axillary flowers singly. These are reminiscent of an inverted sweet pea, though rather more hooded, and are of an extraordinarily deep blue, a colour not often found in the tropics and valued even in temperate regions. White and pale blue forms and doubles also occur, all of which come true from seed. The seed needs soaking overnight in warm water before sowing. When grown in a greenhouse or on a window sill this plant should flower well but may need spraying with liquid derris against red spider mite. It needs a poorish, well-drained soil.

COBAEA (named after Father Bernardo Cobo, 1572–1659, a Spanish Jesuit missionary and naturalist) This is a genus of about eighteen species of which *C. scandens* is the most widely known. It comes from Mexico and western South America and bears fascinating flowers. Each flower consists of a large, 5–7cm (2–2¾in) cuplike corolla which opens pale green,

deepening to mauve, and is held by a saucer-like calyx. The plant's common name is the cup and saucer creeper. It is a vigorous tendril climber reaching 7–10m (23–33ft). The leaves are pinnate with three pairs of leaflets and the mid-rib extended into a much branched tendril armed with tiny hooks. The method by which these circle, or nutate, to find supports to lasso was described by Charles Darwin. In fact many parts of the plant move; the flower stalk bends before the flower opens and again as it dies, and the stamens and style will move if touched. There are forms with deep purple and with white flowers. Raise the plants from seed sown in spring. It can be treated as a half-hardy annual if space will not permit cultivation as a perennial. It only requires frost-free conditions.

ECCREMOCARPUS (from the Greek *ekkremes*, hanging or pendent, and *karpos*, a fruit)
E. scaber, the Chilean glory flower, one of a genus of five South American species, is a native of Chile which will flower from seed in its first year and so is often grown as an annual. If grown under glass as a perennial, however, it will reach 5m (16ft) or more. The form usually seen bears orange bottle-shaped flowers 2–3cm (¾–1¼in)

Gff. Lith. & pic. in Horto Van Houtteano.

long, grouped in axillary racemes among the rather lobed pinnate foliage. There are red and golden forms which come true from seed. This is a tendril climber similar in its climbing mechanism to *Cobaea scandens*. In a cool conservatory it may behave as an herbaceous perennial and die down to the base over the winter. It usually produces copious quantities of winged seeds and self-seeds freely. Provide a well-drained soil.

HARDENBERGIA (named after Franziska, Countess von Hardenberg, sister of the Austrian Carl von Hügel, a patron of horticulture)
The two members of this genus, *H. comptoniana* and *H. violacea*, are slender legumes from Western Australia, where they are called blue coral pea or the native wisteria. They are evergreen, like so many Australian plants, and bear lance-shaped, leathery leaflets in groups of one to three or, rarely, four or five. They twine to 2–3m (6½–10ft) in height. Violet-blue flowers, marked with greenish-white, are held in wisteria-like racemes up to 13cm (5in) long and open in winter and spring. Both species are easy to grow in a cool greenhouse. Like *Eccremocarpus* and *Cobaea*, they will survive outside in very mild areas of temperate countries. Raise from seed soaked overnight in warm water.

HIBBERTIA (named after George Hibbert, 1757–1837, owner of a private botanic garden at Clapham in London)
The genus *Hibbertia* is a group of about 100 species of Australasian and Madagascan evergreens which deserve to be better known. Many are pretty trailing ground-cover plants, but there is a superb climber among them. This is *Hibbertia scandens* (*H. volubilis*), the guinea flower, or guinea gold vine, which is a woody climber, often reaching 7m (23ft) in height under glass and 10m (33ft) in California where it does particularly well. This vine twines and bears glossy, rather fleshy leaves up to 10cm (4in) long which are a rich, dark green. The five-petalled flowers are lemon yellow, up to 5cm (2in) across and densely filled with stamens, giving them the appearance of an open single rose. The flowers open from three-pointed buds in summer and autumn (in Australia often all the year round). It can be raised from cuttings or from seeds – which are scarlet and borne freely in large pods. This twiner is particularly well suited to clothing a pillar where it will form a column of flower.

HIBISCUS (the Greek name for mallow, used by the botanist Linnaeus for this closely related genus)
H. schizopetalus, from tropical East Africa, is a scandent member of a very popular genus of some 300 tropical and subtropical species. It has the usual prominent style

Hibiscus schizopetalus

of these showy flowers but the petals are sharply reflexed and attractively lobed, giving the flower the appearance of a Chinese lantern. Also, the flower stalks are longer than in other hibiscuses, making the plant excellent for training over an arch or across a roof space where the flowers can hang down. It can be raised from seed or cuttings and needs good feeding when in growth in warm conditions.
See also USEFUL PLANTS.

IPOMOEA (from the Greek *ips*, a worm, and *homoios*, similar to, referring to the twisting stems)
There are altogether about 500 species in the genus *Ipomoea*, occurring from the tropics to the warm temperate areas. Some are shrubby or erect, the rest are twiners. They are as a group known as the morning glories, although some flower at other times of the day or night. They may be annual or perennial, and usually have trumpet-shaped flowers which are short-lived but freely produced. The vigorous perennial species often develop root tubers. (Sweet potatoes are in this genus.) All ipomoeas need full sun and will orient their flowers towards it. Unless stated otherwise, most come easily from seed which is best nicked or soaked in warm water overnight before sowing.
I. acuminata, the blue dawn flower or perennial morning glory, comes from South and Central America and the West Indies but is now widely distributed in the tropics. It will reach 13m (44ft). It has heart-shaped or three-lobed leaves and vivid blue flowers 5–8cm (2–3¼in) across which age to purplish during the day. It is propagated by cuttings or layers.
I. alba (syn. *I. bona-nox* or *Caloncytion aculeatum*) delights in the common name of moon flower. This is a night-flowering climber from tropical America which reaches 2–3m (6½–10ft) in height as an annual but up to 13m (44ft) as a perennial. The flowers are a satiny white, scented and up to 15cm (6in) across. It is probably best cultivated as an annual, often flowering only six weeks after sowing. This is one of the finest vines for conservatories which are used as dining areas and is a favourite in the subtropics for planting around restaurants. The flowers close promptly a few hours after daybreak.
I. pes-caprae, the goat's foot vine, is so named after its two-lobed leaves, although its subspecies *brasiliensis* has elliptic leaves. Both have purplish-pink flowers with a darker centre, and will grow well in beach sand or poor soil. It is a vigorous perennial best treated as an annual in a greenhouse. It is best known from the subspecies and is sometimes listed as *I. brasiliensis*.
I. horsfalliae, from the West Indies, is known in cultivation from its large-flowered variety *briggsii*. This is a perennial growing to 8m (27ft) with rather funnel-shaped flowers, narrow and flaring only to 6cm (2½in)

Jasminum polyanthum

across. They are of an unusual magenta colour and rather fleshy, with the calyx and petiole flushed maroon. The leaves are divided into five rather wavy leaflets. This species needs a summer dry eason to flower and then often does so late in the year or over the winter. Raise it from cuttings, not seed.

I. lobata (correctly *Mina lobata*), or Spanish flag, comes from Mexico and South America where its reddish stems climb to 4.5m (14½ft). The three-lobed leaves are handsome and the flowers are orange. They open from scarlet buds and fade to yellow. The flowers are tubular and have exserted stamens with little resemblance to other morning glories. It is best grown as an annual.

I. quamoclit (*Quamoclit pennata*), the cypress vine, is an annual which climbs to 4–5m (13–16ft). It has unusual pinnate leaves with leaflets reduced until they seem skeletonized. The plant bears scarlet, long-tubed flowers from the leaf axils.

I. tricolor (*I. caerulea*) is the annual vine most commonly known as the morning glory. It comes from Mexico, Central America and the West Indies, twines to several metres and produces blue flowers fading to red-purple and up to 10cm (4in) across. There is a good cultivar called 'Heavenly Blue'.

See also USEFUL PLANTS for *Ipomoea batatas*.

JASMINUM (from the Latin form of Persian *yasmin*) The jasmines are a large group of 200–300 sun-loving species, mainly climbers, and mostly Asian in origin. The majority are fragrant and white-flowered although some are yellow and pink. The climbers have simple, trifoliate or pinnate opposite leaves. The best known are the hardy garden species: *officinale*, *nudiflorum*, *beesianum*, *mesnyi* and the hybrid × *stephanense*.

The only species commonly seen as a pot plant is *Jasminum polyanthum*, from Yunnan in China, which is offered for sale on canes or twined around a wire hoop. This is a charming plant for a cool room, with pinnate ferny leaves of five to seven leaflets and very fragrant white flowers, flushed pink outside and borne in profuse clusters of twenty to thirty. It needs a cool season to initiate its flowering, which then occurs in winter and spring. The following are also suitable for a coolish, very light room or greenhouse: *J. abyssinicum*, from Ethiopia, white-flowered and very fragrant with inflorescences of thirty to fifty flowers; *J. angulare* and *J. azoricum*, fragrant and white but with few-flowered panicles and from South Africa and Madeira respectively; *J. dichotomum*, from tropical Africa, with profuse white, fragrant flowers tinged purple and red; *J. dispermum*, from the Himalaya and Yunnan, with very fragrant white flowers backed pink and also pink in bud; *J. grandiflorum* subsp. *floribundum*, from tropical Africa and Ethiopia, with very fragrant white flowers from pink buds; *J. fluminense*, from tropical Africa, Mauritius and the Seychelles (but widely naturalized in the New World), with finely hairy leaves and very fragrant white flowers from greenish and pink buds. Finally, there is *J. odoratissimum*, from Madeira and the Canaries, with alternate leaves and clear yellow flowers, not always fragrant, in groups of ten to twenty.

The more tropical species really needing a warm conservatory to flower are *J. kedahense*, from Malaysia, with fragrant white flowers in groups of seven to fifteen, and *J. maingayi*, from Malaysia, with pure white flowers of an exquisite star shape, though quite scentless and borne in compact terminal heads. *J. rex*, from Thailand and Kampuchea, has white, scentless flowers from pink buds, the largest of any flower in the genus at 5–7.5cm (2–3in) across. It is rightly called the king jasmine.

Kennedia rubicunda

KADSURA (the Japanese name for the plant in Latin form)

The kadsura vines are closely related to magnolias and come from south-east Asia and Japan. There are ten species of evergreen perennial twiners with alternate, waxy leaves. They bear pink, yellow or white flowers 5cm (2in) across, either bunched on the old wood or solitary and axillary. These are followed by globular heads of scarlet berries. *K. marmorata* is grown at Kew, as is *K. japonica* from Korea and Japan. The latter is available commercially from seed. It reaches 3m (10ft) in height and bears small yellowish flowers. The leaves redden in autumn. This species is hardier than *K. marmorata*.

KENNEDIA (named after John Kennedy, 1775–1842, a nurseryman from Hammersmith, London)

This neglected Australian genus of fifteen perennial trailers and twiners has brightly coloured pea flowers. Some are ground-cover plants but the species which are mentioned here also make showy cool greenhouse climbers when trained up against a wall. Several species flower well in the Australian house at Kew where they seem to be remarkably free of the red spider mite which usually affects legumes under glass. Provide a well-drained soil and grow in full sun. They are easily raised from seed. Chip or soak the seed in warm water overnight before sowing in the spring.

K. coccinea, the coral vine, has hairy shoots with clover-like leaves and groups of scarlet flowers marked with a yellow eye. These are borne on long stalks.

K. nigricans has dark maroon flowers marked with gold on the standard (upright) petal and leaves like runner beans. It comes from Western Australia.

K. rubicunda is an eastern Australian plant, vegetatively similar to *K. nigricans* but with reddish flowers.

LAPAGERIA (named after Joséphine Tascher de la Pagerie, 1st Empress of Napoleon)

The Chilean bellflower or copihue, *L. rosea*, is a choice climber of a monotypic genus, and is much in demand. It is the national flower of Chile. The plant has twining stems with lance-shaped leathery leaves, up to 13×7cm ($5\frac{1}{4} \times 2\frac{3}{4}$in) across but usually less. The axillary, bell-shaped flowers, which tend to be tip-borne, reach 8cm ($3\frac{1}{4}$in) in length and are waxy and long-lasting. There are red and white forms, and the seedlings may be marbled or flushed with either of these colours. The flowers are followed by greenish berries which are edible. This species is best grown in a cool greenhouse where it will reach several metres (yards) in height if well grown. Train it across the roof so that the bells can hang down. It is usually commercially available as seed, which is not difficult to raise in an acid, peaty soil.

MANDEVILLA (named after Henry John Mandeville, a British minister in Argentina *c*1837, who introduced *M. laxa*)

The mandevillas are floriferous climbers from a genus of 114 species, from tropical to warm temperate America, which should be grown under glass. All bear simple, paired leaves and flowers with a long tube and fine flaring petals. They are mostly twiners. The following species are commonly available, both of which need rich, moist, but well-drained soil.

M. laxa (*M. suaveolens*), the Chilean jasmine, has white scented flowers 5cm (2in) across in groups of five to fifteen. It is fast-growing, with obovate leaves to 8–15cm (3¼–6in) long which are shed in winter, and is easily grown from seed which is borne in pods reaching 30cm (1ft) in length.

M. (*Dipladenia*) *splendens* was introduced by Sanders and Co. from Brazil and is sometimes sold in the pot-plant trade as *M. sanderi* (or *Dipladenia sanderi*), a closely allied species. This has huge rose flowers, 10–13cm (4–5¼in) across, which grow larger and darker as they age and are held in groups of one to four. The foliage is richly glossy and reaches 8–20cm (3¼–8in) in length. In the greenhouse it will flower between spring and autumn and is easily propagated from cuttings.

Mandevilla laxa

MAURANDYA (*Maurandia*) (named after Catalina Pancratia Maurandy, a Spanish botanist of the late eighteenth century)

The maurandyas are a group of some ten species of slender perennial climbers from Mexico, now included in *Asarina*, but three are usually available from seed under their old name. All of them climb by twining petioles. All the species have roughly triangular leaves and typical foxglove flowers with a long tube and flaring lip. They are easily raised from seed sown in the spring. They will flower well the following winter in a cool greenhouse or conservatory where they give useful colour at a sombre time of year.

MUTISIA (named after J. C. Mutis, 1732–1809, an anatomy teacher from Cadiz who studied South American plants)

The mutisias are climbing members of the daisy family with flowers which last well when cut. They come from temperate South America and do well in a cool conservatory, sun-room or in a bright window. They are evergreen and climb with the aid of the leaf mid-rib which is extended into a branched tendril. Of the sixty known species the two most commonly available from seed have toothed, stalkless, holly-like leaves. Both come from Chile. The seed is borne in dandelion-like heads.

M. ilicifolia has reddish stems, veins and tendrils and a ridged stem. The flowers are pink to pale mauve, centred yellow and are 5–8cm (2–3¼in) across. It will flower nearly all the year round.

M. oligodon is semi-climbing with stems to 1m (3¼ft) long. It has shiny leaves which are white-felted beneath. The buds and young growth are also woolly. The silver-pink flowers reach 6cm (2½in) across.

PANDOREA

PANDOREA (named after Pandora, in Greek mythology the first mortal woman sent to earth by Zeus) The pandoreas are eight to ten species of evergreen twiners from Malaysia and Australia. They have pinnate leaves and many-flowered inflorescences of tubular flowers with five flaring lobes. Both of the following species are vigorous and best suited to a cool conservatory or sun-room. They are raised from seed or cuttings. The most common species is *P. pandorana*, the wonga wonga vine from eastern Australia, Tasmania and New Guinea. It bears small 2cm (¾in) long scented flowers in great profusion from the leaf axils, if given enough light. The flowers are cream to buff-yellow, streaked red and rather hairy. It produces juvenile, fernlike, sometimes bronzed foliage when grown from

(Opposite) *Maurandya barclaiana*
(Below) *Pandorea pandorana*

Bignonia pandorana.

seed. The mature foliage is pinnate, with three to nine leaflets. *P. jasminoides*, the bower plant from Queensland and New South Wales, has larger flowers 6–7cm (2½–2¾in) across. They are usually creamy white or pale pink with a dark pink or purple, hairy throat.

PASSIFLORA

PASSIFLORA (from the Latin *passio*, passion, and *flos*, a flower, referring to the symbolism of the floral parts) The passion flowers are a genus of about 400 tropical and temperate species, most of which climb. They are tendril clingers, and many more species deserve to be cultivated (for both flower and fruit) than *P. caerulea*, which is reasonably hardy outside in temperate countries on a sunny wall. The flower has an intricate structure which has inspired the Christian imagination since the seventeenth century. The passion refers to the Passion of Christ; the five-lobed leaves are thought to represent the hands of the persecutors, the five sepals and five petals the ten apostles at the Cross, the corona the crown of thorns, the five stamens the five wounds of Christ, the central column the scourging post, the three styles the three nails and the tendrils the cords binding Christ to the cross. On a more secular level, most people find the flowers intricate and beautiful. Most species also fruit well and can be raised from seed. They need glasshouse or conservatory conditions to accommodate their size, but many grow well in containers and many species flower well when young. The following are available from seed:

P. cinnabarina, an Australian species with scarlet flowers 6–7cm (2½–2¾in) across.

P. edulis, the purple granadilla or passion fruit from Brazil, Paraguay and northern Argentina, has yellowish-white flowers banded purple, 5–7cm (2–2¾in) across and followed by purple, wrinkled, edible fruit if in a really sunny position. There is also a yellow-fruited form, *flavicarpa*, used commercially in Australia and the West Indies to produce passion-fruit juice.

P. herbertiana is an Australian species with small flowers of an unusual green and orange, reaching 4cm (1½in) across.

P. mollissima, the banana passion fruit, comes from Venezuela, Peru, Colombia and Bolivia. It has downy stems and leaves and pink, pendent flowers 8cm (3¼in) across with a long calyx-tube of equal length. The fruits are covered with yellowish hairs and yield an edible juice. In temperate areas it flowers from August until late November.

P. quadrangularis, the giant granadilla, is of unknown origin but is now cultivated in tropical America, Indonesia and India. It has a winged, four-angled stem and ovate, undivided leaves reaching 10–20cm (4–8in) in length. The flowers are white, flushed purple and pendent, revealing the wavy white and violet corona filaments which some have likened to jellyfish tentacles.

It is a dramatic flower, reaching 10–12cm (4–4¾in) across, and is followed by globular smooth-skinned fruits. These are edible but are not as good as those of *P. edulis*. They ripen slowly.

Among the best red-flowered species, not always easily available, is *P. coccinea*, from Venezuela, Bolivia, Peru, Brazil and the Guianas, with simple, softly hairy, scalloped leaves. The flowers are a magnificent scarlet and reach 7–10cm (2¾–4in) across. It flowers nearly all the year round and bears fruits which are striped and marked in green and orange. This does not do well in a pot and is best allowed to grow away in a conservatory border. The flower of the lovely *P. antioquiensis*, from Colombia, broadly resembles that of *P. mollissima* but is rosy-red. Its fruit is also edible.

PETREA (named after Lord Robert James Petre, 1713–43, a patron of horticulture and botany)
This is a genus of about thirty tropical and West Indian species. *P. volubilis*, the star flower vine or purple wreath, is a West Indian and Central American shrubby twiner of medium vigour, reaching about 3–4m (10–13ft) in height. It bears leaves 5–20cm (2–8in) long. The star-like flowers, 2.5cm (1in) across, are borne in long, wreathing racemes. The colour varies from deep to pale lilac to almost grey. It will take cool greenhouse treatment and can be raised from seed.

Plumbago capensis

PLUMBAGO (from the Latin *plumbum*, lead, referring to its supposed ability to cure lead poisoning)
This genus of about twelve species occurs in the warmer region of the world. *P. auriculata* (*P. capensis*), the South African leadwort, is well known for its vivid sky-blue flowers. It is a scandent shrub but planted out in a south-facing conservatory (north-facing in the southern hemisphere) and trained to cover a wall, it will produce as good a sheet of colour as any true climber. The leaves are lance or spatula-shaped, 2.5–5cm (1–2in) long, and of a fresh, pale green. The flowers resemble those of phlox and reach 2.5cm (1in) across, borne in dense terminal and axillary inflorescences, and of a colour not easy to capture on film. There is also a white form. This plant is easy to propagate from cuttings and seed. Spur-prune the plant after flowering in late summer. It can be kept nearly dry in winter.

PYROSTEGIA (from the Greek *pyr*, fire, and *stege*, a roof, referring to its high-borne mass of richly hued flowers)
P. venusta, from a genus of five species, is a vigorous Brazilian climber with orange flowers, lending it the name of Chinese cracker flower or flame vine. In flower it is one of the most spectacular of all tropical climbers

with profuse terminal and axillary panicles. Like many Bignoniaceae it has pale green leaves consisting of two or three leaflets and a tendril, while the flowers are tubular, about 5cm (2in) long, and flare at the mouth. It is best planted out in a cool greenhouse, and it must have a cool dry period during the winter months to produce its fine floral display.

QUISQUALIS (from the Latin *quis*, who?, and *qualis*, what?, referring to the way the plant changes from a shrub to a climber)

This species, *Q. indica*, known as the Rangoon creeper, from a genus of about eighteen species, is a bushy shrub when young which then develops twining stems with simple, paired leaves. It comes from south-east Asia and is a common ornamental in West Africa and India. The fragrant flowers are borne profusely in the leaf axils and are in groups of twenty or so, opening a few at a time and forming long tubes with five petals at the tips. The colour is white, changing to pink, then to rose and finally to deep carmine over a period of two days, during which time the petals also reflex. The effect is quite charming. The plant is deciduous and develops hooks on the older stems. It flowers throughout the summer and autumn as a greenhouse plant.

Pyrostegia venusta

SOLANDRA (named after Daniel Carl Solander, 1736–82, a Swedish botanist who later became Keeper of the Natural History Department at the British Museum in London)

The solandras, or chalice vines, are a group of around ten species from the New World tropics. Five species are known in cultivation, all woody shrubs with a leaning or sprawling habit requiring some training on to a wall or pillar. The leaves are undivided and attractively glossy, often purplish when young. They make a good foil to the large funnel-shaped yellow flowers borne at the branch tips, which have the curious texture of chamois leather and are scented. All need full sun and rich soil in a greenhouse border, although cuttings have been known to flower in a pot.

S. grandiflora, the silver cup vine, bears 20cm (8in) long flowers which are greenish-white, lined purple within and ageing to yellow. *S. longiflora*, Gabriel's trumpet, has flowers 25cm (10in) long which are fragrant at night. Both these species need more warmth than the fine *S. maxima*, the cup of gold or golden chalice from Mexico, which is the most popular ornamental. The flowers are butter-yellow, cup- rather than funnel-shaped, and up to 15cm (6in) across with purple-brown lines inside. *S. guttata* is similar, but shorter in stature and with finely hairy leaves. These last two species need only a frost-free conservatory or

Solandra grandiflora

greenhouse and will flower best if kept rather dry in winter, even at the expense of the leaves being dropped.

S. *brachycalyx* is the deepest-coloured species with nearly orange flowers and a purple-flushed calyx. Raise all species from cuttings or seed.

SOLLYA (named after Richard Horsman Solly, 1778–1858, a British plant physiologist)
This genus contains two species, of which S. *heterophylla* (S. *fusiformis*) is known as the bluebell creeper. It is a small-growing evergreen from Western Australia which twines to 2m (6½ft), bearing vivid blue nodding bells in groups in summer and autumn among its lance-shaped leaves. The flowers are followed by purple-blue berries 4cm (1½in) long. This climber is easily raised from seed and is best trained on to canes in a pot in a cool greenhouse or conservatory.

STEPHANOTIS (from the Greek *stephanos*, a crown, and *otis*, an ear, said to refer to the petal-lobes)
S. *floribunda*, the Madagascar jasmine or bridal flower, is the only available member of a genus of five species. It

climbs slowly as a twiner and bears smooth, fleshy leaves 7.5–10cm (3–4in) long of a rich, glossy green, an excellent foil to the flowers which are held in clusters of six to eight and are known as pips in the florist trade. They are pure white, waxy, long-tubed and open to 2.5–4cm (1–1½in) across. They have a heavy, rich fragrance. The plant is usually sold in flower, trained around a hoop, where it will hold its flowers for some time and perfume a whole room.

To grow it on, plant it in a larger pot or bed in a conservatory or cool greenhouse where it can be trained across the roof so that the flowers can hang down. The plant needs a winter rest when it should be kept rather dry and quite frost-free until it restarts into growth in the spring. It prefers an acid soil. This plant is produced commercially from leaf-bud cuttings but seed is sometimes available, although it is scarce and expensive because the plant rarely fruits, and when it does the pods are a long time in ripening.

STRONGYLODON (from the Greek *strongylos*, round, and *odous*, a tooth, referring to the calyx-teeth)
The jade vine, S. *macrobotrys*, is one of about twenty species of twiners from Madagascar and the Philippines.

It is a legume with wisteria-like flowers of a luminous jade green, the colour being very rare in the plant kingdom and very difficult to capture accurately on film. It creates a true floral spectacle, the racemes reaching over 60cm (2ft) in length in its native Philippines. The leaves are trifoliate and are cream when young and lax, then turning to violet and hardening and maturing to a deep green. The large ovoid fruits bear short-lived seed. This plant is difficult to maintain in a pot and needs planting out in a warm conservatory in rich, moist but well-drained soil. It will only flower when fully established, but is well worth the wait.

SUTHERLANDIA (named after James Sutherland, c1639–1719, a professor of botany at Edinburgh)

This genus contains six species, of which *Sutherlandia frutescens* is a charming South African scandent shrub reaching 2m (6½ft) in height. It bears the pinnate leaves common to the pea family which are covered with fine hairs, giving it a silvery appearance. They form an attractive background to the scarlet, beaked flowers 3–4cm (1¼–1½in) long, borne in midsummer. The flowers are followed by inflated seedpods of a pale, translucent green. It will do well in a pot of well-drained soil trained up a tripod of canes in a sunny window sill, and is easily raised from seed which has been soaked overnight. It deserves to be more widely known.

SWAINSONA (named after Isaac Swainson, 1746–1812, a London doctor who owned a private botanic garden in Twickenham, near London)

This genus contains more than sixty species, of which *S. galegifolia* is a temperate Australian climber, known there as the smooth Darling pea. It produces soft shoots which reach somewhat over 1m (3ft 3in) in height from a basal perennating rootstock. The leaves are pinnate with small, well-spaced leaflets and the flowers resemble small sweet peas. The flower colour will vary from white, pink or red to brick-red. The spikes reach 20cm (8in) long and are held erectly from the leaf axils. They make good long-stemmed cut flowers. This plant needs tying in loosely to a tripod of canes and will flower all summer if grown in full sun. Prune it hard after flowering and keep on the dry side in winter. The plant is raised from seed soaked overnight in warm water.

TETRASTIGMA (from the Greek *tetra*, four, and *stigma*, the pollen-catching organ of a flower, which in this case has four lobes)

The tetrastigmas or chestnut vines, which form a large genus of some ninety species, are vigorous, woody tendril clingers from the tropical rain forests of south-east Asia. Both the species mentioned here have large, rather fleshy, palmate leaves covered underneath with a brown felt which is especially noticeable on the young

Swainsona galegifolia

growth and all over the stems. They will take over a conservatory if planted in a border or large tub. They will tolerate some shade and are sometimes offered in the pot-plant trade trained up a moss pole or on to a tripod of canes. They make good specimen plants for display in a hallway or living-room. Propagate them from tip cuttings.

T. obovatum comes from the eastern Himalaya down into south-east Asia. The leaflets are more rounded than those of its cousin *T. voinierianum*, from Vietnam, which has rather waxy leaves with three to five leaflets reaching at least 30cm (1ft) across. Both are good foliage plants but *T. voinierianum* occasionally produces greenish flowers dotted with red on the old wood, followed by edible (but acid) grapes.

Both these plants will need regular pruning, repotting and feeding if grown in containers. They require well-drained soil but adequate supplies of moisture to sustain the lush foliage.

Thunbergia laurifolia

THUNBERGIA (named after Carl Peter Thunberg, 1743–1828, a Swedish doctor and botanist who collected plants in South Africa and Japan, later professor at Uppsala)

Most of the cultivated climbing members of this large genus of about 200 species are Asian in origin and are very vigorous twiners bearing long pendent racemes. They all tend to sucker from the base.

T. laurifolia, from south-east Asia, has fine lavender-blue flowers. The most free-flowering form has been named at Kew Gardens 'Augusta's Blue'. It flowers almost throughout the whole year and has laurel-like leaves.

T. grandiflora, the Bengal clockvine, is similar but with more heart-shaped leaves. It has a fine white form.

T. mysorensis, from southern India, has yellow and red flowers borne on the current year's growth.

T. coccinea, from the Himalaya, is a red-flowered species resembling *T. mysorensis* but with smaller flowers marked yellow in the throat.

All thunbergias prefer a dry resting season. They are reliable, floriferous climbers requiring warm conservatory conditions.

TIBOUCHINA (the Guyanese vernacular name in Latin form)

T. urvilleana, the glory bush, is a scandent shrub from tropical South America with great floral value and is a member of a large tropical American genus of more than 200 species. The leaves are lance-shaped and softly hairy, which gives them a grey-green appearance. The five-petalled flowers are borne in terminal heads. They are a superb rich, royal purple, 5cm (2in) across (or more if well-grown) and with prominent stamens. This plant will flower when quite small on a frost-free window sill in full light. If planted out in a conservatory or cool greenhouse border the plant will produce long, light brown, canelike growth which is best trained on to a wall. The main flowering is in late summer to early winter. Provide well-drained neutral to acid soil. Raise from seed, tip or heel cuttings.

TRACHELOSPERMUM (from the Greek *trachelos*, neck and *sperma*, seed)

The trachelospermums are a genus of about thirty species from eastern Asia, of which two are commonly available. They make very good twining evergreens for a conservatory or sun-room where their deliciously scented flowers can best be appreciated. Both species bear glossy dark green leaves up to 6cm (2½in) long and develop whip-like extension growth which will weave tightly into a supporting mesh and will even try to attach itself to brickwork. The white flowers are borne in many-flowered cymes and are slightly twisted and fimbriated. Their scent is of sweet vanilla or jasmine.

T. jasminoides, the star or confederate jasmine from China and Japan, has flowers up to 2cm (¾in) across. It will climb to 4m (13ft) in height. There is a variegated form with grey-green and yellow leaves which are less good as a foil to the flowers.

T. asiaticum from Japan and Korea is similar but is reputedly both faster-growing and slightly hardier. It has yellowish-white flowers. Both species are available in the nursery trade where they are raised from cuttings.

FURTHER INFORMATION

Bibliography

Beckett, K. A., *Climbing Plants* (Croom Helm, 1983)

Bor, N. L. and Raizada, M. B., *Some Beautiful Indian Climbers and Shrubs* (Bombay Natural History Society, 1954)

Darwin, C., *The Movements and Habits of Climbing Plants* (Second edition, John Murray, 1875)

Herklots, G., *Flowering Tropical Climbers* (Dawson-Science History Publications, 1976)

Menninger, E. A., *Flowering Vines of the World* (Hearthside Press, 1970)

PLANTS FOR SPECIAL PURPOSES

MINIMUM TEMPERATURE REQUIRED

Cool (5–10°C [41–50°F])	Moderate (10–15°C [50–59°F])	Warm (16–19°C [61–66°F])
Billardiera	*Bougainvillea*	*Allemanda*
Bomarea	*Hibbertia*	*Antigonon*
Canarina	*Ipomoea* (some)	*Aristolochia*
Clianthus	*Jasminum* (some)	*Beaumontia*
Cobaea	*Mandevilla*	*Clerodendrum*
Eccremocarpus	*Maurandya*	*Hibiscus*
Hardenbergia	*Pandorea*	*Ipomoea* (some)
Jasminum (some)	*Pyrostegia*	*Jasminum* (some)
Kennedia	*Solandra* (some)	*Passiflora* (some)
Lapageria	*Stephanotis*	*Quisqualis*
Mutisia		*Solandra* (some)
Passiflora (some)		*Strongylodon*
Petrea		
Plumbago		
Sollya		
Sutherlandia		
Swainsona		
Tibouchina		
Trachelospermum		

EASE OF CULTIVATION

Suitable for beginners	Moderately easy	Fairly difficult
Clianthus	*Beaumontia*	*Antigonon*
Cobaea	*Billardiera*	*Clitoria*
Eccremocarpus	*Bomarea*	*Hibiscus*
Hardenbergia	*Bougainvillea*	*Lapageria*
Ipomoea	*Canarina*	*Petrea*
Jasminum	*Clerodendrum*	*Quisqualis*
Maurandya	*Solandra*	*Strongylodon*
Passiflora	*Sollya*	
Plumbago	*Tibouchina*	
Thunbergia		

SPACE REQUIREMENTS
An approximate guide in descending order of vigour

Most	Least	Very restricted
Tetrastigma	*Stephanotis*	*Bomarea*
Strongylodon	*Kadsura*	*Canarina*
Aristolochia	*Hibiscus*	*Hardenbergia*
Beaumontia	*Lapageria*	*Eccremocarpus*
Bougainvillea	*Petrea*	*Maurandya*
Thunbergia	*Plumbago*	*Sutherlandia*
Passiflora	*Mutisia*	*Clitoria*
Ipomoea	*Clianthus*	*Kennedia*
Pyrostegia		*Billardiera*
Cobaea		*Swainsona*
Allemanda		*Sollya*
Jasminum		
Pandorea		
Antigonon		
Trachelospermum		
Clerodendrum		
Tibouchina		

DIRECT SUNLIGHT ESSENTIAL FOR FLOWERING

Antigonon	*Kennedia*
Bougainvillea	*Passiflora*
Canarina	*Plumbago*
Clianthus	*Pyrostegia*
Eccremocarpus	*Solandra*
Hibiscus	*Sutherlandia*
Ipomoea	*Swainsona*

LARGE FLOWERS

Allemanda	*Lapageria*
Aristolochia (most)	*Mandevilla*
Beaumontia	*Passiflora* (most)
Canarina	*Solandra*
Clianthus	*Tibouchina*
Ipomoea	

WINTER-FLOWERING

Canarina	*Jasminum* (some)
Hardenbergia	*Maurandya*

LONG FLOWERING PERIOD

Allemanda	*Passiflora*
Clerodendrum	*Quisqualis*
Ipomoea	*Thunbergia*
Jasminum	*Tibouchina*
Maurandya	

PLANTS REQUIRING SEASONAL DROUGHT TO FLOWER

Aristolochia	*Plumbago*
Beaumontia	*Pyrostegia*
Bomarea	*Solandra* (some)
Bougainvillea	*Stephanotis*
Canarina	*Swainsona*
Clerodendrum	*Thunbergia*
Ipomoea (some)	

SCENTED FLOWERS

Allemanda	*Mandevilla* (some)
Beaumontia	*Stephanotis*
Jasminum (most)	*Trachelospermum*

GOOD FOLIAGE

Beaumontia	*Stephanotis*
Clianthus	*Sutherlandia*
Hibbertia	*Tetrastigma*
Maurandya	*Tibouchina*
Passiflora	
Solandra	

ORCHIDS

THE ORCHIDS comprise one of the largest families of flowering plants in the world. More than 700 genera have been described and at least 25,000 species. Although they are all herbaceous plants, they exhibit a great diversity of shape and size, both of plants and leaves. The flowers too are incredibly varied, in their colours, shapes, patterns, scents and size. Many are beautiful, some are extraordinary, others intriguing, but all are appealing and unmistakable flowers.

The greatest numbers occur in tropical lands, but there are species adapted to different wild habitats almost everywhere, even within the Arctic Circle. Many orchids have been brought into cultivation at different times and, to add to the wild species, man has developed more than 70,000 hybrids by artificial cross-pollinations in the greenhouse.

Growing orchids today, both commercially (as plants or cut flowers) and as a hobby, is attracting more interest and attention than ever before. Many people are finding great pleasure in keeping tropical orchids in their homes, or conservatories, or a heated greenhouse where frost-free conditions, or warmer winter temperatures (minimum $10°-15°$C; $50°-59°$F), can be maintained.

The orchid flower has the bilateral symmetry of an iris or a gladiolus flower and, like them, it has three sepals and three petals. The sepals and two of the petals may be similar to each other or rather different in shape and size. The third petal is always different. It is modified to form the lip, or labellum, and it is a prominent and distinctive feature on the lower side of most flowers. Its function is usually to attract an insect pollinator and to provide a landing

(Above) *Lemboglossum cordatum*   (Opposite) *Phalaenopsis schilleriana*

platform for it. In the centre of the orchid flower there is only a single stamen (or two in the slipper orchids) which is united with the stigma and style to form a rather massive structure known as the column. The pollen grains are held together in masses called pollinia near the apex of the column and the stigma is a sticky patch on its surface. As in the iris family, the ovary is behind the flower and is often indistinguishable from the flower stalk, or pedicel, until it begins to develop into a fruit.

This brief description of the orchid flower does not reveal the numerous variations of its different parts. Sepals, petals, lip and column come in many sizes and shapes, plain or patterned, lobed or fringed. The surface often has a lovely texture, smooth but sparkling, and the substance of the flower can be papery-thin or thick and leathery. Orchid flowers are unique in their diversity.

Orchids can be divided into two groups by the way they grow in nature: terrestrial plants which usually grow in the soil, and epiphytes which grow mainly on other plants. They are not parasites as they derive no sustenance from the host tree or shrub, but are merely using it as a place to perch, perhaps to escape the competition from ferns and foliage of the forest floor or to find a position that is closer to the sunlight. Some orchids also grow very well on cliffs or rock faces, and these are called lithophytes. Both these groups have very specialized roots, often completely exposed to the air, which are enclosed in layers of absorptive cells called the velamen. This covering acts like a sponge, absorbing moisture and dissolved food material from rain, dew and clouds.

Many orchid stems are swollen because they have developed into storage organs called pseudobulbs. They are composed of one or several nodes and are found in many shapes and sizes – long or thin, upright or pendulous, short, round or compressed, erect or flattened against the substrate.

The combination of specialized roots and swollen stems which can store water makes it possible for many orchid plants to exist and thrive in the environmental extremes of light and shade, drought and storm which they may experience daily in the tropical forest. In cultivation, the key to successful orchid-growing is the maintenance of healthy roots. The most important single factor is probably adequate aeration. Overwatering is the practice which causes most trouble.

Cultural requirements

In the home: With a little ingenuity, it is possible to provide suitable growing conditions for orchids in almost any room in the house. Temperatures that are comfortable for people are usually suitable for orchids. The light on a sunny window sill is adequate for many species while others prefer a shadier position in another part of the room. Keeping the plants on a trolley which can be moved as conditions change is a good idea.

The greatest difficulty is the provision of sufficient humidity. This is usually achieved by supporting the plants on a grid or on upturned flowerpots in a tray of gravel kept filled with water so that, by evaporation, the micro-environment of the plant is more humid than the rest of the room. It is also helpful to moisten the leaves several times a day with a hand-held atomizer spray, preferably using rain water.

Probably the best method of growing orchids indoors is to keep them in one of the new types of plant cabinet, or a large terrarium, where fluorescent lights can provide extra light as well as warmth. With one or two ferns and foliage plants this can make a very decorative feature.

In the greenhouse: Many people start with a few orchids mixed with other plants in a small greenhouse, but this is not ideal. Small houses suffer from temperature extremes and, as well as the cost of heating a glass structure in winter, one must consider ways of keeping it cool in summer. Solid walls up to the level of the staging help to conserve heat, and an inner lining of polythene, or sheets of 'bubble glaze' under the glass, can drastically reduce fuel costs. Some form of shading over the glass, wooden slats or saran cloth, helps to keep temperatures down from late spring onwards. It will probably also be necessary to break up the light rays by painting the glass with a translucent coating. Both these forms of shading are easily removed in the autumn.

It is helpful to have an earth floor, with shade-loving plants such as ferns, begonias and *Zebrina* growing in it, to help maintain humidity. Good ventilation and an interior fan to create constantly moving air are further requirements.

Unless one can divide the house into two or more sections it will be desirable to choose plants which are either cool-growing ($10°–12°C$; $50°–54°F$ winter minimum temperature), intermediate ($12°–15°C$; $54°–59°F$) or warm-growing ($15°–18°C$; $59°–65°F$). The gentle heat provided by hot-water pipes under the staging is ideal, but a great variety of greenhouse heating equipment can be used successfully, thermostatically controlled electric fan heaters being the most convenient.

Basic cultivation

Containers: A wide range of suitable containers is available. Round or square plastic pots are frequently chosen. Clay pots are equally satisfactory but plants in them will need more frequent watering. Good drainage is essential, and it is often necessary to enlarge the drainage holes provided by the manufacturer. Special orchid pots in plastic and clay with perforated sides are available.

Baskets made of cork-oak bark or slatted teak bars are ideal for plants which need to dry out thoroughly between waterings. Trimmed slabs of cork-oak bark or prepared tree fern fibre make a suitable mounting surface for all epiphytes.

Coelogyne praecox

Pleione praecox

Removal of a naturally rooted offshoot from a *Dendrobium*. The swollen stem has food reserves as well as roots to aid its establishment as a new plant.

Care must be taken to choose a mount or container of an appropriate size for a particular plant. Many dendrobiums, for example, have rather few slender roots and grow best if they are confined to small pots, whereas robust plants like cymbidiums need larger pots for the natural development of their extensive root system.

Composts: A well-aerated compost is essential for all orchids. The composts in use today are mostly based on chips of bark available from specialist suppliers, or on fibrous peat, with the addition of inert material such as grit, perlite or perlag, fragments of expanded polystyrene and pieces of charcoal to help drainage, and occasionally some chopped dried leaves or sphagnum moss to retain moisture. Suitable composts for epiphytic and terrestrial orchids could be made up as follows:

Epiphytes	Terrestrial orchids
three parts washed medium grade bark chips	*three parts fibrous peat*
one part coarse perlag	*two parts coarse perlite*
one part charcoal pieces	*two parts coarse grit*
one part broken leaves or chopped sphagnum	*one part charcoal pieces*

A little bone meal or hoof and horn meal can be added to these mixtures when the plants are potted. Many growers prefer to leave the compost relatively inert and to supply fertilizer to the plants in a dilute liquid feed as required.

Potting: To ensure perfect drainage it is useful to fill one-third of the container with pieces of polystyrene, crock or large stones. The latter may be preferable as they give extra weight to the pot and help to keep it stable. Then the plant is held in the pot with one hand so that the base of the pseudobulbs or the top of the rooting surface is 1–2cm ($\frac{2}{5}$–$\frac{3}{4}$in) below the rim and compost is filled in around the roots with the other hand. It helps to shake the pot gently or tap it against the bench to ensure even distribution of the compost. After potting (and repotting) the compost should be thoroughly moistened and then not watered again for two to three weeks to allow the roots to settle. During this time the leaves need to be misted over frequently to ensure that the plants do not become desiccated.

Repotting: With frequent watering the composts deteriorate and need replacing, sometimes on an annual basis. Plants can grow too large for the container, when they will need dividing or moving into a larger one. During repotting the used compost must be removed and discarded, together with any dead, soft, or brown and shrivelled roots. Healthy roots, which are usually white, should be damaged as little as possible. Old pseudobulbs and divisions can be removed and used to propagate additional plants. Clean pots and fresh compost should be used.

Some orchids seem to resent disturbance, especially those with small or few roots such as *Sophronitis* and many dendrobiums, and these should be repotted as rarely as possible. Properly mounted plants on bark slabs may never need any further attention but if they become loose it may be desirable to transfer them to a fresh mount, holding them firmly in position with nylon fishing line or plastic ties until the new roots establish them securely.

Watering: Learning when and when not to water orchid plants in the home and greenhouse is the most difficult part of starting as an orchid grower. Rain water is best, preferably from a tank in the greenhouse so that it is at the right temperature. It is preferable to water during the morning on sunny days so that the plants will begin to dry out while temperatures are rising. Once every day may be necessary in summer, especially for mounted plants, but twice a week is more usual. This may be reduced to weekly or fortnightly intervals in winter. Misting over the plants, especially the mounted ones, helps to delay drying out and is useful once a day in winter and at least twice a day in summer.

Feeding: Most orchids require extra fertilizer during the growing season. Liquid feeding is the most convenient since it can be combined with watering. Any proprietary fertilizer can be used but it should be diluted to half the strength recommended for pot plants as orchids grow slowly. Foliar feeding is very effective. Some growers prefer to use a high nitrogen fertilizer (30.10.10) early in the season for maximum growth, changing later to a high potash one, such as tomato fertilizer (10.10.30), in order to encourage flower development. Feeding should be regular;

Sophronitis coccinea

once in every two or three waterings is enough in summer and not at all in winter.

Resting: Many orchids are structurally adapted to withstand a period of drought which often coincides with lower temperatures in the wild. They therefore need to dry out and 'rest' at some stage in the annual growth cycle. The resting period may last for a few weeks, with many dendrobiums, for example, or for several months in the case of many Mexican species. It is useless, and may be harmful, to water and feed a plant during the dormant period.

Propagation

Many orchids can be propagated by division, which is easily effected when they are repotted. Cuttings from mature plants can also be taken at this stage. This usually entails removing one or more pseudobulbs from the back of the growing rhizome and, even though they may be brown and leafless, potting them up in the same way as the plants. In many instances a dormant bud at the base will produce a young shoot from which a new plant will develop in a few years.

Sometimes small plantlets will appear on a pseudobulb or stem. Once they have developed a number of aerial roots they can be removed and potted up in small pots for growing on.

Seeds: Orchid seeds are minute, and plants are usually raised from seeds in a laboratory specially designed for micropropagation. The tiny embryos need a source of carbohydrate, usually sugar, and essential minerals for their development. In the wild these elements are supplied by a mycorrhizal fungus. In the laboratory the chemicals are prepared in an agar medium in a sterile flask or jar. After the seeds have been sterilized and sown the containers are kept under controlled conditions while the seedlings develop and until they are large enough to be potted up. This usually takes at least six months, often twelve.

Tissue culture and meristem propagation: The propagation of selected plants from apical meristems or other tissue is also carried out for orchids. It is a routine laboratory procedure in many parts of the world, especially for commercial growers.

Pests and diseases

Orchids are not particularly prone to pests and diseases provided that careful attention is paid to greenhouse hygiene. Dead and decaying leaves and flowers should be removed as soon as possible. Pots and staging should be kept free from weeds. New plants should be carefully inspected to make sure they are free from pests and diseases, and treated if necessary, before being added to the collection. All insecticides and fungicides should be used with care and following the maker's instructions. They can be harmful in high temperatures or left on the plants in sunlight.

Propagation of *Paphiopedilum* by division. With no food reserve these leafy orchids require careful re-establishment in humid conditions.

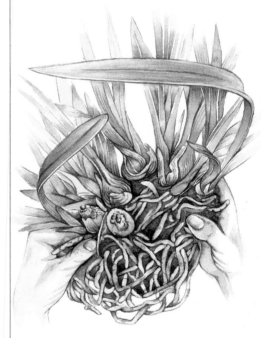

Division of a large *Cymbidium* plant. Each 'backbulb' is able to produce a new shoot and hence form a new plant, but to obtain flowers again quickly several pseudobulbs are left in each clump.

Pests: Aphids (greenfly) are sometimes a nuisance on flower spikes and buds during the winter months. Keep a watch for them and remove with finger and thumb (gently) or spray with malathion as soon as they appear. Malathion is also effective against scale insects and mealy bugs, which may suck plant sap from their hiding place on the undersides of leaves, in sheaths, and near the base of pseudobulbs.

Red spider mites are the worst pest of orchids and difficult to eradicate. A population may become resistant to malathion but can usually be kept in check by an acaricide such as pentac.

Slugs and snails can do considerable damage to buds, flowers and young shoots. Frequent application of bait containing metaldehyde or methiocarb will keep the numbers down. Searching for the marauders at night with a torch and removing them by hand can be more effective.

Diseases: Wrong treatment of plants, such as overwatering, careless repotting, poor ventilation or stagnant air can precipitate fungal or bacterial attack. If black or brown spots appear, or soft watery patches develop and spread very quickly, the best treatment is removal of the affected area as soon as possible. The cut surface can be disinfected with captan or flowers of sulphur. If the rot is far gone before it is detected there is no hope, and the plants should be removed and burned to avoid spreading the infection.

Virus diseases are the worst affliction faced by orchids in cultivation since there is no cure for them. Pale patches on young shoots and leaves should always be regarded with suspicion and a suspect plant isolated. Discoloration can also be a cultural problem, however, caused by mineral deficiencies. It will disappear when the plants are given the correct fertilizer. Suspect plants should not be discarded without expert advice on the nature of the problem.

Guide to purchasing

In orchid nurseries, garden centres, and even in department stores, it is usually possible to choose plants in bud or in flower. Look for a plant which is firmly established, not wobbly, in its pot and which has sufficient space and compost for it to remain there undisturbed for the next year or so. If the purchased plants have been grown in rock wool or oasis, however, which some Dutch growers are now using for orchids, they should be repotted after flowering into your usual compost so that they are easier to maintain in the home. Choose plants with firm unblemished leaves and flowers with clear colours.

Orchids purchased in a completely dormant state, such as *Bletilla* rhizomes or *Pleione* pseudobulbs, should be plump and firm. Avoid those with brown marks, scars or soft patches, which could denote the early stages of disease.

Offset removal from *Vanda*.

Recommended genera

BRASSAVOLA (named after an Italian nobleman and botanist, Antonio Musa Brassavola)

This is a small genus of epiphytic or lithophytic plants, containing about fifteen species, and distributed through tropical America from Mexico to Brazil and Argentina. The slender rhizome lies close to the substrate, and from it one or more slender or swollen stems, each surmounted by a single fleshy leaf, arises each year. The inflorescence arises from the leaf axil and bears one or several cream and greenish flowers which are very fragrant at night. The sepals and petals are similar, long and narrow, but the lip is large, narrow at the base where it enfolds the column, and spreading above to form a broad or narrow, rounded or pointed blade which is sometimes fringed at the edge.

These tough plants require brightly lit conditions and high humidity during the growing season. They grow well in a bark compost in shallow pots or baskets or mounted on cork. The minimum winter temperature is $10°–15°C$ ($50°–59°F$); they tolerate high temperatures in

(Right) *Brassia verrucosa*
(Below) *Brassavola digbyana*

BRASSAVOLA DIGBYANA

summer but require profuse watering and feeding during a warm spell. Less watering is needed during cooler weather and after flowering.

The best known species is *B. nodosa*, which is distributed from Mexico to Panama and Venezuela. It has a fleshy almost cylindrical leaf, and the attractive white lip has purple spots at its base. It is much easier to grow and bring into flower than *B. digbyana* (sometimes placed in the genus *Rhyncholaelia*) which also comes from Mexico. This species has distinctly pseudobulbous stems and broad fleshy leaves with pale green flowers. It has been much used in hybridizing with *Laelia* (× *Brassolaelia*) and *Cattleya* (× *Brassocattleya*) species, or both (× *Brassolaeliocattleya*), because of the large fringed lip.

BRASSIA (named after William Brass, a botanical artist who collected plants for Sir Joseph Banks)
This genus of about twenty species occurs in the tropical parts of the Americas, from Florida to Brazil. The plants are usually rather large epiphytes with a stout creeping rhizome and ovoid or compressed pseudobulbs which bear one to three leaves. One or two inflorescences arise from the base of each pseudobulb and carry showy, spidery flowers, in various shades of cream, yellowish-green or orange, often spotted with brown or purple. The sepals are long and narrow, with similar but shorter petals, the lip much shorter and broader with two or more ridges or crests at the base. It flowers in spring or summer, more than once a year in some species.

The plants become large, producing very many roots, and flower best if rarely disturbed. They need a bark-based compost which drains freely, humid but buoyant conditions and a minimum winter temperature of $15°-18°$C ($59°-64°$F). Water should be given less freely during the winter months but should be sufficient to prevent shrivelling of the pseudobulbs at all times.

Several very spectacular species are widely cultivated. *B. maculata* has greenish-yellow flowers, marked with purple brown. *B. verrucosa* bears pale green or cream flowers, the lip dotted with reddish spots at the base and green warts in the lower half. *B. caudata* produces orange-yellow flowers and in *B. arcuigera* (formerly known as *longissima*) they are orange-brown with large maroon blotches.

Brassia × Rex is a splendid hybrid with large flowers made from *B. verrucosa* × *B. gireoudiana*. Several intergeneric hybrids which have colourful and spectacular flowers and are easy to grow have been made with miltonias (× *Miltassia*), odontoglossums (× *Odontobrassia*) and oncidiums (× *Brassidium*).

CATTLEYA (named after William Cattley, one of the first successful growers of epiphytic orchids in England)
This genus contains about thirty species of showy

Cattleya skinneri

epiphytes and is native to the tropical parts of Central and South America. Thickened pseudobulbs supporting one to three fleshy leaves arise from a basal rhizome which attaches itself to the substrate by numerous fleshy roots. The flowers appear from a sheath at the apex of the pseudobulb, usually one to several, and are large and attractive. The sepals are narrow, the petals much larger and wider, with a lip often differently coloured, large, entire or three-lobed. It flowers in spring or autumn.

Most *Cattleya* species grow best in pots with a freely draining bark-based compost. They require conditions of bright light and high humidity, combined with a buoyant atmosphere. The winter minimum temperature should be in the range of $12°-15°$C ($54°-59°$F). The plants should be watered and fed regularly during the summer months, less frequently in winter.

All the species are easily grown and have most attractive flowers. Those with two- to three-leaved pseudobulbs usually have bigger inflorescences of smaller flowers. These include *C. bowringiana* (rose

Coelogyne cristata

purple or lavender), *C. skinneri* (rose-purple or white), *C. aurantiaca* (orange-yellow or orange-red, rarely cream or yellow), *C. bicolor* (coppery green with a pink lip), *C. forbesii* (pale green and yellow) and *C. intermedia* (white or pale purple with a deeper lip).

Species with only one leaf per pseudobulb have one to five large flowers in various shades of rose purple, usually with a darker lip, e.g. *C. labiata*, *C. mossiae*, *C. gaskelliana*, or yellow with a crimson lip, *C. dowiana*. White forms with a bright yellow patch on the lip occur in many of the species and are often delightfully fragrant. There are some famous and very beautiful white hybrids as well as many other hybrids in a wide range of colours.

COCHLIODA (from the Greek *cochlia*, a snail with a spiral shell, referring to the shape of the callus on the lip of the flower of the first species described)

This genus of about six species is native to highland forests in the Andes of Peru, Ecuador and Bolivia. They are small epiphytic plants with short compressed pseudobulbs bearing one or two leaves at the apex and one or two inflorescences from the base. The flowers are of small to medium size, and rose red or scarlet, with petals broader than the sepals. The lip is attached to the column at its base and is three-lobed in front with fleshy keels or crests on its surface.

These plants are not strong growers and do best in small pots in a compost made up of small particles of bark, perlag and charcoal. They require cool temperatures, with a winter minimum of $10°-12°$C ($50°-54°$F) and a summer maximum of $25°$C ($77°$F), shady conditions in summer and a humid atmosphere with plenty of air movement.

The plants take up little space and are extremely attractive when in flower. The best known species are the rose red *C. rosea*, *C. sanguinea* and *C. vulcanica*, and the scarlet *C. noezliana*. They have been used extensively in hybridizing with odontoglossums because of their brilliant colours. The bright red × *Odontioda* cultivars derived from these crossings are much more commonly grown today than their *Cochlioda* ancestors.

COELOGYNE (from the Greek *koilos*, hollow or concave, and *gyne*, a female, probably referring to the deep-set stigmatic cavity on the column of these species) This genus contains more than 100 species, distributed throughout tropical Asia. The plants are epiphytic and consist of closely set or distant pseudobulbs on a creeping rhizome. The inflorescences usually arise from the apex of the pseudobulb, in the axil of the leaf or leaves, before or after it has finished growing. The flowers are delicately hued but showy, and white, green, pink, ochre or apricot often with yellow markings on the lip. The sepals are narrow, the petals often small, with a conspicuous lip, entire or three-lobed, with two or more elongated keels along its surface.

Many species produce pendulous inflorescences and grow well in baskets in which they create a good display. A compost of bark, charcoal and chopped sphagnum moss is suitable. They come from a wide range of habitats so it is possible to choose species to suit the temperatures available. All species require plenty of water during the growing season and a period with less water when growth is complete.

Cool-growing species include the small *C. ochracea* and *C. flaccida* and the larger *C. corymbosa* and *C. cristata*, which all have white flowers with yellow markings on the lip. Species which require more warmth are the creamy white *C. asperata*, and the green *C. pandurata*. Their attractive hybrid *C.* × Burfordiensis has spectacular green flowers with blackish markings. Other well-known species are the brown and apricot *C. dayana* and *C. massangeana*, the orange- or salmon-flowered *C. tomentosa*, and the variously coloured *C. speciosa*.

CYMBIDIUM (from the Greek *kymbe*, a small boat, referring to the shape of the lip)
This genus of about fifty species, mainly epiphytes, is distributed from India eastwards to Japan and southwards to Australia. The plants are conspicuous by

Cymbidium lowianum

147

their clumps of pseudobulbs enveloped by long, narrow, succulent, or leathery leaves. Inflorescences arise from the base of the pseudobulbs with one to many flowers in a long, upright, arching or pendent raceme. The flowers are variously coloured, often large and showy, with similar sepals and petals. The lip is three-lobed, often with conspicuous reddish margins. It flowers mostly in winter and spring.

Many species are robust plants with a large quantity of succulent roots. They grow best in large plastic pots in a freely draining compost mixture based on peat or bark. A minimum winter temperature of $10°–15°C$ ($50°–59°F$) is needed, depending on the species; hybrids are mostly treated as intermediate. The plants require strong light and good air movement and can be placed outside in a sheltered place in summer when nights are frost-free. They should be watered and fed frequently during summer and given less water in winter.

Cooler-growing species which are easy to flower include *C. tracyanum*, which has striped brown and yellow flowers, and *C. lowianum* (lime green with an orange lip), but these plants quickly become rather large. *C. insigne* is a smaller plant with a long-stalked flower spray in pale pink or white, and *C. tigrinum* has fewer flowers of yellowish green. The smaller plants of *C. floribundum* (often known as *C. pumilum*) and *C. devonianum*, which has pendent inflorescences, make interesting house plants of a more manageable size.

The tropical species, including *C. aloifolium* and *C. finlaysonianum*, require warmer temperatures. They have shorter, more succulent leaves and smaller flowers.

Much more widely grown are the colourful hybrids and many of these, especially the so-called miniatures, are freely available as flowering plants in department stores in the early part of the year.

DENDROBIUM (from the Greek *dendron*, a tree, and *bios*, life, referring to the epiphytic habit of most of the species)

This very large genus with more than 900 species is distributed throughout Asia from India to Japan and south to Australia and New Zealand. The plants are mainly epiphytic or lithophytic and varied in shape, form and size, often with canelike pseudobulbous stems. The leaves are soft, succulent or leathery, one or several on each pseudobulb. The inflorescences are lateral or apparently terminal, with showy, often rather large flowers in a variety of colours. The sepals are varied, the lateral pair united with the foot of the column to form a mentum (or 'chin') which may be spurlike. The petals are wider or narrower than the sepals, and the lip entire to three-lobed, often variously coloured or marked and keeled on its upper surface.

Dendrobium nobile

Because of their widespread distribution, plants of this genus exhibit a wide range of growing requirements, with a winter minimum temperature of $10°–18°C$ ($50°–64°F$). Plants of upright habit are best grown in small pots and pendent ones in slatted baskets or on slabs of cork oak bark. All require good light and plenty of water and fertilizer while growing. Species from India and Australia need to be kept cool and dry in winter, whether they are deciduous or not, in order to flower in the following spring. Species from more tropical parts require moisture throughout the year and a minimum winter temperature of $18°C$ ($64°F$) to flower well. Many species from high altitudes also need moisture throughout the year, cooler temperatures, and shading in summer.

Cool-growing species which require a winter dry period include the rose and white *D. nobile* and many of its beautiful hybrids which are now available in a variety of colours. Also requiring this treatment are a number of golden-flowered species from India, including *D. chrysotoxum*, *D. lindleyi* and *D. densiflorum*, the pink and pale yellow *D. aphyllum*, *D. primulinum* and *D. farmeri*, a group with papery white flowers and stems with black hairs, including *D. formosum* and *D. infundibulum*, the robust Australian species *D. speciosum* and the fragrant *D. canaliculatum*, and many others.

Cool-growing species which need moisture throughout the year include many with brightly coloured flowers from New Guinea: *D. cuthbertsonii* and *D. lawesii* (red), *D. vexillarius* (orange), and *D. violaceum* (pink).

Warm-growing species with spectacular flowers include *D. bigibbum*, *D. phalaenopsis* and *D. superbiens*, and many beautiful hybrids derived from them such as Madame Pompadour and American Beauty which have recently become so familiar among the cut flowers offered for sale in supermarkets.

ENCYCLIA (from the Greek *enkyklein*, to encircle, referring to the way the basal part of the lip enfolds the column)

This is a genus of approximately 150 species which occur predominantly in Mexico and the Caribbean region, with a few in tropical South America. They are epiphytic, lithophytic or occasionally terrestrial plants whose stems form rounded or pear-shaped pseudobulbs clustered together, each bearing one or more succulent or leathery leaves. The inflorescence is terminal, slender or branching with many rather showy flowers. The sepals and petals are similar, and the lip entire to three-lobed, often bearing a callus or crest on its surface.

Many species do best in a bark-based compost in shallow pots or baskets or mounted on slabs of cork oak bark. A winter minimum temperature of $10–15°C$ ($50°–59°F$) is needed, depending on the species. Most

Depending on their natural habitat and its location, the plants require a winter minimum temperature of 10°–15°C (50°–59°F). They grow well in pots in a free-draining compost which is based on bark chips (for the epiphytic species) or peat and perlite. The smaller species with a creeping habit do well mounted on a piece of cork oak bark or tree fern fibre. All the plants require abundant water and fertilizer during the growing period and a drier period after the growth has matured.

Outstanding species which are easy to grow include *E. nocturnum* (white flowers), *E. pseudepidendrum* (orange and green), *E. ibaguense* (orange) and its red-flowered hybrid *E.* × O'brienianum, *E. difforme* (green), the curious pendent *E. falcatum*, and the delightfully scented *E. stamfordianum*.

LAELIA (probably named after one of the vestal virgins)
A genus of about fifty species, *Laelia* species are widely distributed in tropical America with most species in Brazil or Mexico. The plants are epiphytic, lithophytic

(Left) *Encyclia brassavolae*
(Below) *Epidendrum pseudepidendrum*

species require warm temperatures with plenty of water, fertilizer and strong light during the growing season, followed by a dry period during flowering.

Many species were described originally as epidendrums but are now separated from that genus by their lip and column form and by the presence of pseudobulbs. Some of the prettiest include the scented *E. citrina* (yellow), *E. vitellina* (orange-scarlet), and *E. mariae* (lime green and white). There is an intriguing group in which the shell-shaped lip is uppermost in the flower and is striped, reddish violet on cream, which includes *E. fragrans*, *E. baculus*, *E. chacaoensis*, *E. chondylobulbon*, *E. radiata* and *E. cochleata*, the latter having an almost black lip. Beautiful pink-flowered species include *E. adenocaula*, *E. dichroma* and some forms of *E. cordigera*.

EPIDENDRUM (from the Greek *epi*, upon, and *dendron*, a tree, referring to the epiphytic habit of many of the species)
This very large genus with many hundreds of species is found in the New World from North Carolina south to Argentina. They are epiphytic, lithophytic or terrestrial plants, often with conspicuous, slender, reedlike stems bearing many leaves and a terminal inflorescence. The flowers are small or medium sized, insignificant or showy. The sepals and petals are similar, the lip entire or variously fringed or lobed, completely attached to the column in the lower part and thus appearing to arise from the column apex.

or terrestrial with thickened pseudobulbs arising from a basal rhizome and each bearing one or two leaves. The inflorescence is terminal with one to several showy flowers in shades of pink, purple, red, orange, yellow or white. The sepals and petals are similar, or the petals wider, with a differently coloured lip, entire or three-lobed, and often tubular at the base around the column. They are distinguished from cattleyas and encyclias by having eight pollinia instead of four.

The plants are varied in size and grow well in shallow pots, slatted baskets, or mounted on slabs of tree fern fibre or cork oak bark. Brazilian species need a winter minimum temperature of 12°–15°C (54°–59°F) but Mexican species grow at cooler temperatures and can withstand a dry period of several months. Good ventilation, bright light and a buoyant atmosphere are required. The plants should be watered and fed regularly when they are in active growth.

Among the Mexican species, *L. anceps*, *L. gouldiana* and *L. albida* make a spectacular show with their pink or rose-purple flowers in midwinter. The larger-flowered *L. autumnalis* and *L. speciosa* flower earlier.

Laelia harpophylla

Among the Brazilian species there is a wide array of colours, including orange (*L. cinnabarina* and *L. harpophylla*), yellow (*L. flava* and *L. xanthina*), pink (*L. perrinii*), rose-purple, (*L. pumila* and *L. purpurata*), bronze-green with a reddish lip (*L. tenebrosa*), and red (*L. milleri*). There are many small rupicolous species with bright flowers recently brought into cultivation.

Laelia species have been hybridized extensively with *Cattleya* (× *Laeliocattleya*) and other closely related genera. A wide range of colours in small- and large-flowered plants has been derived by selective breeding.

LEMBOGLOSSUM (from the Greek *lembos*, a boat, and *glossa*, a tongue, referring to the boat-shaped callus on the lip)

This genus consists of about fourteen epiphytic species in Mexico and Central America which were formerly classified as *Odontoglossum* but are now separated from that genus by characters of the lip. They have rounded or ovoid pseudobulbs, clustered together, each with one to three terminal leaves. The inflorescences are lateral with showy white, pink or yellow and variously spotted or mottled flowers. The sepals are similar, the petals often wider or differently marked from the sepals. The

lip is narrow at the base, and wide in the central part with a pointed boat-shaped callus.

Most species occur in the wild in highland regions where there is a pronounced dry and cooler season alternating with a warm wet summer. They grow best in shallow pots in a bark-based compost or mounted on cork oak bark. They need a winter minimum temperature of 10°–12°C (50°–54°F) and a summer maximum of 25°C (77°F). The plants should be grown in cool and airy conditions throughout the year, watered well and fertilized during the summer but kept dry as soon as the new pseudobulbs are mature, and in winter.

The best-known species of the one-leaved group are *L. rossii* which has white or pink flowers with brown-spotted sepals, *L. cervantesii*, which is also white or pink and has concentric brown stripes near the centre of the flowers, and the yellow and brown *L. maculatum*. Five species have two or three leaves on each pseudobulb. These include the pure white *L. candidulum*, and two handsome species with tall flower spikes, the many flowers of which usually have a pink lip, *L. bictoniense* and *L. uroskinneri*.

LYCASTE (named after a daughter of King Priam of Troy)

This genus of about twenty-five species is widely distributed in the New World from Mexico south to Peru and Bolivia. Many species have been classified in the past in the genus *Maxillaria*, but they are easily distinguished by their large, plicate, deciduous leaves.

The plants are epiphytic, lithophytic or terrestrial and have a cluster of ovoid or compressed pseudobulbs each bearing two or more large thin leaves at its apex. The inflorescences are usually one-flowered and arise from the base of the mature pseudobulbs. The flowers are large and showy, green, white, pink or yellow, and often fragrant. The sepals are larger than the petals and sometimes differently coloured, the lip three-lobed with a callus on its surface. Flowering is in winter and spring.

The plants need shady conditions with good air movement while the leaves are present. They need large pots with a freely draining compost based on a bark chip or peat mix, and a winter minimum temperature of 12°C

Lycaste skinneri var. *alba*

(54°F). During the growing season (summer) they should be given plenty of water and fertilizer until the new pseudobulbs are fully formed. Then water should be withheld, or provided only lightly, to stimulate flowering and until the new growths form roots.

These plants take up a lot of space when in their summer growth, but it is worth having a few lycastes in a collection for their attractive long-lasting flowers during the winter months. The pale pink and rose *L. skinneri* is a great favourite. Yellow-flowered species such as *L. aromatica*, *L. cruenta* and *L. crinita* flower in spring with great regularity. The green-flowered species *L. leucantha* has a yellow lip and *L. denningiana* an orange one, whereas the orange-red *L. lasioglossa* has a yellow lip. There are also many lovely hybrids, mostly with larger flowers than the species, including some very beautiful pink and red sorts. A few intergeneric hybrids have been made with species of the genus *Anguloa* and these × *Angulocaste* have very large waxy flowers in shades of white and yellow.

Masdevallia coccinea

MASDEVALLIA COCCINEA *Lindl.*

MASDEVALLIA (named after Dr José Masdevall, an eighteenth-century Spanish physician and botanist)
This genus of about 300 species of mostly small, epiphytic plants is widely distributed in the highlands of the New World from Mexico south to Peru, with the greatest diversity in the Andes. The plants consist of a number of slender stems growing in tufts from a creeping rhizome and each bearing a single leaf at its apex. Inflorescences arise from the rhizome and are slender, with one to several showy flowers. The sepals are the most conspicuous part of the flower and are united to form a tube at the base, with the upper parts free and often extending into slender tails. The petals and lip are small and usually hidden within the flower.

The plants grow well in small pots with a peat or bark-based compost which is compact but free-draining. They require water throughout the year and conditions that are cool, shady, and humid with good air movement. They need a winter minimum temperature of 10°–12°C (50°–54°F), and a summer maximum of 25°C (77°F).

Many of the species are brightly coloured and pretty, but others are sombre or almost grotesque. There are many different colour forms of the beautiful *M. coccinea* – rose, yellow, white and scarlet. Other red-flowered species of great brilliance include *M. militaris*, *M. racemosa* and *M. veitchiana*. *M. tovarensis* is pure white, easy to grow, and the flowers are long-lasting.

ODONTOGLOSSUM (from the Greek *odontos*, a tooth, and *glossa*, a tongue, referring to the toothlike projections of the callus on the lip)
As presently regarded, this is a genus of about 100 species which are confined to the mountainous regions of Central and South America. Several well-known species are now classified in other genera, e.g. *Cuitlauzina pendula* and *Osmoglossum pulchellum* (and see also *Lemboglossum* and *Rossioglossum*). They are mostly epiphytic plants with round or ovoid compressed pseudobulbs clustered on a basal rhizome with one to three leaves at the apex. The inflorescence is basal, bearing one to many showy flowers which are variously coloured. The sepals and petals are similar, spreading, and the lip is entire or three-lobed with a conspicuous lamellate crest on its surface near the base.

The plants grow best in pots in a free-draining compost which may be a bark- or peat-based mix. Because the majority of the species come from high altitudes they require cool temperatures, with a winter minimum of 10°–12°C (50°–54°F) and a summer maximum of not more than 25°C (77°F). Moving air is a requirement all the time and the roots should not be allowed to dry out. Heavy shade is beneficial in summer but should be removed during the winter months.

The plants known best in cultivation are some of the

Plate XVII

W.H.Fitch,del.et lith.

Vincent Brooks, Imp.

Andean species and their many colour forms, most notably the Colombian *O. crispum* which has sparkling white, showy flowers, sometimes tinged with pink or yellow and often blotched reddish or purplish brown. It has been hybridized with other species of *Odontoglossum* and with *Cochlioda* species to produce the bright red and yellow cultivars of × *Odontioda* that are so popular with growers. Other intergeneric crosses involving *Odontoglossum* which produce easily grown plants are × *Odontonia* (× *Miltonia* or *Miltoniopsis*), × *Odontocidium* (× *Oncidium*), and some multigeneric hybrids including × *Wilsonara* (*Odontioda* × *Oncidium*) and × *Vuylstekeara* (*Odontioda* × *Miltonia* or *Miltoniopsis*).

There are many well-known and desirable species including *O. hallii* and *O. luteo-purpureum* (yellow and brown), *O. harryanum* and *O. triumphans* (brown, pink and white), and *O. lindenii* (clear yellow). Species with smaller flowers which have long-pointed sepals and petals include *O. cirrhosum, O. lindleyanum, O. naevium* and *O. odoratum*, which are white or yellow with red markings.

ONCIDIUM (from the Greek *onkidion*, diminutive of *onkos*, tumour or swelling, referring to the warty callus which is a characteristic feature of the lip of many of the species)

This is a large genus of over 400 species which are distributed throughout the American tropics and subtropics and the Caribbean. The plant habit is varied and ranges from small to very large. The plants are mainly epiphytic but some species are lithophytic or terrestrial. The pseudobulbs are varied in shape and size and arranged close together or widely separated on a long rhizome. The leaves may be thin or succulent, flat or rounded, and in one group are arranged in an irislike pattern. Inflorescences are often very long and branching and the flowers may be large or very small, commonly yellow marked with brown, but pink, white and brown kinds occur. The sepals are similar, often free or with the lateral sepals partly united, and the petals are usually larger, with the lip the largest part of the flower, held at a right angle to the column, frequently four-lobed and bearing a prominent basal callus.

Growth requirements in this genus are as varied as the plants but nearly all require a brightly lit situation with shade from direct sunlight during the summer. Whether grown in a pot or basket or on a slab they need plenty of water during the growing season and rather less when vegetative growth is complete. The winter minimum temperature varies from 10°C (50°F) to 18°C (64°F), depending on the species.

There are many spectacular and floriferous species that are worth growing. The Variegata group comprises

(Opposite) Odontoglossum luteo-purpureum

small plants with a fan of leaves a few inches high, requiring warm humid conditions throughout the year; *O. pulchellum* is pink, *O. variegatum* and *O. triquetrum* are basically white or lavender and *O. guianense* is yellow. The mule-eared group has a single thick leaf surmounting each small pseudobulb and rather fleshy flowers; *O. bicallosum* and *O. splendidum* have yellow flowers, *O. carthagenense* has pinkish blooms, and in *O. lanceanum* the lip is large and rose-purple contrasting with brownish sepals. Another group has slender swollen leaves shaped like a pencil; these include *O. cebolleta*, which has a bright yellow lip, and the white-lipped *O. jonesianum*.

Many species have clusters of rounded pseudobulbs with one or two apical thin or leathery leaves. Yellow-flowered members of this group include *O. bifolium, O. cheirophorum, O. flexuosum, O. maculatum, O. sphacelatum, O. tigrinum* and *O. varicosum. O. incurvum* and *O. ornithorhynchum* are the most commonly grown pink-flowered species.

PAPHIOPEDILUM (from the Greek *paphia*, referring to Paphos in Cyprus where Aphrodite was worshipped, and *pedilon*, a sandal. Because of the slipper-shaped lip,

Paphiopedilum × Maudiae

they are often known as Venus' or lady's slipper orchids. About sixty species are currently known in the tropical parts of Asia, from India east to Hong Kong and south-east to the Solomon Islands. They are terrestrial or occasionally lithophytic or epiphytic herbs, with a short rhizome from which short upright stems arise, each bearing a fan of green or variegated leaves. The inflorescence is terminal with one to several waxy flowers in a range of rather subdued colours—white, pink, reddish purple, green or brown. The dorsal sepal is erect, large, often spotted or striped, with smaller lateral sepals which are united to form a synsepalum behind the lip. The petals are spreading, usually longer than the sepals, and the lip is slipper-shaped.

All the species grow best in plastic pots in a freely draining compost which is changed annually. Having no storage organs they need to be watered frequently and to be grown in humid conditions. Those with variegated leaves require more shade than the plain green kinds. Plants from cooler regions, e.g. *P. insigne*

and *P. spicerianum*, do best at a winter night temperature of 10°–12°C (50°–54°F), whereas the variegated kinds, e.g. *P. barbatum*, *P. lawrenceanum*, and those with large, thick leaves, e.g. *P. philippinense* and *P. lowii*, do best if kept warmer, always above 15°–18°C (59°–64°F).

Easiest to grow in warm conditions are some of the south-east Asian species such as *P. callosum*, *P. barbatum* and *P. sukhakulii*, and the famous green and white hybrid *P.* × Maudiae. In cooler conditions some of the green-leaved group with yellowish brown flowers, *P. insigne*, *P. villosum* and *P. gratrixianum*, grow without difficulty and flower regularly in the winter and spring. Many spectacular hybrids, with flowers that have a wide range of colours and shapes, have been derived from generations of selective breeding.

PHALAENOPSIS (from the Greek *phalaina*, a moth, and *opsis*, appearance or resemblance, referring to the

Phalaenopsis violacea

mothlike appearance of the white-flowered species)
This is a genus of about fifty species in tropical Asia, distributed from India south-east to the Philippines and with one species in northern Australia. They are epiphytic or lithophytic plants with a short stem bearing two rows of broad, fleshy leaves arranged alternately, and many fleshy roots. The inflorescences arise among the leaves, and are simple or branched, with few to many small or showy flowers, which are variously coloured – white, yellow, pink or mauve with reddish brown markings. The sepals are free and alike, with petals similar to the sepals or much larger and broader. The lip is three-lobed, with the side lobes erect on either side of a distinctive callus.

All the species grow well in pots or slatted baskets in a bark-based compost or mounted on slabs of cork bark. They require humid conditions that are well shaded, with good air movement, and a winter minimum temperature of 15°–18°C (59°–64°F). They should be watered liberally throughout the year and fed while they are in active growth (forming a new leaf).

A genus of great variety in its wild species, there are also very many beautiful hybrids which have been bred by careful crossing and selection. Two white-flowered species, *P. amabilis* and *P. aphrodite*, are the most well known, whereas those with mottled leaves, *P. stuartiana* (white flowers) and *P. schilleriana* (pink flowers), are very attractive plants for a warm situation even when not in flower. One group of species has star-shaped flowers in a variety of colours, including *P. violacea* (pale green and violet), *P. pallens* (white or pale yellow, lined with brown), *P. pulchra* (magenta) and *P. lueddemanniana* (white or cream with purplish spots or bars). The largest species is *P. gigantea*, with greyish green, succulent leaves which may be up to a metre long (usually much shorter in cultivation) and small yellow-green flowers with chestnut markings. A few species are very small plants and quite leafless at times, e.g. *P. parishii*.

PLEIONE (named after the mother of the Pleiades of Greek mythology)

This genus of about fifteen species comes from the temperate forests and high altitudes of Asia, from Nepal eastwards to Taiwan. They are small epiphytic, lithophytic or terrestrial plants which produce an annual round or conical pseudobulb after flowering. The pseudobulbs develop quickly during the warm season, each bearing one to two leaves at the apex, and becoming deciduous in the autumn. The pseudobulbs are dormant during the winter months and short inflorescences are produced at the start of new growth in the spring (or autumn for *P. praecox*). The flowers are large and showy, white, pink, lilac or yellow with reddish brown markings on the lip. The sepals and petals

Pleione limprichtii

are similar, with a three-lobed lip enfolding the column, and with a number of crests or ridges along its surface, often fringed at the margin.

These plants are best repotted every year while they are dormant and they grow well in shallow pans in a bark-based compost. They need good air movement and humid conditions while leafy, and should be watered and fed liberally when they are growing and the roots are active. After the leaves fall they should be kept completely dry and cool until after they have flowered. The winter minimum temperature is 5°–7°C (41°–45°F), and the summer maximum 25°C (77°F).

These are very attractive small plants for cultivation in an alpine house or unheated greenhouse, requiring little attention for the greater part of the year. Most of the species are easily obtained and there is a range of attractive hybrids which have larger flowers in a wide variety of colours. Always popular are the bright yellow species, *P. forrestii* and *P. confusa*, the lilac-coloured *P. yunnanensis*, which is scented, and the autumn-flowering *P. praecox* which comes in a range of colours from white to deep rose pink. Most commonly grown is *P. bulbocodioides* (usually under the name *P. formosana*) whose pink- or rose-coloured flowers appear with the immature leaves.

ROSSIOGLOSSUM (named after John Ross, who collected orchids in Mexico between 1830 and 1840)

This small genus of six epiphytic orchids is distributed

between Mexico and Panama. The plants are easily recognized by the dull grey-blue-green colour of both the clustered ovoid pseudobulbs and their apical leaves. Inflorescences arise from the base of the pseudobulbs with four to twenty large showy flowers which are bright yellow, heavily barred or marked with chestnut brown. The sepals are similar, and the petals wider. The lip is three-lobed, with the side lobes at the base on either side of a curiously shaped callus, and the mid lobe pandurate. They are sometimes known as the tiger orchids because of their distinctive colouring.

These plants grow equally well in a shallow pot or basket in a bark-based compost or mounted on a slab of cork bark. They start their new growth in late spring and early summer and should be kept well watered and fertilized throughout the summer growing season. The flower spike emerges in autumn, and after flowering the plant needs a dry winter rest in good light. These species come from high altitudes and require cool temperatures – a winter minimum of $10°–12°$C ($50°–54°$F), and a summer maximum of $25°$C ($77°$F).

The flowers of these species are rather similar in shape and colouring but vary in size and number. The largest are those of *R. grande*, which is often called the clown orchid because of the shape of its lip callus, whereas those of *R. insleayi* are usually smaller but more numerous. *R. williamsianum* also has smaller flowers with rounder petals. *R. schlieperianum* is more greenish yellow in colour, sometimes with very faint markings. This group was formerly classified in *Odontoglossum*, but they do not hybridize as the other members of the genus and its relatives do, and their appearance is very different.

SOPHRONITIS (from the Greek *sophros*, discreet or modest)

This genus of about seven dwarf species is confined to eastern Brazil and Paraguay. The plants are epiphytic or lithophytic with clustered pseudobulbs each bearing a small dark green or purplish leaf and a short inflorescence. The flowers are showy, one or several, in shades of pink, purple, orange, red or yellow. The petals are broader than the sepals, and the lip is narrow, entire or three-lobed.

These plants are sometimes hard to establish in cultivation. They need shady moist conditions with high humidity, cool temperatures and a buoyant atmosphere. The winter minimum temperature is $10°–12°$C ($50°–54°$F). The plants grow best on pieces of cork bark or in shallow pots in a bark-based compost. Water frequently but sparingly.

The best-known species is *S. coccinea* (sometimes still known as *S. grandiflora*) which has scarlet flowers with a yellow base to the lip. Several distinct varieties have been described, including var. *barboleta* (peach-coloured flowers), var. *pallens* (orange), var. *purpurea* (purple) and var. *rossiteriana* (yellow). The similar *S. wittigiana* has rose pink blooms. *S. cernua* has smaller, rich cinnabar-red flowers borne in clusters of five to nine.

The so-called red cattleyas are intergeneric hybrids with *Sophronitis* in their ancestry. They are usually small plants, easy to grow, and require rather cooler conditions than other members of the cattleya alliance. For best colour the plants should be moved to a warmer and brighter place as the flowers develop.

ZYGOPETALUM (from the Greek *zygos*, a yoke, and *petalon*, a leaf of a flower, i.e. a petal, referring to the thickened callus at the base of the lip which appears to yoke or join the petals together)

This is a genus of about twenty species of epiphytic orchids from the highland forests of tropical South America. The plants are medium sized or large with a cluster of leaf-bearing pseudobulbs growing upright from a creeping rhizome. The leaves are rigid, leathery or plicate. Inflorescences, one to several, arise in the axils of the leaves, bearing one to several showy flowers which are large in a few of the species. The flowers are yellowish green, heavily spotted with dark reddish brown or purple, and with a contrasting three-lobed lip

FURTHER INFORMATION

Bibliography

Bechtel, H., Cribb, P. J. and Launert, E., *Manual of Cultivated Orchid Species* (Second edition, Blandford Press, 1986)

Bristow, A., *Orchids* (Cassell/Royal Horticultural Society, 1985)

Rittershausen, B. and W., *Orchids in Colour* (Blandford Press, 1985)

Williams, B. (Ed.), *Orchids for Everyone* (Salamander Books, 1980)

The *Orchid Review* is the oldest orchid magazine in the world. First published in 1893, it still appears regularly every month, and contains a wide range of articles on various aspects of orchids and orchid growing, fully illustrated in colour. Details of subscription and an introductory copy can be obtained from The Editor, Orchid Review, Katukelle House, Victoria Village, Trinity, Jersey, Channel Islands.

There are many societies in Britain which hold regular meetings, lectures on a variety of topics, shows and visits to orchid nurseries. For details of groups in your area, write to the Sainsbury Orchid Fellow, Royal Botanic Gardens, Kew, Richmond, Surrey, TW9 3AB, England.

which often has violet or bluish striations on a white background. The sepals and petals are similar, and the lip is entire or with very small side lobes at the base.

These robust plants grow easily under the same conditions, or slightly warmer, as cymbidiums. They need large pots for their succulent roots and a freely draining compost which may be bark- or peat-based. They should be watered regularly and fed liberally while in active growth and less frequently during the cooler season. The winter minimum temperature is 10°–12°C (50°–54°F).

Several species are common in cultivation, all with rather similar flowers which are chiefly remarkable for their violet-striped, white lip and for their delightful hyacinth-like fragrance when they are displayed in sunlight. The finest is *Z. intermedium*, which is said to be distinguishable from *Z. mackaii* by its hairy lip, but they are extremely similar. *Z. crinitum* has smaller flowers.

The related genus *Zygosepalum* has only a few species with smaller, compressed pseudobulbs and attractive pinkish brown flowers which have unlobed lips with U-shaped tubercles at their bases.

Zygopetalum crinitum

PLANTS FOR SPECIAL PURPOSES

EASE OF CULTIVATION IN THE HOME	ORCHIDS FOR THE COOL GREENHOUSE OR CONSERVATORY
Suitable for beginners	(Only those which are easily grown and are commonly available from orchid nurseries are shown in this list. All those in the first list would also grow equally well or better in a cool greenhouse and many others could be tried.)
Brassavola nodosa *Brassia maculata* *Cattleya aurantiaca, C. bowringiana, C. intermedia, C. skinneri* *Coelogyne crisata, C. flaccida, C. ochracea* *Cymbidium eburneum, C. floribundum*, miniature hybrids *Dendrobium aggregatum, D. chrysotoxum, D. kingianum, D. nobile* *Encyclia aromatica, E. cordigera, E. vitellina* *Epidendrum* × O'brienianum *Laelia anceps, L. gouldiana, L. pumila* *Lycaste aromatica* *Paphiopedilum insigne* *Pleione formosana* *Zygopetalum crinitum*	*Coelogyne dayana* *Cymbidium* hybrids *Dendrobium densiflorum, D. nobile*, many *nobile*-type hybrids *Encyclia citrina, E. cochleata, E. fragrans, E. radiata* *Lemboglossum cervantesii, L. maculatum, L. rossii* *Lycaste aromatica*, many modern hybrids *Odontoglossum crispum*, many hybrids *Oncidium incurvum, O. ornithorhynchum*, and *Oncidium* alliance intergeneric hybrids *Osmoglossum pulchellum* *Paphiopedilum insigne*, and many hybrids *Pleione* species and hybrids *Rossioglossum grande, R. schlieperianum* *Sophronitis coccinea*
Moderately easy	
Dendrobium phalaenopsis, and hybrids *Oncidium flexuosum* *Paphiopedilum barbatum, P. callosum, P. sukhakulii, P.* × Maudiae, modern hybrids *Phalaenopsis amabilis, P. equestris, P. schilleriana, P. stuartiana*, many hybrids Many other orchids can be grown temporarily in a plant case, while they are in flower, and moved back to the greenhouse for the rest of the year.	

LARGE COLOURFUL FLOWERS		SCENTED FLOWERS
Cattleya *Cymbidium* hybrids *Miltoniopsis* *Paphiopedilum* *Phalaenopsis* hybrids		*Brassavola* *Cattleya* (some) *Encyclia* (some) *Zygopetalum*

TENDER FERNS

JUST TO mention the word fern can bring to mind an image of delicate tracery, a foliage with soothing shades of green and brown. This instant recognition of the plant type is due to the characteristic appearance of ferns, although not all are so easily distinguished.

We know from fossil evidence that the ferns inhabiting our planet today are mostly very different from their ancestors millions of years ago. Even the Carboniferous ferns about 300 million years ago were more advanced than their ancestors of the Devonian period, 400 million years ago, and our present ferns are still in an active state of evolution.

It was of course the ferns and fernlike plants of the Carboniferous era that formed the coal seams so prized as a source of fuel today. These plants grew in profusion and flourished in the ideal conditions of warmth and moisture, many attaining substantial size and girth. It is common today to find the outline impression of stems or leaves (fronds) of these prehistoric plants when breaking open slabs of some coals and shales.

In the familiar hierarchical scheme of classifying the plant kingdom, ferns (or pteridophytes) slot in above the bryophytes (liverworts and mosses) and below the gymnosperms (cycads and conifers), with the angiosperms (the flowering plants) grouped as the most advanced form of plant life.

Although, like the gymnosperms and bryophytes, pteridophytes have not advanced to the stage of producing flowers as a specialized aid to reproduction, they have nonetheless proven very able to compete with the higher plants. This is particularly noticeable in the moist tropics and

(Above) *Pteris quadriaurita* var. *argyraea*   (Opposite) *Davallia solida*

W. Fitch del et lith.

Vincent Brooks, Imp.

Davallia polida Sc.

subtropics where ferns contribute substantially to the flora. It is the constant warmth and moisture of such environments (similar to the Carboniferous period when their ancestors were so dominant) that enables ferns to flourish and develop to exploit the habitats offered in rain forests. Although the moist tropics provide the most advantageous conditions, some ferns have adapted to withstand dryness or cold, and representatives may be found in somewhat inhospitable environments from semi-desert to bleak snow-covered mountain terrain.

Spores

If a fully matured fern frond is examined carefully, a pattern of brown rusty-looking patches may be observed on the underside (or with some species on the frond edge, or apex). Examine one of these patches more closely under a microscope, or with a × 10 lens, and the rustiness will be revealed as numerous reproductive bodies clustered together, sometimes partially covered by a scaly flap. These are called sporangia; the flap, if present, is termed the indusium, and when ripe, the sporangia split along a predetermined line of cells, the annulus, to release their dustlike contents. The granules making up the dust are all similar and are called spores. The sporangia are always grouped in a set pattern of patches according to the species, each patch being termed a sorus. Some ferns have two types of fronds, only one of which is modified to bear spores.

Life cycle

To understand a little more about the ferns, their life cycle must be looked at, for it is quite different from that of the flowering and the cone-bearing plants. The spores, when liberated from the sporangia on the adult plant, are very light and drift about in the air. Many thousands may be produced each year by a mature plant, some of which will alight on a suitable surface. With adequate moisture and other favourable conditions they will start to germinate. From each spore will grow a flattish green disc of cells, commonly heart-shaped and about 5mm ($\frac{1}{5}$in) in diameter, which is termed a prothallus. After the prothallus is mature and fully grown, a tiny fern plant will develop from it, usually emerging from the indented area of the heart-shaped disc. Once the little plantlet has its own rooting system and is established, the prothallus shrinks away and dies. If all is successful this plantlet will grow on, mature and itself produce spores.

A quite ingenious process takes place during the latter part of the life of the prothallus; on its dorsal side, where the micro-climate is more stable (moisture is important), two distinctly different types of structure develop. With the aid of a microscope you will find, among the myriad moisture-absorbing hairs on the oldest part (which incidentally also anchor the prothallus to the substrate), small round projections called antheridia. Towards the growing point you will discern little tubular objects similar to straight-sided drinking glasses; these are called archegonia.

Within each archegonium a single female reproductive cell develops and within each antheridium are produced the male reproductive cells. The male cells are able to move in a film of water and thus reach the archegonium which ruptures when ripe, allowing entry of the male cells, one of which will fuse with the female reproductive cell to form a zygote. This is then able to grow into the new fern plant. The male cells produced by the antheridia and the egg cells produced by the archegonia are collectively termed gametes. From this is derived the name gametophyte generation for the prothallial stage of the fern's life. A fern thus has two distinct parts to its life cycle, the part we can instantly recognize as a fern, the sporophyte stage, and the gametophyte stage, which follows germination of the spore to form a prothallus. A spore is thus quite different from a seed.

Dicksonia antarctica

Habitats and forms

Because the prothallus is dependent upon good conditions for development throughout its growth period (two to three months for some species, well over twelve months for others), ferns are often at a disadvantage when compared to seed-bearing plants. That said, those who have lived in or visited the wet tropics cannot fail to observe the ever-present nature of ferns, some adapting to a terrestrial and others to an epiphytic habitat.

Most green plants have roots, stems and leaves, and the majority of present-day ferns are no exception. Although many are compact, low-growing, and exhibit a herbaceous growth pattern, some have developed much larger proportions. The best known of these are the tree ferns, which can extend their main stem or caudex in some cases many metres in height. They are found throughout the tropics and subtropics, especially in Australia, Tasmania and New Zealand. In parts of New Zealand tree ferns form a conspicuous entity within forested terrain. The main genera are *Dicksonia* and *Cyathea*. Other ferns produce giant fronds rather than tall stems, the most notable being *Angiopteris*. In complete contrast some ferns have comparatively diminutive proportions. This is especially true within the delicate and specialized group containing the filmy ferns in the family Hymenophyllaceae. Many of these species are epiphytic, some choosing the adventitious root mass produced by tree ferns, especially *Dicksonia*, as their home. It is interesting to observe this phenomenon in New Zealand where the fronds of *Hymenophyllum lyallii* and *Trichomanes venosum*, like emerald jewels, clothe the dark chestnut outer root mass of the *Dicksonia* stems.

Taxonomic study reveals that there are some 10,000 to 12,000 different species and varieties of ferns alive today, with by far the greatest numbers concentrated within the tropics. Even so, comparatively few have been consistently cultivated and even fewer have been actively taken up as house and garden plants. It was during the Victorian period that the great interest in growing ferns both indoors and in the garden became fashionable. The Victorian fern craze developed into such a cult that some wild populations of ferns throughout the British Isles became seriously depleted through overcollecting. Indeed it is well documented that considerable quantities of ferns, both whole plants and root stocks, were sent by rail and road to London and other cities in Britain for sale. It was a very profitable occupation and such was the demand that some species, including the royal fern *Osmunda regalis, Ophioglossum lusitanicum,* and the Tunbridge Wells filmy fern *Hymenophyllum tunbrigense,* together with numerous exquisite varities of other ferns, were collected almost to extinction. This fashionable craze was actively pursued for some thirty years from the 1850s to the end of the 1880s.

Just as the Victorians valued the fern for its soothing colour and fineness of form, a less intense though quite definite resurgence of interest in these plants has occurred from the late 1960s to the present day. As during the previous fashion, fern motifs have appeared on fabrics, utensils, china and the like. Although we now generally have smaller gardens and there is a tendency towards smaller homes without gardens, we satisfy our need to have plants around us by growing them indoors where they also complement home furnishings and décor. Ferns as house plants have become fashionable and provide a lucrative business for the commercial producer.

Cultural requirements

In the home: Conditions provided in our homes are not always conducive to the well-being of most plants. The levels of humidity fluctuate but are generally low. There can also be considerable fluctuations in temperature, often aggravated by central heating which warms and dries the air and is the cause of a dramatic drop in the temperature at night when the system switches off. These conditions tend to limit the range of plants that can be grown indoors and nowhere is this more pronounced than with ferns.

The main problem when attempting to grow ferns is to prevent the plants from drying out. The majority have a comparatively fine fibrous root system and a short rhizome or stem with fronds emanating from around the growing tip. Most ferns have no means of water storage and are therefore dependent on a regular supply of moisture to the soil. Combined with this, most fern fronds (apart from the mid–rib or rachis which is the upper part of the frond stalk) are composed of soft and often quite delicate tissue, the cells of which, if allowed to lose moisture to any great extent, may well desiccate and shrivel to the point where even if water is copiously applied they are unable to recover. Often the rhizome stock will survive and new fronds will be produced, but visually the plant is ruined for a matter of weeks or months until it can recover. This tendency to suffer so drastically if allowed to dry has been the major limiting factor that has restricted the greater use of ferns as plants for home decoration.

In the greenhouse: The problems of drying out can be lessened, if ferns are grown in a conservatory, greenhouse or sun-room, by providing some form of shading during the summer months. Ferns can be grown in association with other plants and will also tolerate the shady environments beneath taller subjects or under benching. There are a number of devices and systems that can provide an automatic supply of moisture, along with small humidifiers which moisten the air a little.

A conservatory or greenhouse can provide a recuperation area for ferns or other plants that become 'tired' if grown too long indoors. Take care when moving ferns to ensure that they are not taken from a poorly lit situation indoors and then placed in too bright a place in the conservatory or greenhouse, since this could have damaging consequences to foliage already adapted to lower light levels. Comparatively few ferns are able to withstand strong sunlight, especially through glass, and as a general rule a position in good light but screened from direct sunlight is always preferable. Equally, as bright sunlight should be avoided, so too should the

Osmunda regalis

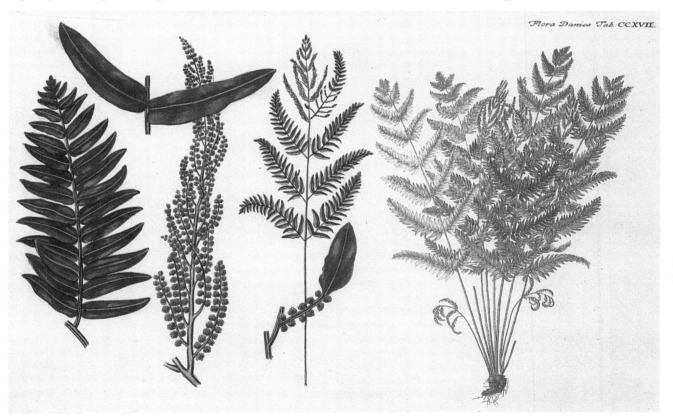

Many epiphytic ferns can be grown on pieces of cork oak bark. This method of cultivation is particularly successful with platyceriums. A layer of sphagnum moss should be placed between the plant and the piece of bark before the plant is secured into position with nylon line.

darkest corners of a room where the level of daylight may not be sufficient for the fronds to manufacture enough food to provide the plant's needs; this may be more noticeable during the short days of winter.

Basic cultivation

Pots and containers: There is often much debate over the use of clay or plastic plant pots, but, providing you remember that plastic containers lose water far less rapidly than clay pots, for the majority of ferns one is as good as the other. Because clay plant pots weigh more than plastic they have the advantage of providing stability for bulky subjects and are more attractive in appearance. In general, if plastic pots are used the compost should be more 'open', with coarse peat and larger grist sand or grit.

Most ferns which are indoor plants are not over-fastidious with regard to compost, nor are they gross feeders. The all-important factor is that there should always be sufficient moisture available to the roots of the plants, but if the compost is allowed to become waterlogged it will induce consequences just as dire as drought. Therefore use a compost which will hold moisture and yet allow excessive water to drain through it to leave a reasonably aerated substrate. The composts available are of two basic types: those that contain loam (soil-based composts) and those without loam content (usually peat-based). The former are able to retain more water and plant foods and are heavier so that in plastic pots they will give better stability. The danger is that they can become over-wet, 'sour' and thus cold in winter, which will discourage root activity. Peat-based composts, on the other hand, are better aerated even when wet; they are generally warmer but do not give physical stability and retain less plant food, so that additional feeding is essential. A compromise can be reached by mixing three parts by volume coarse peat, one part sharp sand and one part loam, which will provide good drainage, stability, some food source and the reserve of moisture that is so important. No additional fertilizer need be added at the time of potting but once the plant roots have permeated the compost a proprietary brand of balanced liquid plant food should be given every three weeks at a rate slightly less than that recommended for most other house plants.

Some of the epiphytic species of fern will grow well and look most attractive if grown within a metal or wood lattice basket. This method of accommodating plants proves ideal for almost all of the *Platycerium* species and varieties; for most of the *Davallia* group and for certain *Nephrolepis*, *Adiantum* and other polypodiaceous plants. The baskets need to be lined with moss and a fibrous but free-draining loamless compost used. Once the plants settle in their rhizomes will spread in and around the basket structure, the fronds able to hang gracefully in the air.

The art of using ferns, especially *Davallia* species, as basket plants to produce an almost perfect sphere of greenery was practised by the Japanese some years ago. These spheres were termed 'fern balls' and demanded much dedicated care by way of training and tying or pegging-in the rhizomes to the surface of the basket in order to create a complete cover of plant growth.

One or two species may usefully be tried in the ordinary wire hanging baskets and when placed in a porch or alcove are quite appealing. Indeed, potted subjects such as *Drynaria*, *Cyrtomium* etc., placed in a macramé plant hanger, make very pleasing decorative features – see *Nephrolepis* on page 180.

Watering: To help maintain a little more humidity in the air around the base of each plant it is useful to stand the plant pot on sharp grit or gravel held in a saucer or shallow dish. When watering, a little water can be poured over the gravel from where it will gradually evaporate and be carried up around the plant. This is particularly beneficial for the more delicate varieties of *Adiantum* and *Nephrolepis* and for species of *Davallia*, *Hemionitis*, *Anemia*, etc. Take care, however, not to bring the water level above the top of the gravel as the pots should not stand in water.

Care: Provided the fern is positioned sensibly in the room and watered as necessary it remains only to remove the older fronds as they yellow and to check the plant for any pest or disease problems. It is also useful to turn the plant every week or so, to prevent it from becoming lopsided in appearance, which will happen over a period of time, especially if it receives light from one direction only.

Potting-on, division or propagation of ferns should not be attempted during the winter months since most ferns drastically slow down their growth rate during this time. This work is best carried out in spring or early summer. Even those species which normally continue to grow throughout the full twelve months in their native tropical habitat will have a period of slower growth in temperate countries, almost certainly as a response to fewer hours of daylight and reduced light intensity.

Propagation

Division: It is possible to increase the numbers of some ferns by division, the easiest and simplest method of propagation. This is especially so where the plant naturally produces a number of growth points at compost level as with many of the maidenhair species and cultivars (*Adiantum* spp.); *Nephrolepis* spp. and cultivars; *Pellaea* spp., some *Doodia* and *Asplenium* etc.

First, remove the plant from its pot. To do this, turn the plant pot upside down and, holding the plant and root ball securely with one hand, tap the pot rim sharply on some firm surface like a bench edge in order to dislodge the root mass. This action may well need to be repeated several times to free a well-rooted

Asplenium scolopendrium

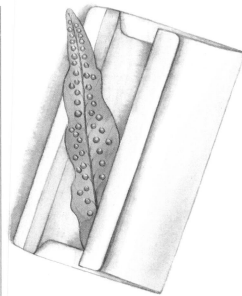

Fern fronds, with ripe sporangia on the underside, can be removed from the plant and placed inside an envelope. The envelope should then be transferred to a warm dry room where the spores will be shed naturally.

The dustlike spores are sown on to the surface of prepared pots of sterilized compost.

individual. The number of new plants obtainable from the original will depend on its species, age, and growth condition. Two to six viable divisions from a well-established 13cm (5in) pot of *Adiantum raddianum*, for instance, can usually be obtained, although the more one divides the stock plant the smaller each division will be and in consequence each plant will take longer to re-establish itself.

To obtain the divisions simply slice through the rhizome mass and compost with a sharp knife or small saw. Trim straggly fronds and remove some of the old root ball, then repot. It may be wiser to make only two or three divisions from a 13cm (5in) pot plant until you are more familiar with the idiosyncrasies of a particular species or variety. Once divided, thoroughly water in the newly potted plants. Those ferns which have thicker rhizomes, *Davallia* and *Polypodium* for example, can be increased by using a rooted section of rhizome which is then given support using a wire peg to hold it to the new compost. It should then be placed into the closed environment of a propagator until sufficiently rooted.

Spores: Ferns may also be propagated from spores. Take off a piece of frond which has ripe sporangia. In most cases these will appear dark in colour and glossy. If they are dull brown and scaly the spores will have been shed and if green or greenish yellow the sporangia are unripe. A ×10 hand lens may prove helpful to examine them. Place the selected piece of frond in an envelope and allow it to dry in a warm room. The spores will be shed by the sporangia as they dry and will be ready to sow.

Prepare a 7.5cm (3in) clay pot for each sowing by boiling it for twenty minutes in a saucepan of water. It is preferable, however, to use new pots for spore sowings. Compost for sowing can be made up of two parts loam, two parts peat and one part sand, although the ratio can be varied somewhat without detriment. It must be sterilized and this can be done by placing a quantity of the moist compost in a baking tray lined with aluminium foil which should be wrapped over it to encase it, then place it in an ordinary oven. The steam generated will do the sterilizing and should be allowed to penetrate the compost for twenty minutes. A temperature of 82°C (180°F) is required to ensure harmful organisms such as pathogenic fungi and bacteria are killed. When cool the compost may be stored in a closed polythene bag.

To make the sowing, place a piece of broken pot over the drainage hole in the 7.5cm (3in) pot, fill the pot with compost, and firm it down with the base of another pot, leaving 12mm ($\frac{1}{2}$in) between the compost and the pot rim. Surface sterilize the pots and compost by pouring boiling water over them using a small clean metal watering can with a rose attachment. Place a square of window glass over each prepared pot. Surface sterilize the glass squares in the same way as the pots, immediately replace them and allow them to cool.

Shake a quantity of spores from the collecting packet or

envelope on to a clean sheet of writing paper. Carefully spread these over the central area, tipping back any excess. A fine dusting of spores will be left adhering to the fibres of the paper. Remove the glass square, invert the paper over the pot and tap with the hand to deposit the spores on to the surface of the compost. Immediately replace the glass square. *Do not* cover the spores with more compost.

Place the sown pots in a tray containing 12–20mm ($\frac{1}{2}$–$\frac{3}{4}$in) of distilled water in a warm shaded situation indoors or in the greenhouse. Germination may occur after three weeks, and will show as a green flush over the compost surface and on the inside rim of the pot. In some species this may take up to one year after sowing.

The plant is now at the prothallus stage and, as growth progresses, the prothalli will develop their sexual organs. Following fertilization the little sporophytes will eventually be seen, pushing their first small fronds above the prothallial mat. Once these appear, the glass square can be slightly moved to allow air to be admitted to the surface. Only after a further two to four weeks, or until a sufficient number of young sporophytes have developed, can the glass be removed completely.

Once the little fronds have reached 5–10mm ($\frac{1}{5}$–$\frac{2}{5}$in) in height, the next process can be carried out. Using the same compost mixture as that for the sowing, fill a number of 7.5cm (3in) pots. Lightly firm and leave a flat surface. With the blade of a knife or a sharpened small split cane, gently lift a small patch containing prothalli and little sporophytes and set them carefully into the compost in the prepared pot. Several of these little patches can be set in the new pot. From this procedure comes the term patching-off. The newly set patches should be thoroughly watered in and placed in a propagator. Cover for one or two days to allow the small ferns to recover, then place on greenhouse benching which should be screened from strong light at all times. Eventually the patches can be potted-on, or, in the case of tree ferns, the plants in each patch can be separated and potted individually. From this point it is necessary to repot only when required.

The pot should be covered with a sheet of glass to ensure the compost surface remains moist.

Fern spores normally germinate within one to two months. Each spore produces a prothallus. When growing clustered together these appear as a green mass on the compost surface.

Pests and diseases

Although ferns are not usually troubled with pests or diseases, there are a number of common 'nasties' that will attack them. Cultural difficulties can also cause them to look unhappy. Unfortunately most ferns are sensitive to many of the chemicals available for insect and disease control, and unless care is exercised in their usage, as much damage can be caused to the plants from them as from the initial pest or disease. By following a few simple rules, however, it should be possible to produce reasonably trouble-free plants. The first essential is to make sure that when obtaining new plants they are healthy and free from pests, and if

Within a short space of time the prothallus will produce a frond, which is recognizably the developing fern plant.

there are plants already in the home, conservatory or greenhouse which are harbouring problems, the newly obtained ferns should not be placed with them until these problems are dealt with.

Always try to treat a pest or disease quickly before it becomes severe. It is best to check over the plants, removing any yellowing fronds and other signs of trouble, at each watering.

Pests: Aphids form colonies of small green, greenish yellow or black insects which may clothe newly developing fronds, especially clustering on the unfurling 'crozier' of the frond. Initially, wash them off with clean water from a pressurized pump sprayer. If the insects persist use a very mild solution of washing-up liquid – a few drops in a gallon of tepid water. Apply by pressurized sprayer.

Mealy bugs appear usually as small groups of white, mealy-covered, slow-moving insects, and are usually located on the underside of fronds and also among developing fronds. Try to dislodge and wash them off with clean water through a pressurized sprayer. If they persist, spray with a weak solution of malathion prepared according to the manufacturer's instructions. Some species of mealy bug will colonize the root areas. Should this occur, drench the root ball with a malathion solution.

Several species of scale insect may attack ferns, from the small brown disc type to even smaller but more elongated 'snow' scale. The latter causes white areas to develop on the frond in the immediate area where the insect is feeding. Whereas young scale insects colonize other parts of the plant, the adults of all species are immobile and, protected by their outer scale, they attach themselves to the plant, in order to suck the sap. They are difficult to eradicate. Picking off the larger species by hand will help, plus careful wiping of the stems and tougher areas of the plant with a soft sponge, using clean tepid water. If persistent, spray with malathion or diazinon liquid.

Hand pick slugs and snails or use a proprietary bait. They can be a problem in conservatories and greenhouses.

Diseases: Sooty mould occurs when areas of frond become sticky with 'honeydew' – the excreta of aphids, scale insects, mealy bugs, etc., on which a black fungal mould develops. Wash or wipe off the foliage with clean tepid water and control the insects which are causing the honeydew secretion.

Botrytis is a grey fungal mould prevalent where the air circulation between plants is poor and the humidity too high. It is not often a problem of ferns in the home but is more likely to be encountered in the greenhouse and conservatory. Remove the infected foliage and space out the plants. Increase air movement if possible and keep conditions a little drier.

Cultural problems: Drought is potentially the most damaging of all cultural problems. Depending on the severity, a few or all the fronds may be killed and even slight drought in some instances would have the same effect. Many ferns will smell of dry grass

Pteris cretica

when suffering from drought. Should this occur plunge the plants as soon as possible into a bucket of just tepid water and allow them to soak until all the air bubbles are out of the compost. Remove, drain and after a day or so cut back any black shrivelled fronds to leave a length of stem above the stock. If the damage is too severe the whole plant may die but most ferns will produce new fronds in due course, although they may take several months to recover fully.

Overwatering occurs most frequently during the winter months. The plants may lose their glossy green colour and the fronds may become limp with dark or even blackish areas. The plant will feel heavy and if tapped out of its pot the compost may smell of decomposition. Reduce the amount of water and if possible move the plant into a slightly warmer environment. Do not repot immediately if the problem occurs in winter, although this could be done in summer. Should matters deteriorate rapidly, however, repotting even in winter may be worth trying. It is often more difficult to effect a successful recuperation from overwatering than from drought.

Blechnum brasiliense

Guide to purchasing

Visit your local garden centre, florist or city department store and look at the ferns that are offered there; in general, most will offer a similar selection. Those most commonly offered include: *Pteris*, especially *P. cretica* and its varieties; *Nephrolepis* especially *N. exaltata* 'Bostoniensis' (the Boston fern); *Blechnum*, a number of species including *B. gibbum* and *B. brasiliense*; *Platycerium* (the stag's horn fern), mainly the smaller fronded types especially *P. bifurcatum* and cultivars; *Asplenium* especially *A. bulbiferum* (the hen and chicken fern from New Zealand) and *Adiantum* (maidenhair ferns) especially cultivars of *A. tenerum* and *A. raddianum*.

It will pay dividends to purchase your plants from a reputable retail outlet where plants are generally better grown and looked after prior to selling and the selection a little more adventurous. Unless the aim is to obtain a reasonably mature plant for a particular setting in the home or conservatory it is better to look for healthy younger plants so that they can be grown on in your care. When selecting ferns check that they are free of plant pests, especially scale insects (*Coccus* spp.) and mealy bugs. The odd aphid, slug etc., though better if not present, can be more easily controlled than the aforementioned. Look for signs of previous drying out, damage to fronds (brown or dead areas), and if possible check for healthy root activity around the top of the pot or emerging from the base. Plants should be of good colour and compact. Yellow foliage or legginess usually means that the plant has been poorly cultivated by the production nursery, or that the plants have been on the sales display shelving too long.

Recommended genera

ADIANTUM (from the Greek *a-*, not, and *diantos*, wettable, referring to the water-repellent nature of the fronds)

This genus is geographically widespread, spanning the tropics where it is most prevalent but also occurring in temperate climes. It contains about 200 species and numerous cultivars, all known as maidenhair ferns.

Adiantum species are highly prized for their graceful foliage, and many have fronds which support soft, green, delicate, airy arrangements of pinnules on a glossy black stalk or stipe. Their foliage is often used as background for single flowers made up as buttonholes or in arrangements such as corsages. The fronds selected for such purposes have to be mature to give enough rigidity to the foliage and therefore the more open foliage types, especially *A. raddianum* or *A. tenerum*, are preferred.

They all demand sufficient water at their roots, since the foliage will become flaccid through lack of moisture if the roots are allowed to dry out. If this condition persists for even a couple of hours the delicate segments of foliage will be unable to take up moisture and will certainly die. Almost all actively growing ferns can be affected, although it is *Adiantum* that will more often be damaged to a greater degree. Because of this problem the genus has been labelled troublesome in cultivation, but it need not be the case. Use a loam-based compost or make up your own using one part loam, two parts peat, one part sharp grit. For *A. capillus-veneris*, which is a lime-lover, add crushed mortar rubble or ground limestone roughly in the proportion of one tablespoon to the quantity of compost held in a 25cm (10in) pot.

Of the remaining myriad species and cultivars *A. raddianum*, the delta maidenhair, is much favoured for its wide selection of good forms. These include *A. raddianum* 'Decorum', similar to the straight species in shape and form but easier to grow; *A. raddianum* 'Fritz Luth' is a neat and fairly compact yet attractive fern with a feathery and layered appearance to its foliage. For an even more delicate tracery of foliage 'Gracillimum' is ideal, its new fronds showing markedly pink pigment when young. 'Pacific Maid' is one of the best of the compact fronded plants, the pinnae or segments of each frond touching and slightly overlapping each other.

Another species which encompasses a number of cultivars is *A. tenerum*, and in general most of these plants require more warmth in winter than the *A. raddianum* group, needing a minimum temperature of 10°C (50°F). *A. tenerum* is native to Florida, the West Indies, through

Adiantum raddianum 'Fritz Luth'

Asplenium bulbiferum

ASPLENIUM (from the Greek *a-*, not, and *splen*, the spleen, referring to its supposed medicinal properties) Commonly known as spleenworts, this group is very diverse, and is represented worldwide from the lowland tropics to the harsher temperate zones. The genus contains some 700 species, varying in size and form and encompassing epiphytic and terrestrial plants, along with plants which have adapted to living in rock crevices or rooting into old brick wall mortar. Of the extensive number of spleenworts no more than eight to ten species are commonly encountered for sale as house plants. The most commonly offered for sale is *A. nidus*, the bird's nest fern. In the wild it is normally epiphytic, but nevertheless will adapt itself well to pot cultivation. It is unusual in that the fronds are entire, being strap- or tongue-like, whereas most spleenworts have divided fronds, some extremely so. There are a number of species similar in form in the *A. nidus* complex, although the one most often seen is the plant which has almost vertical fronds forming a narrow funnel or vase of growth. Cultivation is easy. A peat-based compost should be used and a temperature of 15°C (59°F) provided. It makes an attractive house plant if given a reasonably light situation.

A. bulbiferum is the hen and chicken fern, possibly the most usual of the dissected foliage spleenworts to be seen in conservatories and decorative plant collections. In cultivation for many years, it is viviparous, producing little ferns from bulbils on the mature fronds and is easily propagated by this means. Native to New Zealand and Australia, it tolerates cool conditions and succeeds with a minimum temperature of 4.4°C (40°F).

BLECHNUM (a classical Greek name for a now unknown species of fern)
Mostly tropical or subtropical, this genus contains about 200 species of rather coarse terrestrial ferns. It shows a great diversity of shape and form, from *B. gibbum*, which is proportioned almost like a small tree fern, and to some extent *B. brasiliense*, to the miniature stature of *B. penna-marina*, a southern-hemisphere native which has fronds 5–25cm (2–10in) long.

One or two species do lend themselves as house plant subjects, including *B. gibbum* which is readily available commercially. After a number of years of growth it will produce a tough upright caudex 50–70cm (20–28in) in height, with a cluster of fronds around the top. The plant is somewhat variable as it is possible to find clones which are able to develop additional growth points at intervals up the caudex. These growth points help to give the plant a much enhanced appearance as they will clothe the stem with foliage. *B. gibbum* adores plenty of humidity, so when placing the plant indoors put the pot in a suitably sized bowl or tray filled with gravel or peat which can then be kept moist. This will help to create a

Mexico to Peru, and although the true species is seldom grown, one or two cultivars can be obtained. *A. tenerum* 'Farleyense' is possibly the most common, and has broadly triangular fronds with overlapping pinnae. It is brilliant green and holds some of its foliage in good condition throughout the year. *A. tenerum* 'Fergusonii' is another plant to be recommended, with narrowly triangular fronds and pinnae much more widely spaced than on 'Farleyense'; it is an altogether more erect and tougher-looking plant.

Most maidenhair ferns appreciate a good level of atmospheric humidity and are often happiest in a bathroom or kitchen. Do not, however, place them near a central-heating radiator, but in good light, though shaded from direct sunlight.

Propagation can be by division of the rhizome-covered root mass or from spores. Division provides mature individual plants quickly, although if a greater number of plants is required, raising from spores is much the better way. Division of the plants is best carried out in spring before the onset of active growth. The majority of maidenhairs slow their growth rate throughout the winter, especially the outdoor-tolerant species.

humid micro-climate around the plant, to the benefit of its softer foliage. An occasional spray with tepid rain water or distilled water, directed especially over the caudex, will encourage adventitious roots, usually noticeable at the base of the stem. If these can be sustained the plant will respond more favourably through the winter. This is a challenging plant to grow in centrally heated rooms but worth the trouble.

B. brasiliense can also be found on general sale and is a coarser growing subject, not developing such a tall caudex as *B. gibbum* but having longer fronds, up to 1m (3ft 3in) in length, which show markedly pink

Blechnum gibbum

coloration during unfurling and for a few days afterwards until chlorophyll masks the pigment. It is possibly a better plant for the warm greenhouse or conservatory than the home, although if space is available it will make a good feature specimen when well-grown. No special treatment is required, apart from ample water and the need for moderate to high atmospheric humidity. The minimum temperature required is 18°C (64°F).

CYATHEA (from the Greek *kyatheion*, a little cup, referring to the shape of the sorus)
Some of the most imposing and beautiful tree ferns are contained within this very large genus. It has 300 or

more species native to the tropics and subtropics, and its correct nomenclature is still debated. *C. arborea*, of West Indian origin, is the plant upon which the description of the genus was based. This plant, along with *C. fugax*, *C. contaminans* and others, will extend its caudex or stem many metres giving the plant treelike proportions. Though it has a single crown only, *C. arborea* can reach 15m (50ft) in its ideal rain-forest habitat.

Some tree ferns, such as *C. smithii*, one of the New Zealand species, retain their dead fronds which form a skirt below the crown. However, it is more common for the old fronds to fall away leaving a spiral pattern of scars on the stem. Almost all of the *Cyathea* species produce adventitious roots from their stems, more abundantly over the metre or so immediately above the ground. These should be encouraged in cultivation by providing a gaiter of plastic mesh or similar around the stem, leaving some 8cm (3¼in) of space between the gaiter and stem. This should then be filled with coarse peat, bracken litter or moss, the aim being to retain moisture, so that the roots grow and form a thick mat. If this can be achieved, when the plant has grown tall and ungainly it can then be severed completely at soil level and lowered into a new planting space or retubbed as desired. This procedure has proved satisfactory for *C. arborea*, *C. contaminans*, *C. fugax* and others, and means that mature plants can be retained longer, in some cases for many years. Development from spores, the other alternative, would require at least five years to produce plants of 1.5–1.8m (5–6ft) in height.

Some small *Cyathea* species are suitable for house plant use, and the New Zealand species are again more frequently seen. *C. smithii* is one of the smallest of these. *C. medullaris*, the black tree fern or mamaku (its Maori name), has very dark frond mid-ribs and stipes while the area around the crown is clothed in papery, blackish-brown scales. It will grow very tall, although young plants are easily maintained.

Better suited to the home is *C. cooperi*, a native of Australia. It is a plant of good form and robust constitution, making a fine specimen which does not outgrow its space too quickly.

The minimum temperature for *Cyathea* should be 10°C (50°F) and the plants appreciate a light misting-over in summer.

CYRTOMIUM (from the Greek *kyrtos*, arched, referring to the arching fronds)

There are some twenty species in this genus, natives of the tropics and subtropics.

C. falcatum, the Japanese holly fern, is one of the more common ferns cultivated for the home, but a more decorative plant, known as *C. falcatum* 'Rochford-ianum', is also available. Originally produced by Rochford's, formerly a well-known pot plant nursery, it has deeply serrated margins to its pinnae. Both are handsome ferns with dark green glossy foliage, which is quite coarse to the touch. *C. falcatum* will tolerate a range of conditions and temperatures, but it will do better if kept out of direct sunlight, and if the temperature is not allowed to drop below 10°C (50°F). A good general potting compost will suffice. It should be propagated by spores.

C. caryotideum is a plant of rather lax habit, with fronds having fewer but larger and more irregular pinnae. *C. fortunei* is smaller than *C. falcatum*, dull green in colour and with narrower pinnae.

DAVALLIA (named after Edmond Davall, 1763–98, a Swiss botanist)

This genus of forty species, mostly native to the Old World tropics and subtropics, consists of small- to medium-sized epiphytic ferns, many with hard fleshy rhizomes covered with scales, which become detached and are shed after a number of years. Almost all *Davallia* species shed their fronds each year, although with *D. solida* and *D. solida* var. *fejeensis* this period without fronds may be short, lasting only one or two weeks in late winter or early spring. *D. canariensis*, on the other hand, grows through the autumn, winter and spring, resting during the summer. In its native Canary Islands, the rhizomes of *D. canariensis* can become quite flaccid from moisture loss during drought, although this appears to do little harm to the plant which soon becomes turgid again after rain. All these species prefer a coarse, well-drained substrate, which can be provided with a mixture of coarse peat, crushed bark, perlite, perlag or something similar. They may be grown in pots or make good hanging-basket subjects, looking exceptionally effective in wooden lattice baskets.

Temperatures need not be excessive, and a minimum of 16°C (61°F) will prove suitable for most of these plants, although *D. canariensis* can be grown successfully at 9°C (48°F). Propagate by spores, or by using slices of rhizome pegged out on to pans of peat, or a peat and perlite mixture.

DICKSONIA (named after James Dickson, 1738–1822, a British nurseryman much interested in botany)

There are about thirty species of tree ferns in this genus, of which the most often cultivated are *D. antarctica* (a species native to Tasmania and Australia), *D. squarrosa* and *D. fibrosa* (both New Zealand ferns with interesting Maori names, *wheki* and *wheki ponga* respectively).

D. antarctica is a very robust fern with a crown of strong fronds held aloft on a stout trunk. This tough trunk contains much lignified and hardened tissue. The outermost layer is formed from a mass of aerial roots which will eventually completely cover the frond bases to form a tight water-absorbing and strengthening mat.

In its native habitat it will grow to well over 10m (34ft) in height. However, as with the majority of *Dicksonia* species, it is slow in gaining height, and therefore small plants will not outgrow their allotted space too quickly.

D. antarctica has a very pleasing shape or form. It will tolerate very cold conditions and can be grown outdoors in milder areas of temperate countries. If kept indoors, it should be placed in good light, in a loam-based compost which can be improved by the addition of coarse peat. It is best for the large conservatory or greenhouse. Keep the compost moist and mist over the crowns and root-clad trunks at least once a day in summer. *D. fibrosa* and *D. squarrosa* require similar attention, although they demand humidity of at least 60 per cent or above to grow successfully.

DIDYMOCHLAENA (from the Greek *didymos*, twin, and *chlaina*, a cloak, referring to the indusium or sporangia cover)

Now quite common in cultivation, this genus contains only one species, *D. truncatula*, which is an attractive terrestrial plant. The fronds form a shuttlecock effect, growing upwards and slightly outwards from a low stock. Fronds of *D. truncatula* can attain a height of 90cm (3ft) on older plants. The young fronds exhibit the pleasing pink pigment common to a number of fern genera.

It is relatively easy to grow as a house or conservatory plant, although attention must be paid to ensuring that the roots do not dry out. Should this occur the slightly leathery pinnate fronds will shed some or all of their pinnules, leaving them skeletonized. Use a loam-based compost with added peat, perlite or both, and place away from strong sunlight but in good light. Mist over occasionally in summer. The temperature should drop no lower than $15°C$ ($59°F$).

DIPLAZIUM (from the Greek *diplazios*, double, referring to the paired sporangia)

This is a large group of ferns, mostly tropical but also spreading into northern temperate areas. The genus is similar to *Athyrium* in general frond shape and texture and even in the arrangement of the sori. A number of species are cultivated, including *D. esculentum* and *D. proliferum*. *D. caudatum*, a native of southern Spain, is also worthy of wider cultivation. The fronds of *D. esculentum* are used as a green vegetable in parts of Malaysia.

The plant produces a short trunk up to 60cm (2ft) in height, although the fronds can be lax and floppy. *D. proliferum* is possibly the best plant for pot culture, with its strong upright fronds less dissected than the majority of these plants. It also produces small plantlets on the surface of the fronds which can be removed and used for propagation. The minimum temperature should be

Diplazium proliferum

above $15°C$ ($59°F$) and the humidity 65 per cent or above. *D. caudatum* has dissected foliage up to 90cm (3ft) and it will grow successfully in cooler conditions with lower humidity then *D. proliferum*. Use a general peat-enriched potting compost. This species can be propagated from spores.

DRYNARIA (from the Greek *drys*, oak, referring to the sterile fronds which resemble the leaves of certain oak species)

The twenty species in this genus are fascinating epiphytes from the tropics of the Old World, usually found growing on rain-forest tree boles or branches, and also on rocks. They are commonly termed oak leaf ferns because of the distinct, small, leaflike fronds which sit upon the fleshy, scale-covered rhizome. These fronds are persistent in that they do not fall, even though they soon lose their green colour. They are designed to give some degree of protection to the rhizome, and by trapping moisture and debris, help to prevent excessive water loss. In all species the spore-bearing fronds are larger, and after completing their spore-bearing and photosynthesizing functions are shed by the plant.

(Above) *Drynaria rigidula* 'Whitei'
(Right) *Hemionitis arifolia*

Species occasionally offered for sale are *D. quercifolia*, *D. rigidula*, *D. rigidula* 'Whitei' and *D. sparsisora*.

All are best grown in wooden lattice baskets, though they can be accommodated in large clay pots or half-pots. Because they are epiphytic the compost should be open, well-drained and consist of coarse peat, perlag, charcoal and pieces of bark. Temperatures should be above 15°C (59°F) and good light is essential, although direct sunlight should be avoided.

HEMIONITIS (from the Greek *hemionos*, a mule, referring to its former use by herbalists to induce sterility or to prevent pregnancy in women)
These small-fronded, low-growing terrestrial ferns are found mostly in the American tropics although they also occur from India to the Philippines. Only five species are known and of these the two most often seen are *H. arifolia* and *H. palmata*. Both like a moist, humid environment and can therefore be used as subjects for bottle gardens and terrariums.

H. arifolia produces narrow, arrow-head shaped fronds on thin black wiry stems, some 15–20cm (6–8in)

177

high. *H. palmata*, also called the strawberry fern, produces a clump of fronds, the surfaces of which are covered in fine short hairs. Provided sufficient humidity is present, young plantlets will develop in the axis of the frond and stalk and around the base of the parent plant.

Propagate by potting up the young plantlets or grow from spores. Do not place in strong sunlight, although gloomy situations should also be avoided. A good open potting compost will suffice. Keep moist.

LYGODIUM (from the Greek *lygodes*, willow-like, an oblique reference to the twining or climbing rachides) This group of some forty species of ferns from the tropics and subtropics have adapted themselves as climbing plants. In the wild they are to be found scrambling through and over other shrubby plants in order to reach the light. Each climbing 'stem' is, in fact, a single frond.

L. japonicum, the Japanese climbing fern, is probably the most useful for temperate climates. It will grow successfully with a minimum temperature of 5°C (41°F) and may even succeed out of doors in favourable situations, provided the root and rhizome mass are protected from frost. The plant forms a delicate green lacy effect as it climbs the wires or cane supports provided for it. It can reach 5m (15ft) or more. When

well established it produces a new flush of fronds from the base of the plant each year in early spring. Old fronds should be cut and removed before the new ones commence their climb. Use a good loam-based compost with added peat and grit.

Other *Lygodium* species that may be available are *L. flexuosum*, *L. microphyllum* and *L. palmatum*, although all of these require more warmth with a minimum temperature of 15°C (59°F). They will all accept strong light, although it is advisable not to have them growing immediately behind unprotected glass in summer.

MICROLEPIA (from the Greek *micros*, small, and *lepis*, a scale, referring to the small scalelike indusium or sporangia cover)
Of the thirty or more species in this genus, natives of the Old World tropics, Japan and New Zealand, only four are usually grown and of these *M. platyphylla* is the most decorative and most often seen. It has fronds exhibiting a blue-green coloration; this is more pronounced if grown away from strong light. In cultivation, when grown in pots the fronds do not extend more than 90cm (3ft), but if planted in a greenhouse bed or given ample

(Below) *Lygodium japonicum*
(Opposite) *Microlepia platyphylla*

Nephrolepis cordifolia

exalata 'Bostoniensis', the true Boston fern, have made this plant sought-after as a favourite subject to adorn the home, especially for the bathroom, hall or living-room. It is usually very tolerant of occasional neglect, although frequent periods of drought can often have disastrous results.

The rapid production of many thousands of identical young plants became commercially possible with the advent of laboratory techniques using sterile culture methods. These developments gave growers the ability to satisfy a demand that was rising around the same time for elegant evergreen plants to complement and enhance the interior decor of people's homes. Placed in a macramé or cane hanger, the Boston fern is unequalled for its striking effect.

Other available species include *N. exalata*, also called the sword fern, possibly because its fronds are held more upright; it is the species from which the true Boston fern was selected in America many years ago. *N. cordifolia* is another species almost as prolific as *N. exalata* in the number of cultivars it has produced. Sometimes called the fishbone fern, it produces fronds up to 60cm (2ft) long and is somewhat stiffer in appearance than *N. exalata*. One cultivar, *N. cordifolia* 'Duffii', is interesting in that it has very narrow, rounded pinnae clothing the frond stems, while each frond apex is divided into a number of segments, giving an almost crested appearance. The fronds may be 40cm (16in) tall but only 12mm ($\frac{1}{2}$in) wide.

Nephrolepis thrive in a peat-enriched potting compost, and should be occasionally repotted into a slightly larger container. This is best done in the spring when new growth is just emerging. Propagation can be from young plants produced from stolons which root into the parent plant's compost; these should be sliced out together with a wedge of substrate and potted separately. They may take two to three months to establish satisfactorily and initially need considerable care.

space they can grow to twice this size. The plant tends to rest during the winter when few, if any, new fronds are produced.

Of the other species *M. speluncae* will also grow rather large. If given suitable conditions it will reach over 90cm (3ft), and the fronds will have a slight coarseness to the touch. *M. strigosa* is a very useful pot plant in that it can be kept potbound and thus the fronds will remain smaller. It is evergreen, its growth light and airy, and can be used as a filler plant or background to more colourful flowering subjects. Good general loam-based compost with added coarse peat is all that is required and one must never allow the plant to dry out at the roots.

NEPHROLEPIS (from the Greek *nephros*, a kidney, and *lepis*, a scale, referring to the shape of the indusium or sporangia cover)
The genus contains about thirty species of scrambling or tufted ferns native to the tropics, Japan and New Zealand.

Various factors have combined over the past decade or more to push this particular group of ferns to the front line of potted indoor foliage plants. More particularly the arching and cascading fronds of *N.*

OSMUNDA (said to be named after Asmund or Osmundus, an eleventh-century writer who furthered the cause of Christianity in Sweden; alternatively from the Latin *os*, a mouth, and *mundare*, to purify)
Although it contains relatively few species this genus has representatives in both tropical and temperate climes. The royal fern, *Osmunda regalis*, is a native of the British Isles, although it was almost collected to extinction during the Victorian era when the craze for growing ferns around the home and garden was at its height. Other species that may be obtained are *O. cinnamomea*, the cinnamon fern, and *O. interrupta* (syn. *O. claytoniana*), the interrupted fern. After a number of years and after making several crowns they will all form a large rootstock.

Pellaea rotundifolia

O. *regalis*, which also has several varietal forms, can extend its fronds to 1.5–1.8m (5–6ft) in height when in a good situation out of doors and near water. The tightly curled fronds emerge in spring clothed in a mat of woolly hairs, making them look as much animal as vegetable. The fronds have a distinctive reddish colour when first produced, but this is masked by chlorophyll as they mature. With the royal fern the topmost area of frond is reserved for spore production and is very characteristic. O. *cinnamomea* has separate fertile fronds which are produced in spring, followed a little later by the sterile ones. The fertile fronds are relatively short-lived, and wither away after the spores are shed. They give the plant its common name, being reminiscent in colour to sticks of cinnamon when the spores are ripe. O. *interrupta*, like the royal fern, produces its spores on a section of the normal frond, though here the area selected is sandwiched near the centre of the frond, with sterile pinnae above and below the fertile area. Of the three species O. *regalis* is the most suitable for indoor cultivation, growing successfully in containers. A loam-based compost with added peat is required, and the plants prefer good light. All three can be used as interesting cool greenhouse plants.

PELLAEA (from the Greek *pellaios*, dark, referring to the purple to blackish frond stalks)
Relatively small, these often low-growing ferns are sometimes known by their common names of cliff brake or rock brake. They are mostly found in America and South Africa. A number are in cultivation and have been popular for many years, including *P. atropurpurea*, purple cliff brake; *P. falcata*, Australian cliff brake; *P. rotundifolia*, the button fern or New Zealand brake; and *P. viridis*, together with its variety *P. v.* var. *macrophylla*. They are, in general, natives of rocky areas and rather poor soils, often found with their fronds pushing out from rock crevices; they are plants able to withstand great fluctuations of temperature. The stipes or leaf-stalks are generally of a wiry nature, often dark brown to black, but with many there is an unfortunate tendency to fracture if knocked or handled too vigorously, and so it is necessary to support them with a split cane or wire.

The purple cliff brake, *P. atropurpurea*, has fronds up to 25cm (10in), its purple stems holding outward the very decorative grey to blue-grey fronds. *P. falcata* produces a mass of fronds from a creeping, underground stock. The fronds grow to 35cm (14in) in length, and the main rib is clothed in two rows of dark green pinnae. Old fronds should be removed by severing the leaf-stalk at its base. *P. rotundifolia* is similar but with round shiny pinnae held like little buttons (hence the common name), sitting in two rows down the wiry mid-rib of the frond.

These ferns are very easy to cultivate and seem to thrive best in a slightly alkaline soil. A loam-based compost, which has added to it a proportion of grit and hard coarse peat, suffices. Do not overwater and as a general rule keep the crown at or a little above soil level. Grow in good light, although strong sunlight through glass should be avoided. Temperatures need not be high; 7°C (45°F) at night is sufficient, rising to 15°C (59°F) or so during the day.

PLATYCERIUM (from the Greek *platys*, broad, and *keras*, a horn, referring to the shape of the outward-facing fronds)
The stag's horn, or sometimes called elks' horn or moosehorn ferns, are a widely distributed group of most unusual looking epiphytes. In the wild they are confined to the tropics and of the eighteen or so species, only one is found in the New World. Some have been in cultivation for many years, although these tend to be the plants that tolerate cooler and drier conditions. They are also somewhat less spectacular than the very large species, which need higher temperatures, and retain completely evergreen clasping and fertile fronds throughout the year.

The species most frequently available commercially are *P. angolense*, also known under *P. elephantotis* (elephant's ear fern); *P. bifurcatum* and its numerous varieties and *P. vassei*, also known as *P. alcicorne*. All these ferns produce two distinct types of frond – clasp or nest fronds – which in the wild bend back to clothe the branch on which the fern is growing, lifting outwards a little above the crown of the fern so that any debris from the host tree can be caught and, after eventually rotting, any nutrients can be utilized. The more flamboyant, outward-facing fronds take the shape of stags' antlers, which are fertile and bear the spores.

Platycerium alcicorne

These plants need a minimum temperature of 15°C (59°F), although *P. bifurcatum* will survive at a temperature of 10°C (50°F) or even 7°C (45°F) so long as these conditions are experienced only occasionally and the plants are not kept too wet. For best results grow in a very open spongy compost consisting of coarse peat, sphagnum moss and crushed bark or coconut husks. The aim should be to provide adequate stability with perfect drainage.

The plants may be set within a clay pot or container placed so that they are facing to one side; they should not be flat on the compost surface. Alternatively, they may be grown in slatted wooden baskets or mounted on slabs of cork bark or hardwood; it is best here to use plastic-covered wire or nylon line in order to secure the plants on to the support. They do well located on a wall mounting, provided that the siting allows for easy removal of the plant for watering and is free from draughts and in good light. A useful idea is to fix a decorative board (a bread-board perhaps) to the wall, on to which is secured a metal loop. Then, if cork bark is used to hold the plant, it can also have a metal 'tongue', which will insert into the metal loop on the board. This will enable easy removal of the plant for watering or other attention. However, always allow the plant to drain well before placing it back on the board. Water once a week throughout the year but less in winter, especially if the temperature is low.

POLYPODIUM (from the Greek *polys*, many, and *pous/podos*, a foot, referring to the freely branching and rooting rhizomes)

This has traditionally been one of the largest groups of ferns and although much taxonomic work has been done to clarify nomenclatural problems further research is needed on the family Polypodiaceae in general. They are found throughout the world in the tropics, subtropics and temperate regions alike. These plants are rhizomatous, most are epiphytic and many have rather leathery fronds, often entire and straplike, though not always so.

One of the tropical species most commonly seen as a pot plant is *P. aureum*, also known as *Phlebodium aureum*, the rabbit's foot fern. It has a fleshy rhizome clothed in light brown papery scales. The fronds are dark green, simply divided with pinnae on either side of the central stem or rachis. The sori are scattered over the undersurface and appear as little golden brown mounds, each consisting of numerous sporangia. Because the sori are conspicuous they are often mistaken for a disease or plant pest.

There are a number of cultivars and varieties of *P. aureum* available, including *P. aureum* var. *glaucum* which has a rather special blue-green bloom over its fronds, and *P. a.* 'Cristatum', in which the segments of the

Pteris cretica 'Albo-lineata'

fronds are further divided towards their tips. Some botanists now separate plants once grouped under the genus *Polypodium* into twenty or more different genera, including *Campyloneurum*, of which *C. angustifolium*, the narrow-fronded strap fern, is the most commonly seen. *Microgramma*, in which *M. lycopodioides* can be found, is a most useful small robust fern with glossy, 10cm (4in) long, entire, narrowish fronds produced from a brown scaly rhizome. It is a good plant for clothing the base of tree ferns, palms, cycads or similar and may be grown as a basket plant. *Microsorum* is another generic grouping of, in this case, ferns from the Old World. *M. punctatum* and *M. p.* 'Cristatum' are also suitable as subjects for the living-room or conservatory. Dark green, glossy foliage emerges from tightly packed rhizomes at or a little below soil level. It requires a minimum of 15°C (59°F). They should be placed in good light in winter but protected from strong sunlight in summer.

PTERIS (from the Greek *pteron*, a wing, referring to the shape of the pinnae composing the fronds)

A native of the tropics and subtropics and containing well over 200 species, this genus, together with *Nephrolepis*, is one of the most popular for indoor and greenhouse use. They are commonly known as table ferns or brake ferns, with some having individual common names. The ones more frequently offered for

FURTHER INFORMATION

Bibliography

Foster, F. Gordon, *Ferns to know and grow*
  (Hawthorn Books Inc., 1971)
Goudey, Christopher J., *Maidenhair Ferns in
  Cultivation* (Lothian Publishing, 1985)
Holttum, R. E., *Ferns of Malaya* (*Flora of
  Malaya* Vol. II), (Government Printing
  Office, Singapore, 1968)
Hoshizaki, B. J., *Fern Growers Manual* (Knopf,
  1979)
Kaye, Reginald, *Hardy Ferns* (Faber & Faber,
  1968)
Macself, A. J., *Ferns for Garden and Greenhouse*
  (Collingridge, 1952)
Perl, Philip, *Ferns* (Time-Life Books, 1979)
Swindells, P., *Ferns for Garden and Greenhouse*
  (Dent, 1971)

Societies

The American Fern Society
Dr David S. Barrington
Department of Botany
Vermont (University)
Burlington, VT 05401
USA

The British Pteridological
Society
Secretary
Mr A. R. Busby
Croziers
16 Kirby Corner Road
Canley
Coventry CV4 8GD
England

Fern Society of South Australia
P.O. Box 711
G.P.O.
Adelaide
South Australia 5001

International Tropical Fern
Society
8720 Southwest 34th Street
Miami, Fla 33165
USA

Los Angeles International Fern
Society
c/o 14895 Garden Hill Drive
La Mirada, Calif 90638
USA

The Nippon Fernist Club
Department of Forest Botany
Faculty of Agriculture
Tokyo University
Japan 113

sale are the small- to medium-sized species and varieties, which have fronds produced in clusters from stubby stocks that do not grow much above soil level. The fronds of most species exhibit various patterns of division, with some particularly intricately divided. Usually the first pair of pinnae on each frond splits so that one segment of each is held horizontally, leaning slightly downwards, while the other two are invariably angled forward.

Pteris cretica, the true table fern or ribbon fern, is a robust plant with fronds which may reach 60cm (2ft) or more in height. It has rather tough, papery leaflets and is relatively easy to grow. *P. c.* 'Albo-lineata' and 'Albo-lineata Cristata', lovely names to roll off the tongue, are striking plants, where the centre of each frond segment is pale silver. The latter plant is crested at the tips of each frond as well. Neither grows as strongly as the straight species. Its cultivars 'Rivertoniana', 'Wilsonii' and 'Wimsettii' are also often seen and are all good decorative, easily grown plants. 'Rivertoniana' has shortish, feathery, green fronds while 'Wilsonii' is again a crested fern.

P. ensiformis is rather a meagre plant but good stock is available of its cultivar 'Victoriae', which like 'Albo-

(Opposite) *Rumohra adiantiformis*

lineata' is silvery white along the middle of each pinnae. Commonly called the silver lace fern, it makes a striking plant. Of the other available species, *P. tremula* has a pleasing open habit of growth, its frond segments quivering and trembling upon the slightest movement, hence its common name, the trembling fern. *P. quadriaurita* and *P. q.* 'Argyraea' are both larger ferns, with the latter having silver to white linear markings on all divisions of the frond. They are all terrestrial plants and are easily grown using a loam-based compost with added peat. Temperatures need not be excessive as most will grow well enough with a minimum of 10°C (50°F). *Pteris cretica* will tolerate 7°C (45°F) or lower if not overwatered.

RUMOHRA (named after Dr Carolus de Rumohr Holstein)
The common name of leather fern is most apt for this genus of one species from the warm areas of the southern hemisphere, its fronds being extremely tough and much valued by floral artists since they do not wither or wilt quickly.

R. adiantiformis produces fronds from an underground rhizome, reaching some 60cm (2ft) in length. Pot in a loam-based compost with added peat and provide a minimum temperature of 15°C (59°F).

PLANTS FOR SPECIAL PURPOSES

MINIMUM TEMPERATURE REQUIRED

Cool (5–10°C [41–50°F])	Warm (10–19°C [50–66°F])
Adiantum capillus-veneris, A. pedatum *Asplenium bulbiferum* *Blechnum penna-marina* *Cyrtomium caryotideum, C. falcatum* *Dicksonia antarctica* *Lygodium japonicum* *Osmunda regalis* *Pteris cretica*	*Asplenium nidus* *Blechnum brasiliense, B. gibbum* *Cyathea arborea, C. contaminans* *Davallia solida* and var. *fejeensis* *Didymochlaena truncatula* *Diplazium proliferum* *Microlepia platyphylla* *Platycerium* (most will grow best in warm conditions)

EASE OF CULTIVATION

Suitable for beginners	Moderately easy	Fairly difficult
Adiantum raddianum *Asplenium nidus* *Cyrtomium falcatum* *Dicksonia antarctica* *Nephrolepis cordifolia, N. exaltata*, and cvs *Pellaea rotundifolia* *Phlebodium aureum* *Platycerium bifurcatum* *Pteris cretica* and cvs	*Blechnum brasiliense* *Davallia canariensis* *Lygodium japonica* *Microlepia platyphylla* *Osmundia regalis* *Pellaea falcata* *Rumohra adiantiformis*	*Diplazium proliferum* *Drynaria* *Hemionitis*

LIGHT REQUIREMENTS

Shady situation

Adiantum capillus-veneris, A. venustum   *Pteris cretica*
 Cyrtomium falcatum

Direct Sunlight

A word of caution is necessary here in that the effect of strong sunlight through unprotected window glass can be very damaging to ferns. Though the plants listed will take good light, strong sun on them for long periods should be avoided.

Asplenium bulbiferum   *Dicksonia antarctica*
 Davallia canariensis   *Osmunda regalis*

ATTRACTIVE FOLIAGE

Adiantum, most species and cvs
 Blechnum gibbum
 Cyathea (most)
 Davallia solida
 Cyrtomium falcatum
 Didymochlaena truncatula
 Microlepia platyphylla
 Pellaea rotundifolia

USEFUL PLANTS

ALL PLANTS are useful; green landplants supply oxygen to the atmosphere, bind soils, circulate water and nutrients, and serve as food for animals. The non-green plants break down other plant and animal material and contribute to chemical cycles in nature too. Without plants animal life could not exist.

Useful or economic plants are those which provide a benefit such as a crop. Crops are obtained from fruits, nuts, seeds, stems, roots, leaves, bark, and include products that are eaten, fibres used in cloth and papermaking, oils for industry and cosmetics, and timber for building. Of the exotic tender crop-plants which are the subject of this section, some will not produce edible fruits because of their very special growing requirements, but growing them will give some appreciation of their importance in other areas. On the other hand, the plants are ornamental and some will flower and produce good fruits.

Many crop plants are large when they become productive. If they were potted-on every time they filled a pot with roots, they would soon outgrow the space available in greenhouse or home. Restricting them and repotting only when this becomes essential will keep them small for a number of years. Replacing an inch or so of the soil surface every year will feed the roots and allow slow development. They are then effectively grown as indoor bonsai, and if their shape is managed with careful pruning they can be very attractive.

Many of the warm-region crops come from areas with a Mediterranean climate, and these are more suitable here than the tropical kinds. Some are well-known house plants, but are not usually recognized as of economic

(Above) *Pelargonium graveolens* 'Variegata'   (Opposite) *Carica papaya*

importance. Some are insignificant in a temperate region, but very valuable in tropical areas.

Cultural requirements

It is not by accident that most good house plants come from warm regions. Garden plants from colder climates would be attractive inside but do not tolerate indoor conditions for long. In order to ornament our houses with growing things we have to choose plants which need warmth. Many tropical plants have very precise demands for flowering and fruiting, but tolerate a wider range of conditions for growth; freedom from frost is all that is needed for some. Living-room conditions, however, provide just about the worst environment for most plants, especially in winter, because of the very dry atmosphere resulting from central-heating systems, and because the human inhabitants could not tolerate the humidity level best for the plants. Winter conditions are also wrong because some plants need a dormant period just when we want warmth. Poor light, the shock of sudden exposure to direct sun, draughts which remove moisture from leaves, and sudden changes in temperature, are all hazards for plants indoors.

Crop plants have been selected over long periods to obtain good varieties for various climates. Examples include avocado, peanut and citrus. Fortunately this means that some varieties will tolerate indoor cultivation, although others fail. It is not always possible to tell which varieties will be best, but if one kind of avocado, for example, fails, then another might succeed.

Some exotics flourish in constantly high temperatures and humidity but still grow reasonably well if chilling is avoided. A hot, dry atmosphere will damage leaves even of very tough species. Standing potted plants on trays of gravel and keeping water in the gravel will moisten the air around them, but the pots must not stand in water or the compost will become waterlogged and the roots of most kinds of plants will rapidly deteriorate.

Success with many exotics depends on keeping the evergreen kinds growing as slowly as possible during the winter, and keeping the deciduous ones cool and nearly dry to prevent growth from starting too soon. The good house plants are really those which need glasshouse protection but which tolerate living-room conditions.

Basic cultivation

Atmosphere: Plants will flourish in the same atmosphere as people, but prefer somewhat higher levels of carbon dioxide and lower oxygen. They are badly affected by fumes and like a higher level of humidity than people do.

Light: Light is vital, and strong indirect sunlight is usually best, but is often lacking indoors. Sunlight affects the temperature and moisture needs of plants as well as their health. Direct sunlight can damage delicate leaves, but very shady conditions are also detrimental to most plants. Some, however, like the Norfolk Island pine, asparagus ferns, *Chlorophytum*, ferns and ivies, do well in shady places. If a plant is not getting enough light its leaves turn pale and the stems become spindly and weak. Artificial lighting helps, and fluorescent sources are best. Ordinary light bulbs are too hot when close enough to be of value.

In conservatories depending on natural light alone, light is usually inadequate in winter and excessive for some plants in summer. The latter can be countered by shading.

Water: It is often difficult to know when to water a plant and when to leave it alone; experience is the only good teacher.

Some plants grow in waterlogged soil, and these are normally originally found in water or boggy areas. In all others waterlogging cuts off air from the roots which rapidly deteriorate. Once damage of this sort has occurred the only course of action is to allow the plant to dry out, remove all rotten roots, and repot in compost which is only very slightly moist. The plant will have to produce new roots before it can take up water and nutrients again, and this can take a long time.

Complete drying of the soil will cause wilting and possibly loss of leaves, but is less likely to kill.

Water needs depend on the condition of the plant and its rate of growth, light intensity, temperature, air movement, atmospheric moisture, and on the kind of compost and pot. One way to tell if a plant needs water is to feel the soil 2cm ($\frac{3}{4}$in) or so below the surface. If it is moist, no additional water is needed.

Rain water is best but tap water often has to suffice. Good compost will balance such water problems as alkalinity, at least in the short term.

Food: Liquid fertilizer can be used when the plants are growing well. It is not needed when they have been repotted into fresh compost, and must be avoided when they are resting or in poor condition. If such food is given when the roots cannot take it up from the compost, salt concentrations in the soil will increase and cause serious damage.

Composts and containers: Composts used for house plant production are usually peat-based products with no loam in them. They are easy to handle, light, and contain essential plant foods. If they dry out they can be difficult to moisten, and they do not last long. If a plant is to be grown for several years in one container, it is best in a loam-based compost with plenty of horticultural sand and some leaf mould or well-rotted manure. This sort of growing medium will support growth for much longer.

Plants which grow tall are safer in loam-based compost in clay pots. Plants in light composts in plastic pots tend to topple over if they grow upwards or to one side. Clay pots are somewhat less likely to become waterlogged than plastic ones.

Musa basjoo, showing the false stem formed from the bases of the leaves. The inflorescence is divided into male and female parts. The female flowers, and ultimately the fruits, are carried in basal clusters. The male flowers terminate the inflorescence.

Cocos nucifera

Plants should be handled gently, but firmly enough to avoid dropping them. Bruising leaves and stems can lead to rotting or deformity. Root damage can cause a considerable setback, needing weeks of careful treatment for recovery. Branches which are broken during repotting should be carefully pruned.

Repotting is usually best done at the beginning of the growing season so that new growth has plenty of time to mature, and any damage can heal properly. Dead roots can be removed at this time and root damage will not so easily lead to rotting.

Pruning: Some plants are poisonous (*Dieffenbachia*, for example), others have irritant sap (such as philodendrons and euphorbias) or hairs, some taste objectionable (such as aloes). When pruning plants, it is best to avoid contact with the sap and to wash your hands thoroughly after handling them. Avoid rubbing eyes, or face, with dirty hands. The sap of aloes will not be forgotten if it gets on to food, and some uncommon ones are poisonous.

Propagation

Seeds and cuttings are common means of propagation. The former can produce a good number of plants. Most kinds are best sown in spring to allow a long growing season. Large seeds and oily ones, like those of mangoes and lychees, should be planted immediately after being removed from the fruits.

Cuttings are very much a matter of trial and error for many plants grown indoors. If they fail, layering or air-layering (see page 117) might succeed. Layering involves bending a shoot down to the ground, and cutting some of the bark away from the lower surface before covering it with compost. Air-layering uses an upper shoot. The bark is cut away from about a third of the stem circumference, and about 1cm ($\frac{2}{5}$in) wide. The wound is then bound round with damp moss and wrapped with polythene which is tied into place. When roots have formed from the wounded area, the newly rooted stem can be separated from its parent plant and potted. The plant will need plenty of humidity for establishment, and the new roots must not be damaged.

In addition to seeds and vegetative propagation from stems, the underground parts of many plants provide an ideal means of growing interesting specimens. The tubers, corms, fleshy roots and bulbs which are imported for consumption are usually alive and can grow when given warmth and moisture.

Pests and diseases

Some pests are extremely difficult to eradicate, and it is important to avoid infestation. Inspect new plants thoroughly for pests and potential disease in damaged areas before adding them to a collection, and if an infestation appears, isolate the host plants immediately. Some kinds of pests can be removed by hand, or reduced by cutting off infested parts. Chemical treatment is possible, but seldom practicable or safe indoors.

Glasshouse whitefly are resistant to many chemicals. *Encarsia formosa*, a minute wasp parasite of the pest, is a very effective means of control in glasshouses, and one which could work indoors during the summer.

Scale insects and mealy bugs have waxy coats which protect them from water and some chemicals. Contact insecticides will work if applied when the very young insects are moving around. Alternatively, use a systematic insecticide.

Aphids can be killed by contact insecticides, but it is safer to remove infested shoots and burn them.

Deficiencies

Yellowing of the leaves often indicates that the plant cannot take up what it needs from the soil, but can follow physical damage from drought, draughts, temperature shock or waterlogging. Plants which naturally grow in acid soils deteriorate in alkaline soil, and their leaves often lose their strong green colour. The addition of acid peat, or well-rotted leaf mould can correct the problem, and watering with rain water usually helps.

Mineral deficiencies are best corrected by repotting into a suitable compost.

Guide to purchasing

Many exotic crops are first noticed as unusual fruits or vegetables on shop counters. Fruits often contain viable seeds, or plants can be grown from tubers, stems or crowns. Growing such pieces provides a free bonus to the crop we consume. Seeds of others are obtainable from seedsmen, but some kinds should be avoided because the seeds live only a short time and will not survive drying out; these include Para rubber and cocoa.

It is worth obtaining fruits from different geographical regions, particularly with avocados, because some varieties are better suited to home cultivation than others. Sometimes a seed produces more than one plant; this happens in mangoes and citrus and is known as polyembryony.

Some crop plants are sold as house plants, but not all are ideal. Young coconut palms are offered with the seeds still attached. It is possible but not easy to grow them well, but if they flourish they will outgrow the available space very rapidly; if they fail, the result is disappointment.

In buying plants the purchaser should look carefully for signs of pests or diseases, check the compost for excessive wetness, and try to ascertain that the plants have been properly cared for. The best protection is to ask the supplier about his plants, or go to well-established growers.

Mangifera indica

Actinidia deliciosa

Recommended genera

ACTINIDIA (from the Greek *aktis*, a ray, referring to the radiating styles)

This genus of about a dozen climbers originates in Asia, but various species are grown in areas with a Mediterranean climate.

They are deciduous woody climbers with attractive leaves. The fruits contain more vitamin C than citrus fruits, and breeding work aims at producing hardier plants for more widespread cultivation. In cooler climates the plants are hardy and will flower, especially in mild areas. Frosts can cause damage to the tips of young growths, and cold weather is not good for crop production. The plants need cool glasshouse protection for regular fruiting.

A well-drained deep fertile soil is best and the stems can be trained against a south-facing wall, or over pyramids of stakes. Pruning is done when the leaf buds begin to grow. Old wood should be removed every year to encourage development of new shoots, with cuts made just above strong buds. There are separate male and female plants and pollination is essential for fruiting. Fruits are picked in the autumn after the leaves have fallen, and light frost will not damage them.

Plants can be raised from seeds, but the progeny are not necessarily good for fruit production. Nurserymen offer male and female plants of named cultivars, and established plants can be increased by layering long shoots in late autumn. Actinidias need a lot of room but can be trained on a conservatory trellis.

A. deliciosa (*A. chinensis*) is the Chinese gooseberry, also called the Kiwi fruit because of crop development in New Zealand. *A. arguta* and others are used in breeding more productive plants, and *A. kolomikta* is important for its hardiness. This species is well-known as an ornamental climber; its green leaves have pink and white tips.

AGAVE (from the Greek *agauos*, stately, referring to the erect, tall flowering stems; commonly known as century plants)

There are about 300 species from warm areas of the Americas. All form rosettes of tough leaves, most with strong spines on their margins or tips. There are small species, but many produce leaves over 2m (6½ft) long. The large species are called century plants because they take a long time (about twenty-five to fifty years) to reach flowering size. An individual flowers only once, producing an enormous flower shoot with hundreds of flowers. The plants then depend on side-shoots, bulbils from the flower stem, and seeds for continuation.

A. sisalana is a large species producing the fibre sisal,

used to make ropes, matting and fishing nets. In some areas, the leaf-tip thorns of agaves are stripped from leaves with the long fibres still attached, and used as needles and thread.

The plants need well-drained compost, plenty of water in summer, and as much sun as possible. They should be kept cool and almost dry in winter. Growing the plants in pots keeps them small; if they are potted-on regularly, they soon become too large for house plant use. The leaf-tip spines are very strong and sharp, but can be cut off from leaves where people walk.

Variegated forms of *A. americana* are attractive but large. A smaller very ornamental species is *A. victoria-reginae*, with dark green leaves and clear white lines marking the angles.

See also CACTI AND OTHER SUCCULENTS.

ALOE (from *alloeh*, the early Arabic name for this genus)
This genus of succulents has almost 300 species from Africa, the Middle East and Madagascar.

They range from rosettes hugging the ground to tree-like forms. Most have attractive red or yellow tubular flowers on branched flowering shoots. Unlike the

Aloe vera

agaves which are monocarpic, the aloes flower and then continue to grow.

A. vera (*A. barbadensis*) is called Barbados aloe because the medicinal drug aloine (bitter aloes) is extracted from plants introduced to the West Indies. It is also known as the burn plant because its sap relieves the pain of burns. Other species also produce a purgative drug.

Like other succulents the aloes need plenty of sunlight and very well-drained compost. They need plenty of water in summer but little or none in winter when protection from frost is essential. Most species are easy to propagate from stem cuttings in summer. The cut surfaces should be allowed to dry before cuttings are planted in a very sandy mixture kept only slightly moist.

The sap of such plants is called bitter aloes, and it is important not to handle food with dirty hands after dealing with them. The sap of a few uncommon kinds is poisonous, but the taste of any is unforgettable.

Many species are grown in collections of succulents and some, such as *A. variegata*, the partridge-breasted aloe, are very ornamental and suitable for sunny window sills. Some will flower regularly if they have enough light.

See also CACTI AND OTHER SUCCULENTS.

AMARANTHUS (from the Greek *amarantos*, not withering, referring to the long-lasting flowering shoots; commonly known as love lies bleeding)
The genus comprises about fifty tropical and subtropical annuals, some reaching 2m (6½ft) tall. The soft hairy leaves sometimes show the reds and reddish-purples of the flowers.

The edible seeds of many species are used for food, and some species are important vegetables.

A rich loamy soil is best for strong development of the plants raised from seeds sown in heat in April. When large enough to handle, seedlings should be potted separately, and transplanted regularly to encourage rapid growth. High temperatures, good light and plenty of water are necessary to produce strong plants with good flower and leaf colour.

A. caudatus, love lies bleeding, and *A. hypochondriacus*, prince's feather, from India and Asia, are used as half-hardy annuals in summer bedding. These and the North American *A. retroflexus* supply useful grain crops, and the leaves of the last two are used as vegetables.

ANANAS (from the Brazilian Indian name for pineapple)
There are eight tropical American species, but only *A. comosus* is well known.

Most bromeliads are epiphytes, growing on tree branches. Almost all originate in tropical America, and form rosettes of tough evergreen leaves. Roots usually only serve the purpose of anchoring them, and moisture is absorbed by the leaves. The pineapple is one of the few terrestrial bromeliads, with flowers in a complex mass producing a compound fruit. Many cultivars have been raised in the tropics, and pineapples were an important glasshouse crop in Britain until it became cheaper to import them.

Tops of fruits can be cut off carefully and placed on sandy compost after the cut surface has been dried. They cannot grow if the centres are cut out. The compost should be only slightly moist until roots form, and this will occur quite rapidly at 26°C (79°F). A compost of loam, peat and well-rotted manure is suitable, and the plants need full sun and a moist atmosphere in spring and summer. A minimum temperature of 18°C (64°F) is necessary. Plants can fruit at two years old, but take longer indoors. Such house plants will flower and fruit if they grow strongly. Liquid fertilizers can be provided until the fruits start to ripen, and then the plants need

very little moisture. The fruits take about six months to develop.

A. comosus 'Variegatus' and the similar *A. bracteatus* 'Striatus' have yellow-margined leaves flushed with red when young, and are popular house plants.

See also BROMELIADS.

ANNONA (A Latinized version of a South American Indian name)
There are about a hundred species in this genus, most from tropical America and Africa, and introduced to other tropical areas. The majority are small trees growing to about 5m (16ft) tall. The fruits generally have rough surfaces around soft, whitish, usually sweet pulp in which large dark brown seeds are embedded. Some cultivars are almost seedless.

Ananas cosmosus 'Smooth Cayenne'

Annona reticulata

and earthnuts. The specific name means underground and refers to the fruits which form in the soil. The plants remain close to the ground, and produce many yellow flowers. The seeds contain an edible olive-oil substitute also used in margarine and soap-making. The seed pulp is a valuable cattle food.

This species is very successful as a house plant. Seeds are planted singly in small pots of peaty compost in spring. A temperature of 15°C (59°F) is sufficient for germination, but more warmth promotes strong, rapid development. Little water is needed before germination, and then the plants must have a constant supply, and full light.

They should be transplanted frequently, and the final 15–20cm (6–8in) pots will allow space for fruit formation. The seeds will germinate easily if kept warm and moist. Fertilizer can be applied to advantage after the flowers open. The plants will start to die down as fruits ripen in the soil.

It is important to obtain fresh seeds for growing which are complete in their pods (obviously, avoid prepared or cooked samples). The seeds can be planted in their pods, or separated before sowing.

CAMELLIA (named after G. J. Kamel, a seventeenth-century Jesuit priest and botanist)
This is an Asiatic genus of a hundred or so species of evergreen shrubs. *C. japonica*, *C. reticulata*, and *C. saluenensis* have produced many hardy and half-hardy ornamentals. Another, of great value as a beverage, is *C. sinensis* (or *Thea sinensis*), the origin of tea. It comes from south-east Asia and cultivars have been raised in many regions. A few varieties can survive outside in cooler climates, but do not grow strongly enough to produce a crop.

Tea plants can be grown indoors and need fairly humid conditions, good light, but shade from direct sun, and freedom from frost. An acid compost with plenty of well-rotted leaf mould is suitable. An annual mulch with acid peat and leaf mould will keep the roots healthy, and prevent yellowing of the leaves which usually indicates alkalinity. Root disturbance should be avoided.

Seeds can be sown in a standard seed compost kept moist and given bottom heat. A temperature of about 26°C (79°F) is sufficient for germination and 24–26°C (75–79°F) for subsequent growth. Seedlings should be potted-on carefully and gradually given less warmth to harden them off before winter.

CARICA (the Latin name for a kind of fig, from the Greek *karike*)
There are about forty species in this genus of small, evergreen trees from warm American regions, but, as with many crop plants, the exact origins are unknown.

Seedlings can be placed in a standard compost, and will need plenty of water once a good root system has formed. The plants will grow satisfactorily indoors but a dry atmosphere damages the leaf-tips; strong growth is achieved only in warm glasshouses. A winter minimum temperature of 10°C (50°F) and just enough water to keep the leaves turgid would be tolerated, but winter care of this sort usually leads to gradual deterioration. Flowering and fruiting occur only in a warm conservatory.

A. reticulata is the custard apple; *A. squamosa*, sweetsop; *A. cherimola*, the cherimoya; and *A. muricata*, the soursop, of which the fruits can weigh two kilos (4½lb). The fruits of *A. squamosa* dry on the tree and can, if they fall into a river or on to a beach, be carried across the ocean from the Americas to the beaches of western Europe.

ARACHIS (from the Greek *arachis*, without branches)
There are about fifteen species in this genus which comes from South America. Only *A. hypogaea* is of economic importance. This is an annual cultivated in most tropical countries for the seeds known as peanuts, groundnuts

The species that produces the pawpaw is now an important crop in many tropical areas.

C. papaya reaches 6m (20ft) in height but some selected forms in India fruit prolifically at less than 1m (3ft 3in) tall. The fruits can be eaten fresh or preserved, and these and the leaves contain important enzymes useful in cooking. Meat is tenderized by being wrapped in the leaves. The enzymes also have medical uses.

Seeds germinate easily but the seedlings are subject to damping-off disease, and need careful watering. The plants grow rapidly and, given a temperature of 21–26°C (70–79°F), can flower and fruit in eighteen months from seed. Their leaves attract such unwelcome pests as glasshouse whitefly and red spider mite, but regular spraying with tepid water will help to reduce the danger of infestation.

The closely related mountain pawpaw, *C. pubescens* (also known by its synonym *C. cundinamarcensis*), comes from the high regions of Ecuador. It produces smaller fruits but is more suitable for higher altitudes in the tropics, and is also better for indoor cultivation in cooler latitudes.

Pawpaw plants are usually either male or female, and both kinds have to be grown for fruits to be produced. Seeds normally produce a mixture, but growing conditions can affect the sex of individual plants. The dwarf cultivar 'Solo' is hermaphrodite and commercially available.

CERATONIA (from the Greek *keras*, a horn, referring to the plant's hard pods)

There are only two species in this genus – both small trees. The one commonly in cultivation is the well-known *C. siliqua*, the carob tree, locust tree or algaroba bean, an evergreen member of the pea family reaching about 15m (50ft) in height, and common in the Mediterranean region.

The pods grow to about 20cm (8in) long and are used for cattle food and human consumption. Fermented pods provide a beverage, and the husks are, by some, assumed to be the locusts of John the Baptist. The seeds are the original carat weights of jewellers, and are also used as a chocolate substitute.

The tree is hardy in the mildest areas of temperate countries, but generally needs cool glasshouse protection. Specimens are best grown in pots to restrict development, and if trained and pruned carefully they can grow into attractive bonsai. They need well-drained compost, plenty of light, and adequate water in summer. In winter they should be kept cool and only just moist, to prevent loss of leaves. A minimum temperature of 7°C (45°F) suffices. More warmth tends to encourage growth to continue during the winter and the shoots will become weak and spindly in the poor light.

CHLOROPHYTUM (from the Greek *chloros*, green, and *phyton*, a plant)

This genus in the lily family has about 200 species from warm regions; only two are commonly grown and are known as spider plants.

C. comosum and *C. elatum* are attractive, variegated house plants, producing no tangible crop. They are included because of their ability to clean the atmosphere. These plants take in and metabolize atmospheric pollutants and use them as food, thus reducing or eliminating some toxins. United States space research shows that they remove carbon monoxide and formaldehyde, as well as nitrogen, from the air.

The plants are best grown in rich, sandy loam, and are tolerant of a wide range of composts. They should not become waterlogged, but their fleshy roots enable them to survive considerable periods of drought. They grow well in shady places and, provided they are not subjected to frost, temperature is not too important.

The flowers are white and insignificant but flowering shoots produce small plants where the flowers have been. These can be left hanging on the flower shoots, or they can be taken off and grown separately.

Other house plants which remove atmospheric

Ceratonia siliqua

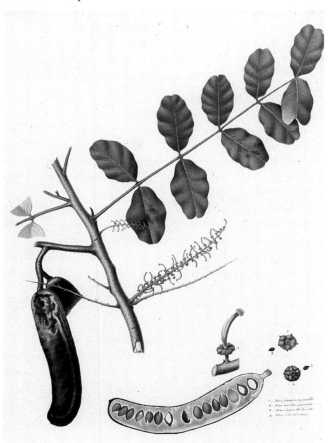

pollutants include *Scindapsus aureus* and *Syngonium podophyllum*.

CITRUS (the Latin name for the citron)

This genus has twelve species, most of which originate in the drier monsoon areas of subtropical south-east Asia. Many are grown in areas with a Mediterranean climate. Most are small, evergreen, thorny trees, but thorns do not always appear. The flowers are white and sweetly scented.

Seeds often start germinating inside the fruits, and can be planted in well-drained compost. Ungerminated seeds can be sown immediately or kept until spring, when most will still grow. Temperature is not critical for germination and seedlings can be produced very easily on window sills. The young plants should be potted separately when they can be handled easily, and need slightly acid, well-drained sandy compost with peat or well-rotted leaf mould. Yellowing of the leaves results from soil alkalinity or from starvation, when plants have been left in the same pots for too long. Once the plants have grown large enough for the space available they can be kept in large pots for many years, provided that some topsoil is replaced with good compost annually. Liquid manure can be used during the summer.

Such plants will tolerate a fairly dry atmosphere but this can damage the leaves and young shoots. A humid atmosphere with good light and ventilation is best, with indirect sunlight in summer and the best available light in winter.

Pruning consists of removing dead wood whenever it is noticed, and cutting back straggly branches to encourage development of fruit-producing side shoots. Flowers grow on one-year-old wood, and pruning before spring growth begins will allow new shoots to ripen in summer. The tips of growing shoots can be pinched out once or twice a year to encourage a more twiggy kind of growth.

The plants can stand outside in summer, but they must be brought in before the change in conditions becomes too extreme and could shock them. In winter a temperature of $10°-12°$C ($50°-54°$F) is sufficient, and just enough water should be given to prevent wilting.

Specially selected cultivars are propagated by bud grafting on to specially selected rootstocks. Most *Citrus* varieties are self-compatible, and fruits will form without artificial pollination. In the open, insects pollinate the flowers, but using a small paintbrush on indoor plants assists pollination and ensures fruit setting.

Citrus medica

The time taken for a particular plant to reach flowering size varies a lot with growing conditions; regular flowering can start between three and ten years old, but seedlings will sometimes flower much earlier. Grapefruits usually take longer than oranges and lemons.

Scale insects are a serious pest on citrus plants and their sticky secretions encourage the development of sooty moulds on the leaves. Young scales are not easy to spot, but new plants added to a collection should be inspected carefully to try to prevent infestations. Scales are often found near the leaf veins. They can be wiped off and destroyed, or very young insects can be killed by using a contact insecticide on plants outside in summer.

The following are some important kinds (hardiest first):

> *Fortunella japonica*, kumquat
> *Citrus reticulata*, satsuma, tangerine, mandarin (all distinct forms)
> *Citrus sinensis*, various oranges
> *Citrus × paradisi*, grapefruit
> *Citrus medica*, citron
> *Citrus limon*, lemon
> *Citrus maxima*, pomello or shaddock
> *Citrus aurantium*, Seville orange; subsp. *bergamia* produces oil of bergamot
> *Citrus aurantiifolia*, lime
> × *Citrofortunella microcarpa*, calamondin

COCOS (from the Portuguese *coco*, grimace, referring to the base of the shell which resembles a face)

This genus is probably of Melanesian origin, but the important *C. nucifera*, the common coconut, is widespread in tropical areas. There are hundreds of varieties, some reaching 30m (100ft) in height, and dwarf kinds reaching only 8m (26ft). This palm is so useful that plants have been distributed by man for many centuries. The seeds or shells disperse naturally on ocean currents.

Every part of the palm, at almost every stage of development, can be used. It supplies beverages from seeds and flower shoots, foods from seeds and buds, oils, fibres, cooking and eating utensils. In Europe the plant is only of relatively minor significance, supplying food additives, fibre for matting, and enjoyment at fun-fairs.

House plant suppliers offer seedlings which can survive for a few years but are not really suitable for growing indoors. They need constant high temperatures and humidity to keep the leaves in good condition, and if a plant grows well it will soon outgrow the space available.

Imported seeds will sometimes germinate, but removal of the outer husk makes germination unlikely. Fresh seeds can be placed on damp peat, with the broad face downwards, and need a temperature of $24°–27°$C ($75°–81°$F) for germination. Plants obtained with seeds attached are best left in their original containers until the connection with the seed shrivels, unless they can be potted without disturbance. Sometimes a spherical structure is found attached to the flesh inside a nut – this is the 'coconut apple' which transfers stored food to the developing embryo. It is very unlikely that an opened nut could grow successfully.

COFFEA (from the Arabic *kahwah*, coffee)

There are about forty tropical species in this genus, mostly from Africa. The plant is of considerable economic importance in Africa and South America because of the demand for the beverage containing the stimulant caffeine. *C. arabica* is the most important source, but *C. canephora*, robusta coffee, and *C. liberica*, Liberian coffee, are also used.

The plants are evergreen shrubs growing to about 3m (10ft) in height with dark green shiny leaves, and sweetly scented white flowers. The seeds are short-lived and will not survive for long stored dry. They must be sown when fresh and will germinate at $20°–29°$C ($68°–85°$F). The beans available from coffee retailers have been cleaned and dried slowly ready for roasting and will not germinate.

A loam, peat and sand compost is suitable and the plants need constant warmth and high humidity. A winter minimum temperature of $16°$C ($61°$F) is sufficient, and less water is needed in winter than during the summer growing season. Such pot plants can be grown on kitchen window sills but would not produce a crop sufficient for use. Fruit development takes several months, and the berries are picked when red. They then need slow drying and further treatment before they can be turned into coffee.

Coffea arabica 'Nana' produces a dwarf compact plant ideal for pot culture. Viable seeds are commercially available.

CORCHORUS (from the Greek *korkhoros*, stye, referring to the plant's medicinal value in the treatment of this eye condition)

The genus has about forty species from tropical regions, but only two Indian annuals, *C. capsularis* and *C. olitorius*, supply important products. Both provide the fibre jute, and the latter species is eaten as a spinach-like vegetable in the eastern Mediterranean region.

Mature plants can reach 3m (10ft) in height, but much less in containers. The fibres are valuable in cloth-making, but cotton alone is more important.

The seeds should be sown in spring, and need well-drained seed compost and a temperature of about $16°$C ($61°$F) for germination. Seedlings can be transferred to 12cm ($4\frac{3}{4}$in) pots, three per pot, when large enough to

(Opposite) *Coffea arabica*

handle, and need humid tropical conditions for good growth. Plenty of water must be provided and the plants can be fed when flowering starts. They can be repotted once into 20cm (8in) pots, which allow sufficient space for mature growth.

CYPERUS (from the Greek word for sedge)
There are over 500 species in this genus which occur in many areas. *C. papyrus*, the Egyptian paper sedge, originated in swampy Nile areas, but also grows elsewhere in Africa. The leaf stalks grow from a large rootstock and contain the material that is made into papyrus – the original writing material of the ancient Egyptians. The plants look rather like grasses but have leaves and flowers on the stem tops. Papyrus stalks can grow to 3m (10ft) tall; other species are much smaller.

Papyrus plants can be grown in large pots of standard compost kept very moist. Pots can stand in trays of water, or the plants can be grown in corner beds of large heated pools. A winter minimum temperature of 16°c (61°F) is sufficient, and a summer temperature of 21°–27°c (70°–81°F) is adequate for strong growth. Old stems tend to topple over.

C. esculentus var. *sativus* is about 30cm (1ft) tall and hardy. It yields the tubers known as tiger nuts.

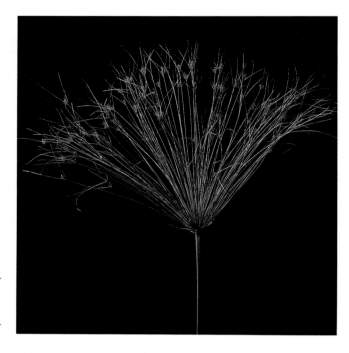

(Above) *Cyperus papyrus*
(Below) *Cyphomandra betacea*
(Opposite) *Eichhornia crassipes*

CYPHOMANDRA (from the Greek *kyphoma*, a tumour or hump, and *aner*, a man, referring to the humped anthers)

There are about thirty species in the genus which comes from warm areas of the Americas and West Indies, but only the Brazilian *C. betacea*, the tree tomato or tamarillo, is important. This small evergreen tree, related to tomatoes and potatoes, is grown extensively in New Zealand and other suitable areas for the fruits which must be allowed to ripen to orange or red before being eaten.

Fruiting-size trees can be grown in large pots, but they are better planted in glasshouse borders. The plants start to flower at ten to twelve months, and crop regularly for five years or more. A standard potting compost is suitable, and repotting is usually done in spring. Standing the plants outside in summer encourages development of strong shoots, but like other tender plants they must be brought in before the autumn cold causes damage. A winter minimum temperature of 7°C (45°F) suffices. High humidity is not needed, but a very dry atmosphere causes leaf damage. It is natural for old leaves to fall, leaving the branches somewhat bare except for leafy tips. Careful pruning will keep the plants more leafy, but hard cutting back encourages production of many soft shoots.

The plants grow well from seeds, but the progeny are variable, and fruit production may not be as good as in selected cultivars.

EICHHORNIA (named after J. A. Fr. Eichhorn, 1779–1856, a Prussian statesman)

There are about seven aquatic species in this genus, coming from warm areas of the Americas, but only one, *E. crassipes*, is well known. This plant originated in tropical America, but is now an extremely injurious weed in many tropical freshwater areas. The name *crassipes* means thick or fleshy footed or stemmed and refers to the inflated leaf stalks. Spikes of attractive pale lilac flowers are produced, and it is commonly known as the water hyacinth or lilac devil.

The plants are eaten by hippopotami and cattle. They are rich in potash and, therefore, valuable as fertilizers. They remove large amounts of plant foods from water and have been used in cleaning polluted water. They grow very rapidly and the large amounts of green material can be rotted to produce gas.

The plants need warm water and will flower in large aquaria. A water temperature of about 27°C (81°F) is suitable. Lower temperatures are tolerated but cause deterioration in winter.

FICUS (the Latin name for the fig)

This very large genus has perhaps a thousand species of tropical woody plants. *F. elastica* is the popular India rubber plant. It is native to India and tropical Asia, and forms a 30–40m (100–130ft) tree with enormous buttress roots and aerial roots descending from the branches. It usually starts from seeds lodged on branches

Ficus religiosa

of other large trees, gradually strangles the supporting tree and then becomes independent. The latex has been used commercially, but is almost insignificant when compared with true or Para rubber, *Hevea brasiliensis*.

The cultivars of *F. elastica* are good house plants. They prefer warmth but will tolerate cool conditions if draughts are avoided. Good light is needed, but not direct sunlight. The plants can be stood on trays of damp gravel, but dryish soil causes less damage than waterlogging. The tough, long-lasting leaves can be sponged with tepid water to remove dust, but the waxy surface should not be scratched.

A well-drained compost is best and repotting can be done in the spring, if the roots have filled the pot. The top of the stem can be shortened to encourage the development of side shoots, which will produce bushier specimens. If allowed to grow without pruning, these plants will become too tall for living-rooms and will need cutting back. It is possible to root the pieces but air-layering (see page 117) is more likely to succeed.

Other important *Ficus* species include *F. carica*, the hardy fig tree which sometimes produces good crops in temperate climates; *F. bengalensis*, the banyan tree; and *F. religiosa*, the sacred peepul tree of India. *F. pumila*, or *F. repens*, is a creeping or trailing pot plant much used in the home. Most species are sensitive to fumes from gas fires which may cause premature leaf drop.

GOSSYPIUM (an ancient Latin name which possibly derives from the Arabic word for soft material)
This is a genus of about twenty tropical shrubs or herbaceous perennials, closely related to *Hibiscus*. The shrubby kinds are treated as annuals and their seeds are harvested for cotton; most have yellow flowers, some with purple centres. The seeds are covered in long fine hairs – the source of cotton.

An acid compost is best but the plants will grow in various soils. The seeds should be sown in late winter, with two or three to a 7.5cm (3in) pot, and kept at a temperature of 18°–21°C (64°–70°F). They need shade until germination starts, and then plenty of sun. The young plants should be repotted regularly to keep them growing strongly, until they are in 25cm (10in) pots. They can reach nearly 2m (6½ft) in height, but rarely grow taller than 90–120cm (3–4ft) in pots.

Flowering and fruiting depend on adequate warmth and humidity. Additional food can be supplied during the summer.

Cotton is the world's most important textile fibre; the main species are *G. barbadense* and *G. hirsutum* from the Americas, and *G. herbaceum* from the East Indies. Growing the plants as annuals in tropical areas helps to reduce trouble from insect infestations.

HIBISCUS (the Greek name for mallow, used by the botanist Linnaeus for this closely related genus)
There are about 200 species in this genus, mostly tropical evergreen shrubs, but some are annuals, and a few species are hardy. Products of economic importance from this genus in the tropics include fibres, vegetables, and edible flowers and fruits.

The plants grow well in a coarse compost of loam, peat and sand, and are best in warm, humid glasshouses. Once flowering is over the perennials need less water for the winter resting period. Pruning the shoots in spring, and increasing heat and moisture, promotes strong growth for flowering. The seeds should be sown in spring and most kinds germinate well at about 24°C (75°F); cuttings taken in spring or summer will root in a heated propagator. Sudden changes in temperature or water supply will cause the buds and leaves to fall. A humid atmosphere is best for most of them, but the tougher-leaved kinds will tolerate drier conditions.

Important annuals include the Indian *H. cannabinus*, also grown in Africa for kenaf, a valuable textile fibre; *H. esculentus*, now more correctly placed in the genus *Abelmoschus*, from West Africa, the source of okra or ladies' fingers, the young fruits used as a vegetable; *H. sabdariffa*, rozelle, from the West Indies, a fibre plant of which the fleshy sepals are used in pickles and jellies. *H. tiliaceus* is a small tree found in tropical coastal areas which provides a valuable fibre for ropes.

H. rosa-sinensis has produced many hundreds of highly ornamental cultivars and is the species most widely cultivated for its attractive blossoms. *H. schizopetalus* is a thin-stemmed semi-scandent species with very attractive red pendent flowers. *H. syriacus* is a hardy deciduous shrub with several cultivars.

See also TENDER FLOWERING CLIMBERS.

IPOMOEA (from the Greek *ips*, a worm, and *homoios*, similar to, referring to the twining stems)
There are about 500 species in this genus, mostly originating in tropical and subtropical regions. The most important is the tropical American *I. batatas*, the sweet potato, which takes its Latin name from the native name for this useful vegetable.

The pink-skinned tubers contain large amounts of starch and sugars, and many of the cultivars are grown in tropical areas for food. The leaves may be entire and heart-shaped, lobed or deeply fingered, green or purple.

(Below left) *Gossypium herbaceum*
(Below) *Hibiscus esculentus*

Ipomoea batatas

The leafy stems normally creep over the ground; they rarely climb but can be trained over trellis-work. A minimum temperature of 18°C (64°F), and a rich, well-drained compost are needed. Very little water should be given in spring but plenty until autumn when the stems die back to leave the tubers dormant for the winter.

The tubers produce shoots very readily if warm enough, but the size of the tubers deteriorates unless tropical conditions are provided.

See also TENDER FLOWERING CLIMBERS.

LAWSONIA (named after Dr Isaac Lawson, an eighteenth-century Scottish army doctor and patron of Linnaeus)
The tropical *L. albida*, or *L. inermis* (meaning white and non-thorny), is the only species in this genus. It is a shrubby tree cultivated particularly in India, Egypt and Sudan. When powdered, its leaves produce the dye henna, which is used for colouring hair and finger nails. The small white flowers are sweetly scented.

The plants can be grown in sandy peat and loam mixtures, and tropical glasshouse conditions are best. In the tropics the shoots are clipped annually to produce the orange-yellow dye used in cosmetics. The seeds are sown in spring in ordinary seed compost kept at about 21°C (70°F). As house plants they grow very slowly.

In some tropical regions the plants are used for hedging.

LITCHI (the Chinese name for the fruit; also known as *Nephelium*, an old name for burdock, because the fruits look similar)
This genus contains about twelve species (thirty if included in *Nephelium*) from south-east Asia. *L. chinensis* is Chinese and is a subtropical tree reaching 15m (50ft) in height. It is the most widely cultivated species, although

others also produce useful fruits. It has evergreen pinnate leaves and clusters of small greenish-yellow starry flowers. It is commonly known as the lychee.

The seeds should be planted immediately after removal from the fruits because they will not survive drying. They can be placed individually in pots of peaty compost, and need constant warmth and moisture for germination. The plants may grow for several years, but rarely persist and are very unlikely to flower or fruit indoors. Some smaller cultivars might do so in tropical glasshouses. The long, rather narrow, pointed, glossy leaflets will turn brown in a dry atmosphere. Spraying the plants daily with tepid water and standing the pots on trays of damp gravel increases humidity. Artificial fertilizers can be applied in summer.

Nephelium lappaceum is a large Malaysian tree producing rambutans; *N. longana* is a 6m (20ft) tall Indian tree producing longans.

MANGIFERA (from the Tamil name, plus the Latin *ferre*, to bear)

There are about forty species in this genus, which is best

Litchi chinensis

known for producing the mango fruit, but only *M. indica* is important for crops, and hundreds of cultivars of this species have been selected for tropical areas. The tree is native to the East Indies, where it reaches 20m (65ft) in height. The fruits vary in size, texture, flavour and colour, and are eaten fresh or cooked.

Mangoes often contain good seeds, and their viability can be tested by dropping them into water; those that sink are likely to contain embryos and those that float are useless. The seeds should be planted immediately in peaty compost, and should be kept warm and moist. Germination usually occurs within three weeks. The seedlings should be potted-on during spring and summer whenever the roots fill the pots, and a minimum temperature of about 18°C (64°F) should be provided. The leaves are evergreen and fairly tough, but will suffer damage in dry air.

The plants can flower in tropical glasshouses, but fruiting is very rare and they are best grown just for their ornamental foliage. The flowers must be pollinated, and this can be done using a paintbrush; cross-pollination from one plant to another is not necessary. Shoots can be pinched back during the growing season to keep the plants compact.

The seeds are polyembryonic, and several seedlings can grow from a single seed.

MUSA (named after Antonius Musa, physician to the first Roman Emperor, Augustus)

There may be forty species in this subtropical genus which includes the various types of banana, but their history in cultivation is very long, and some supposed species are probably cultivars.

The plants are herbaceous perennials with shoots arising from basal suckers. There is no woody tissue and, in spite of their appearance, they are not trees, but have stems which die down after flowering. Various species and many hundreds of cultivars are useful for fruits eaten either green or ripe, and for fibres. Bananas are the most prolific food plants; the starch in the fruits is very nutritious and more easily digested than that of cereals. The skins contain various plant foods and are valuable in compost.

Bananas can be raised under glass in temperate climates and an area of 5 × 5m (15 × 15ft) is sufficient for four clumps of small varieties. Small plants in pots make handsome foliage house plants. A fairly well drained, slightly acid compost with a high organic content is ideal, and the beds should be mulched with farmyard manure in spring. Additional plant food can be given during the growing season. Copious watering, preferably with rainwater, is necessary. High atmospheric humidity is essential, and temperatures of a minimum of 18°C (64°F) in winter to a maximum of 24°C (75°F) in summer are sufficient. The plants will stand full sunlight, although partial shade helps to maintain high humidity.

Propagation of edible kinds must be by taking suckers, because they are clones and some are also triploid varieties (i.e. with three sets of chromosomes) which cannot produce seeds. One very popular cultivar is *M.* 'Dwarf Cavendish' which will fruit in 60–90cm (2–3ft) square tubs. Fruits should be left on the plant until they are fully formed, when the branch is cut and left hanging in the same environment until the fruits ripen. When the stems have finished fruiting they should be cut down to near ground level to encourage the growth of new suckers. Although the shoots grow and flower within one season in the tropics, they take longer in cooler climates even when grown indoors or under glass.

The seeds of non-edible kinds should be raised in rich seed compost, and kept warm and moist. Some are hardier than the fruiting sorts.

M. basjoo, the Japanese banana, will grow out of doors in milder areas and produces an important fibre in the tropics. *M. textilis*, from the Philippines, produces manila hemp.

M. ensete, or *Ensete ventricosum*, the Ethiopian banana, is hardy in very mild areas of temperate countries.

OLEA (the Latin name for the olive)

There are about twenty species in this genus, which comes from various warm regions, but only the southern European *O. europaea*, the olive, is commercially important. This is a long-lived evergreen tree growing to about 10m (30ft) in height, producing attractive timber. The fruits are crushed to extract olive oil, a very high-grade salad and cooking oil, and are also eaten as preserves.

The plants grow best in well-drained loamy soil, but they are tolerant of a range of conditions, and can be planted against south-facing walls in mild areas. They are best grown as glasshouse specimens in cooler climates, and can make very good indoor bonsai. The seeds should be sown in spring, with the tender young plants raised under glass and then stood outside in summer. Cuttings root quite easily if placed in sandy soil in a shaded frame during the summer.

It is important to keep such near-hardy plants cool enough during the winter to prevent formation of soft shoots at that time, but still to protect them from frost. Watering must also be controlled carefully, to prevent the roots from drying out but to avoid waterlogging when the trees are taking very little moisture from the soil.

OPUNTIA (named in 1754 after an ancient name for a thistle growing around Opus, a town in Greece inhabited by the Locri Opunti tribe)

This genus of between 200 and 350 species (dependent on which botanical work is followed) of cacti comes from North, Central and South America. Some are naturalized in other warm regions, such as Australia and southern Europe, and have in some places become serious weeds.

The plants form flattened or rounded stems covered in tufted spine clusters representing much reduced leaves. The stem sections vary considerably in size; stems of the kinds which produce edible fruits, prickly pears, reach 20–30cm (8–12in) in length. Strong-growing kinds have been used for hedging in subtropical regions, and spineless forms have been specially selected for cattle fodder in dry areas. The fruits can be eaten fresh or made into jam (the Aztecs used the plants as vegetables). *O. ficus-indica*, the Indian fig, and others, produce the edible fruits.

Fresh seeds are easy to grow in pans of well-drained seed compost, and germinate rapidly at 18°C (64°F); stored seeds will grow, but take longer to start. These cacti must have well-drained compost and although they can use plenty of water when growing, they tolerate extremes of drought and are better grown rather dry. Full sun is needed whenever available. Cut stem sections root very easily if they are placed in barely moist sandy compost during the summer. Excessive moisture will cause rotting.

Some species are hardy outside in temperate climates, but the stems are often disfigured by rain or hail.

See also CACTI AND OTHER SUCCULENTS.

ORYZA (from the Greek *oryza*, rice, from an ancient Oriental word)

There is probably only one species, *O. sativa*, but about twenty kinds have been described separately, and many thousands of cultivars have been raised.

This important crop plant is native to the East Indies, but it is widely cultivated in wet tropical regions where rice feeds more people than any other food plant. It is a vital source of starch in Asia, and has been introduced to South America, the West Indies and southern Europe. It was probably first cultivated in India 4000 years ago, and the exact origins of the species are uncertain. There are perennial wild relatives but *O. sativa* is grown as an annual.

Seeds should be sown in temperate climates during the spring in a loam, peat and sand mixture in pots or pans standing in water. A temperature of 24°–26°C (75°–79°F) is best for germination, and when the seedlings are about 5cm (2in) tall they should be planted out at three or four to a 20cm (8in) container. Established plants need to be fed frequently and must have constant warmth and moisture if they are to flower

(Opposite) *Olea europaea*

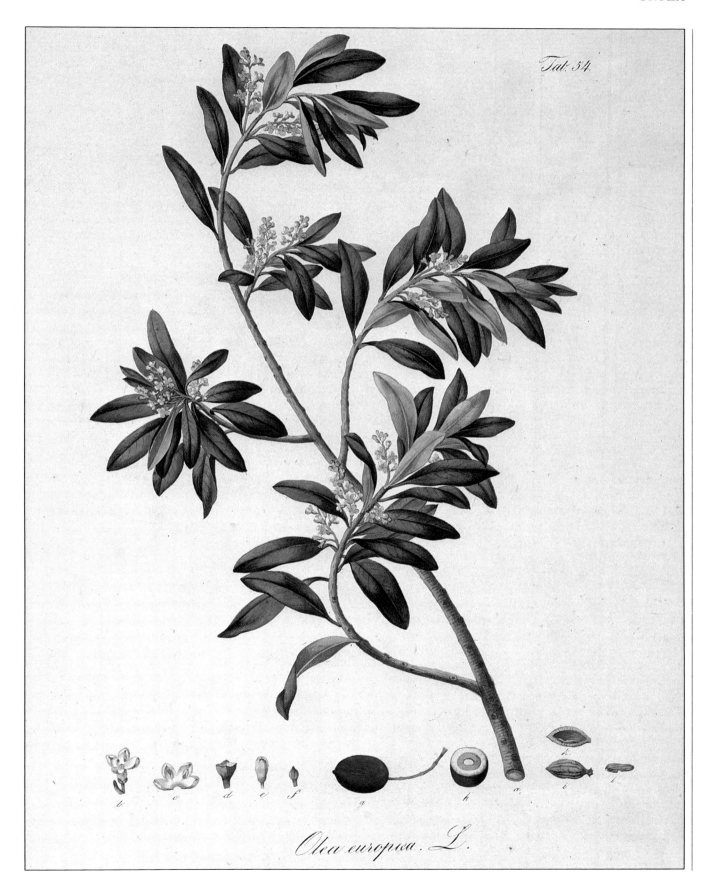

Tab. 54.

Olea europæa. L.

Oryza sativa

and produce seeds for a following season. When the seeds are nearly ripe the water should be drained away.

In India and eastern Asia rice straw is dried, pressed and used to make attractive pictures.

PELARGONIUM (from the Greek *pelargos*, a stork, referring to the beaklike fruits)
Almost all 250 species in this genus, commonly known as geraniums, are South African, but a few come from other warm regions. Several are widely cultivated for oils distilled from the highly scented leaves.

The plants are succulent-stemmed, and many can survive periods of drought in a leafless state. Their attractive flowers and patterned leaves make them ornamental. They need very well-drained compost and full sun. Some are suitable as house plants but they grow best in a conservatory where the sun will heighten the leaf scents, and induce bud formation. They are best cut back and kept fairly cool and almost dry during the winter, but if the growing area is warm they will need more water to prevent wilting. The important species for oils include *P. graveolens*, *P. radula*, *P. roseum* and *P. capitatum*.

Seeds of some species produce flowering plants in less than a year, but oil-producing kinds are best propagated from cuttings which root easily in sandy compost.

The following are some of the scents available:
    Apple, *P. odoratissimum*
    Apricot, *P. scabrum*
    Lime, *P. nervosum*
    Orange, *P. citriodorum*
    Lemon, *P. graveolens*, *P. crispum*
    Almond, *P. quercifolium* 'Pretty Polly'
    Filbert, *P. concolor*
    Ginger, *P. torento*
    Peppermint, *P. tomentosum*, *P. denticulatum*
    Pine, *P. filicifolium*
    Rose, *P. graveolens* 'True Rose', *P. capitatum*

PERSEA (the Greek name for an Egyptian tree which is, however, unrelated to this genus)
There are about 150 species of small trees in this genus of the laurel family, but *P. americana* from tropical America is the avocado from which hundreds of cultivars have been developed for cultivation in tropical and subtropical areas.

The seeds should be planted soon after being cleaned. The seed coats contain germination inhibitors and it is important to put them into well-drained compost and to water them regularly. Germination will take place in ordinary living-room temperatures and the seedlings grow rapidly.

Cultivars from drier areas, such as Mexico, tolerate cool, dry situations better than those from the West Indies. If the leaf margins become brown, it is likely that the plant is of moist tropical origin, and not suitable for cultivation in cooler climates.

The plants should be transplanted in spring but only if the present container is full of roots. A 30cm (1ft) diameter container is the largest needed and this would suffice for several years' development if liquid feed is provided during the growing seasons. Pruning should be done in early spring, cutting back the stems to side shoots or buds. Regular pinching out will produce bushy specimens. They will occasionally produce their greenish-yellow flowers, but are unlikely to fruit because the flower mechanism prevents self-pollination.

Avocados are the most nutritious fruits known, containing vitamins A, B and E, and highly digestible oil. They have very high energy value, some containing over 1000 calories per pound.

PHOENIX (from the ancient Greek name for this palm)
There are about seventeen species of *Phoenix* or date palms, which come from tropical and subtropical Asia and Africa. The most valuable is *P. dactylifera* from North Africa. It is extremely important in such arid regions, and was cultivated in Mesopotamia in 3000 BC.

(Above) *Persea americana*
(Right) *Phoenix dactylifera*

It reaches 30m (100ft) in height and has long pinnate leaves. The palms produce suckers which are important for propagating productive specimens. Dates form an extremely important carbohydrate food in most Arabic regions.

Date palms flourish around the Sahara, and in the Middle East. Rain prevents pollination in other tropical areas, and the fruits will only ripen in very dry climates. The palms are dioecious (with separate male and female plants), and in plantations one male is grown with every fifty females.

The seeds germinate within a week if planted in small pots placed on a radiator. The seed produces a coleorhiza from the centre of the rounded surface, and this extends 10–20cm (4–8in) before the first leaf and roots appear from its tip. The seedlings grow best in well-drained sandy compost. The first leaves are narrow, but later ones are pinnate.

Although these palms come from arid regions, a very dry atmosphere can damage the leaf tips. Growing palms in pots dwarfs them, which is an advantage if they are to be used as houseplants. Date palm leaves reach 2m (6½ft) long on ten-year-old plants. The palms can take a

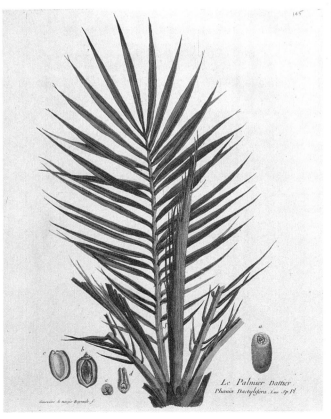

Le Palmier Dattier
Phœnix Dactylifera .Lun .Sp.Pl.

Le Grenadier a fruit.
Punica granatum. Linn. Sp. Pl.
Ital. Melagrano. Esp. Granadas. Angl. Balaustine-tree. Allem. Granatopffel.

Genevieve de Nangis Regnault. f.

long time to recover from disturbance and when they are repotted the roots should not be damaged.

Only *P. canariensis* can grow outside in milder temperate regions. Mature *P. dactylifera* specimens are sometimes planted outside and their thick stems protect the growing points for some years, but they gradually decline, and cold winters kill them.

PUNICA (from the Latin *malum punicum*, the Carthaginian apple)

There are only two species in this genus, *P. granatum*, the well-known pomegranate, and a very rare Socotran endemic, *P. protopunica*. *P. granatum* is a deciduous, shrubby tree reaching about 7m (23ft) in height. It occurs wild from the Balkans across to the Himalaya, but is widely cultivated. The plants provide a beverage as well as fruits.

The seeds should be sown in sandy compost in spring and will germinate at 13°–18°C (55°–64°F). When the young plants have grown for a season and are hardened off, they can be planted outside in sheltered south-facing (north-facing in the southern hemisphere) sites, but they are unlikely to fruit except under glass. Pruning can be done in spring when growth starts, and full sun is needed for ripening of the wood. The plants can be grown as indoor bonsai, but must be kept cool and fairly dry in winter.

There is a miniature, often semi-evergreen, form *P. granatum* 'Nana', which is an ornamental pot plant easily raised from seed to flowering size in under a year.

QUERCUS (the Latin name for the oak tree)

There are over 400 kinds of oak in temperate and warm regions, many important for timber, and some for bark extracts used in tanning. *Q. suber*, the cork oak, is a small, southern European species, reaching 10m (33ft) or more in height. It has an unusual bark structure which forms a dense light, corky layer, and the trees are cultivated in Spain and Portugal for the production of cork. There are strict laws controlling cutting to ensure constant supply and to protect the trees. The first, virgin, cork is cut at twenty to twenty-five years old, and the next harvest is nine years later for reproduction cork which does not have the same rough surface.

This tree is hardy in milder temperate areas, but like the olive is probably best as an indoor bonsai. It needs to be kept very cool in winter, but pot-grown plants must not freeze and should have enough moisture only to prevent shrivelling of the twigs. Such plants are best pruned in late spring.

SECHIUM (possibly from the Greek *sekos*, an animal enclosure)

There is only one species in this genus, commonly known as chaco or christophine, which probably originated in tropical America, but which is grown in southern Europe, tropical Africa, America and elsewhere. The fruits are edible and are also used for fattening pigs. The root is cooked and eaten like a yam.

This is a perennial herbaceous climber in the cucumber family, with fleshy roots weighing up to 10kg (22lb). The 10cm (4in) long fruit has a single large seed, which can germinate inside the fruit. It should be planted in a rich well-drained compost, and needs humid, warm conditions. The stems grow to 3–4m (10–13ft) or more in height and need support.

SIMMONDSIA (named after F. W. Simmonds, a nineteenth-century naturalist and traveller)

The only species in this genus is *S. chinensis*, commonly known as jojoba, which comes from the Sonoran desert in Arizona, California and north-west Mexico. It is an evergreen dioecious shrub growing to about 3m (10ft) tall, and is related to box. It flourishes in areas of very little rainfall; about 30cm (12in) annual precipitation is sufficient for the growth and establishment of seedlings.

Oil from the seeds is an excellent substitute for sperm whale oil, which is important in industry. It is also used in cosmetics.

(Opposite) *Punica granatum*
(Below) *Simmondsia chinensis*

The plants grow well in dry conditions and need well-drained coarse compost. They grow naturally on coarse clay and gravel and need full sunlight to keep the leaves and stems tough. If they are grown too soft the shoots and young leaves become rather delicate. The plants could be used as indoor bonsai, but would probably only flower if given adequate space to develop. They take about five years to reach flowering size and are then productive for eighty to a hundred years. Fruiting depends on the presence of both male and female plants.

La Macre ou Chataigne d'Eau
Trapa natans, Linn. Sp. Pl.

Trapa natans

TRAPA (from the Latin *calcitrappa*, a four-spined weapon used to stop cavalry progress, referring to the shape of the fruit)
The one variable species, *T. natans*, which is sometimes treated as a range of distinct kinds, comes from warm areas of Eurasia and Africa and is commonly known as the water chestnut.

This attractive aquatic has rosettes of toothed floating leaves and submerged rootlike leaves. The horned fruit contains a large edible sweet seed.

Some forms are hardy in temperate countries, but the plants are best as warm-water aquatics suitable for medium to large aquaria. The water temperature required depends a lot on the area of origin, but a fairly wide range is tolerated by most forms.

The plant known as *T. bispinosa* is the Singhara nut, which has two-spined fruit, instead of the usual four.

ZINGIBER (said to be corrupted from a Sanskrit word meaning a horn, probably referring to the shape of the rhizome)
There are about eighty species in this genus which are found in Malaysia, the East Indies, and nearby areas. *Z. officinale* is the source of ginger, and other species contain useful flavouring materials in the rhizomes.

These plants are herbaceous perennials with stout

PLANTS FOR SPECIAL PURPOSES

EASE OF CULTIVATION				LIGHT REQUIREMENTS	
Suitable for beginners	**Moderately easy**		**Fairly difficult**	**Shady Situation**	**Direct Sunlight**
Actinidia	*Ananas*	*Lawsonia*	*Cocos*	*Camellia*	*Agave*
Agave	*Annona*	*Mangifera*	*Cyperus*	*Chlorophytum*	*Aloe*
Aloe	*Camellia*	*Musa*	*Litchi*	*Coffea*	*Ceratonia*
Amaranthus	*Carica*	*Oryza*			*Cocos*
Arachis	*Coffea*	*Phoenix*			*Olea*
Ceratonia	*Corchorus*	*Punica*			*Opuntia*
Chlorophytum	*Eichhornia*	*Quercus*			*Pelargonium*
Citrus	*Gossypium*	*Sechium*			*Phoenix*
Cyphomandra	*Hibiscus*	*Trapa*			
Ficus	*Ipomoea*			**ATTRACTIVE FOLIAGE**	
Olea					
Opuntia				*Aloe*	*Musa*
Persea				*Chlorophytum*	*Pelargonium*
Pelargonium				*Cocos*	*Persea*
Simmondsia				*Coffea*	*Phoenix*
Zingiber				*Cyperus*	

ATTRACTIVE FLOWERS				SCENTED FLOWERS OR LEAVES	
Actinidia	*Citrus*	*Gossypium*	*Opuntia*	*Citrus* (flowers)	*Pelargonium* (foliage)
Amaranthus	*Coffea*	*Hibiscus*	*Pelargonium*	*Coffea* (flowers)	
Camellia	*Eichhornia*	*Ipomoea*	*Punica*		

rhizomes. The leafy stems grow to about 90cm (3ft) in height, but the flower shoots with their yellowish-bracted conelike flower spikes are much shorter.

Pieces of rhizome sold for culinary use are usually alive and will grow if planted in well-drained peaty compost and given warmth and moisture. A temperature of 24°C (75°F) is ideal, and the compost should be only just moist until the first shoot appears. Plenty of water is needed during the growing season. When the leaves start to die late in the year, watering should be reduced, and the rhizomes kept dry for the winter.

The plants will flower if the growing conditions are suitable, but pot-grown specimens seldom do so. Even in tropical glasshouses flower spikes are infrequent.

FURTHER INFORMATION

Bibliography

Purseglove, J. W., *Tropical Crops* (Volume 1 Monocotyledons, Volume 2 Dicotyledons, Longman, 1968 and 1972)
Masefield, G. B., Wallis, M., Harrison, S. G. and Nicholson, B. E., *The Oxford Book of Food Plants* (Oxford University Press, 1969)
Lötschert, Wilhelm and Beese, Gerhard, *Collins Guide to Tropical Plants* (Collins, 1983)

COMMON NAMES AND PRODUCTS

In the descriptive section the subjects are arranged in generic order. Since these generic names may not be familiar to many readers the following list of products and popular names may be used to locate the plant required.

Common name	Genus
Algaroba bean	*Ceratonia*
Alligator pear	*Persea*
American aloe	*Agave*
Aquatics	*Cyperus, Eichhornia, Oryza, Trapa*
Aromatic oils	*Pelargonium*
Avocado	*Persea*
Banana	*Musa*
Bark	*Quercus*
Bergamot oil	*Citrus*
Beverages	*Camellia, Coffea, Punica*
Bonsai	*Ceratonia, Olea, Punica, Quercus, Simmondsia*
Carob	*Ceratonia*
Century plants	*Agave*
Cereals	*Amaranthus, Oryza*
Chaco	*Sechium*
Cherimoya	*Annona*
Chinese gooseberry	*Actinidia*
Christophine	*Sechium*
Chocolate	*Ceratonia*
Cork	*Quercus*
Custard apple	*Annona*
Date palm	*Phoenix*
Drift seeds and fruits	*Cocos, Annona*
Dyes	*Lawsonia*
Fibres	*Agave, Cocos, Corchorus, Gossypium, Hibiscus, Musa*
Fig	*Ficus*
Fruits	*Ananas, Annona, Carica, Citrus, Cyphomandra, Hibiscus, Litchi, Mangifera, Musa, Olea, Opuntia, Persea, Phoenix, Punica, Sechium*
Geranium	*Pelargonium*
Ginger	*Zingiber*
Grain	*Amaranthus, Oryza*
Groundnut	*Arachis*
Henna	*Lawsonia*
Jojoba	*Simmondsia*
Jute	*Corchorus*
Kiwi fruit	*Actinidia*
Lemon	*Citrus*
Lemon scent	*Pelargonium*
Locust tree	*Ceratonia*
Longans	*Litchi*
Love lies bleeding	*Amaranthus*
Medicines	*Aloe*
Mountain pawpaw	*Carica*
Nuts	*Arachis, Cocos*
Oak	*Quercus*
Oils	*Pelargonium, Olea, Simmondsia*
Olive	*Olea*
Papaya	*Carica*
Paper	*Cyperus*
Papyrus	*Cyperus*
Pawpaw	*Carica*
Peanut	*Arachis*
Perfumes	*Pelargonium, Simmondsia*
Pineapple	*Ananas*
Pomegranate	*Punica*
Poncirus	*Citrus*
Prickly pear	*Opuntia*
Rambutan	*Litchi*
Rice	*Oryza*
Roots and tubers	*Ipomoea, Sechium*
Rubber	*Ficus*
Seeds, edible	*Arachis, Ceratonia, Trapa*
Singhara nut	*Trapa*
Soursop	*Annona*
Sperm whale oil	*Simmondsia*
Spices	*Zingiber*
Spider plant	*Chlorophytum*
Sweetsop	*Annona*
Tea	*Camellia*
Tiger nut	*Cyperus*
Timber	*Olea, Quercus*
Tree tomato	*Cyphomandra*
Vitamins	*Actinidia, Persea*
Water chestnut	*Trapa*
Water hyacinth	*Eichhornia*
Weights (seeds)	*Ceratonia*
Yams	*Sechium*

GLOSSARY

Adventitious   plant organs arising at an unusual point on the plant.

Agar   a crude, polysaccharide extract from some red algae which can be used to solidify growth media for the culture of bacteria, fungi and tissue and meristems.

Algae   Uni- or multi-cellular lower plants, e.g. seaweeds. Distinguished from other closely related plants by the presence of chlorophyll.

Angiosperm   a flowering plant; members of the class Angiospermae characterized by their true flowers and the development of the seeds within a usually enclosed carpel or ovary.

Annual   a plant which completes its life-cycle from seed to seed in one growing season.

Annulus   in ferns, the row of thickened cells which encircle the sporangium.

Anther   in flowering plants, the pollen-containing part of the stamen.

Antheridium   the male organ of reproduction in lower plants, ferns for example.

Apical   referring to the tip or growing point, as in apical shoot or root.

Archegonium   the female organ of reproduction in lower plants, ferns for example.

Areole   in cacti, a usually well-defined area which bears spines, and sometimes glochids.

Axil   the upper angle formed by the junction of a leaf petiole or branch and the stem that bears it.

Biennial   a plant which completes its life-cycle from seed to seed over two growing seasons.

Bifoliate   consisting of two leaflets.

Bigeneric   pertaining to two genera, e.g. bigeneric hybrid: one between two species from different genera.

Bipinnate   a compound leaf with pinnate leaflets attached to a central stalk.

Bract   a modified leaf which subtends an inflorescence or flower.

Bryophyte   a primitive plant belonging to the division Bryophyta, principally mosses and liverworts.

Bulbil   a tiny bulb or bulblike organ produced on the stem or in the inflorescence.

Bulblet   a tiny bulb produced around the mother bulb.

Calyx   the collective name for the sepals.

Callus   A raised or uneven swelling found on the lips of the flowers of some orchid species, or the un-differentiated tissue produced around a cut surface.

Campanulate   bell-shaped.

Capillarity   the movement of water in an upwards direction due to the phenomenon of capillary attraction, whereby water moves through the minute spaces between soil particles.

Capitate   compact and in the form of a head.

Carpel   the female reproductive organ of flowering plants, consisting of ovary, style and stigma.

Caudex   a thickened stem base at or below ground level, which often acts as a food/water storage organ.

Cephalium   a woolly swelling usually at the top of certain cacti, where the flowers are produced.

Chimaera   plants containing adjacent groups of cells, or tissue, which are genetically different.

Chlorophyll	the green pigment in plants which traps light energy during the process of photosynthesis.	**Dorsal**	the back or outer surface of a part or organ, e.g. the lower side of a leaf.
Clone	all of the plants derived from a single individual by vegetative propagation, and all genetically identical.	**Epiphyte**	a plant growing upon another plant without deriving any nourishment from it.
Coleorhiza	the protective sheath which surrounds the radical (first) root in seedlings.	**Etiolation**	the production of long, spindly stems and reduced leaves lacking chlorophyll due to exclusion or reduction of light.
Column	the structure within an orchid flower formed by the fusion of the style and stigmas to the stamens.	**Filament**	the stalk of a stamen, which bears the anther at its tip.
		Flexuous	sinuous or wavy.
Compost	any substrate devised for the cultivation of plants. It normally consists of several ingredients.	**Floriferous**	free flowering.
		Gamete	a mature haploid reproductive cell, which is either male or female.
Cordate	heart-shaped.		
Corm	a shortened, flattened underground stem surrounded by scalelike leaves.	**Gametophyte**	the phase in the life cycle of a plant when the gametes are produced; in the case of ferns this is a structure known as a prothallus.
Cormlet	a small corm.		
Corolla	the collective name for the petals.	**Germination**	the beginning of the growth and development of a spore or seed.
Corona	petals or stamens modified into the shape of a crown.	**Glochid**	a tiny barbed spine, often arranged in tufts, found in many cacti.
Cultivar	a variant of horticultural worth; plants selected from a species in the wild or in cultivation and distinguished from the type by one or more characteristics.	**Graft**	the method of vegetative propagation where the aerial part of one plant (the scion) is attached to the lower stem and roots of another (the stock).
Cutting	a piece of plant material used in vegetative propagation.	**Gymnosperm**	a group of higher plants characterized by the production of seeds which are not covered by an enclosed protective structure as in angiosperms. The majority are conifers but they also include cycads, *Gnetum* and *Ginkgo*.
Cyathium	a cuplike structure enclosing a flower or flowers. This is the characteristic inflorescence arrangement of euphorbias.		
Deciduous	referring to a plant which loses its leaves at a certain season.	**Half-hardy**	plants not hardy to frost. In temperate climates they are grown outside only during the summer.
Decumbent	growing along the ground for most of the plant's length, but erect near the tip.	**Haploid**	having a single set of unpaired chromosomes in the nucleus; the condition of sex cells before fertilization.
Dentate	toothed; often applied to leaf margins.		
Dioecious	having male and female flowers or cones on different plants.	**Hardy**	plants tolerant of freezing temperatures.

Herbaceous	referring to a non-woody perennial which dies down to a resting rootstock during the winter.
Hyaline	transparent or translucent.
Hybrid	the offspring resulting from a cross between two plants with a differing genetic composition.
Indeciduous	evergreen.
Indusium	in ferns, the protective covering of the sorus, enclosing the sporangia (see also sorus).
Inflorescence	a group or arrangement of flowers.
Intermediate	mid-way in characteristics between two extremes.
Labellum	the lower middle petal or lip of an orchid flower; it is generally greatly enlarged and brightly coloured.
Lamellate	chambered, made up of thin transverse plates.
Lanceolate	shaped like a lance.
Lignify	to become impregnated with lignin.
Lignin	a complex compound produced by plants which, when deposited in plant cells, causes them to become strong and rigid.
Lithophyte	a plant naturally growing in rocky situations.
Loam	a descriptive term for a particular soil type containing a balance of clay, sand and silt. It has particularly good structural and nutritive qualities.
Lobe	a rounded segment of a leaf, petal or sepal.
Mentum	an extension to the base of the column, found in some orchid flowers.
Meristem	undifferentiated plant tissue capable of cell division.
Monocarpic	plants which flower and fruit only once and then die.
Monstrose	a divergent form in which the shoots of the plant are often folded and distorted; generally applied to cacti and succulents.
Mucilage	a gelatinous secretion produced by many plant organs, which swells on contact with water.
Mulch	a material placed on the surface of the soil to suppress weed growth and conserve moisture. It can either be inorganic, e.g. polythene, or organic, e.g. manure.
Mycorrhizal	an association between various species of fungi and the roots of numerous types of green plants; generally mutually beneficial (symbiotic).
Node	the point of attachment of one or more leaves or branches to the stem.
Nutation	the movement of plant parts in response to internal or external stimuli.
Oblanceolate	reverse lanceolate, with the broadest part of the leaf towards the tip.
Offset	a lateral shoot which develops from the base of a stem, affording a means of vegetative propagation.
Ovary	the structure within the flower which contains the ovules.
Ovate	with the outline of a hen's egg, attached at the broader end.
Ovoid	as ovate, but a solid body.
Ovule	the immature seed, before fertilization.
Pandurate	fiddle-shaped.
Panicle	an inflorescence in which the flowers develop into a complex branched arrangement.
Papillate	bearing nipple-like protuberances.
Pappus	a hair or bristle which is attached to the fruits of members of the daisy family and provide a method of dispersal.

Pectinate — comblike.

Pedicel — the stalk of a flower.

Perennial — a plant which lives for more than two years.

Perianth — the outer parts of the flower which enclose the carpels and stamens; normally differentiated into a calyx and corolla.

Petal — a member of the inner whorl (corolla) of the perianth; generally conspicuous and colourful.

Photosynthesis — the production by plants of sugars from water and carbon dioxide, using light energy.

Pinna — the primary division of a compound leaf or frond.

Pinnate — a compound leaf or frond with leaflets or pinnae arranged on either side of the central axis, or rachis, often terminated by an individual leaflet or pinna.

Pinnule — division of the pinna in a bipinnate leaf or frond.

Pistil — the collective name for the female reproductive parts in flowering plants.

Plicate — fanlike, folded longitudinally.

Pollination — the transfer of pollen from the anther to the stigma.

Pollinia — the cohesive masses of pollen grains produced by orchids and milkweeds.

Polyembrony — having more than one embryo in an ovule and therefore capable of producing several seedlings from one seed.

Propagation — the reproduction of a plant by sexual or asexual (vegetative) means.

Prostrate — trailing along the ground.

Prothallus — a flattened heart-shaped structure which is the gametophyte generation of ferns, being the intermediate stage between the spore and the young fern plant.

Pseudobulb — the green bulbous stem-base produced by some orchid species.

Pteridophyte — a fern.

Pubescent — covered with short soft hairs.

Raceme — an unbranched inflorescence consisting of individual flowers attached to a central axis by pedicels.

Rachis — the central axis of a compound leaf or frond or inflorescence.

Radicle — the part of the embryo that develops into the primary root.

Reticulate — consisting of a netlike pattern or arrangement.

Rhizome — a thickened, often elongated, horizontal stem, underground or on the surface.

Rugose — having a coarse, wrinkled texture.

Rupicolous — growing in rocky places.

Sagittate — shaped like an arrowhead.

Sap — the liquid content of plant tissue, normally a mixture of water and dissolved nutrients.

Scandent — with climbing stems which are not rigid and may need support.

Sepal — a member of the outer whorl (calyx) of the perianth which encloses the flower when in bud.

Sessile — stalkless.

Sorus — collectively the kidney-shaped structures (sporangia) found on the underside of the fronds of ferns, and containing the spores.

Spadix — a fleshy spike-like structure bearing the flowers, often surrounded by a large bract (spathe), characteristic of the family Araceae.

Spathe — a large often showy bract at the base of a flower or inflorescence and which may enclose it.

Spathulate — spoon-shaped.

Sporangium one of the club-shaped organs in the sorus on a fern frond and containing the spores.

Spore a reproductive cell in ferns and other primitive plants.

Sporophyte the adult asexual spore-producing form of the fern plant.

Sport a spontaneous mutation arising from a cultivated plant, often more vigorous than the original.

Spur-pruning a form of pruning in which the stems are cut back to short lateral growths.

Stamen the male pollen-producing organ of a flower, consisting of an anther borne on a filament.

Stigma the receptive part of the style. Pollen grains adhere to the surface, which is often sticky.

Stipe the stalk of a fern-frond.

Stolon an above-ground stem, developing sideways and producing a new plant at the tip, and sometimes at the nodes.

Striate with longitudinal stripes or ridges.

Style the piece of connective tissue between the stigma and the ovary.

Substrate the material on which plants grow.

Subtended supported underneath.

Succulent any plant which stores water in fleshy stems or leaves.

Sucker ultimately an erect shoot developing from a bud on roots or underground stems of plants, sometimes emerging at some distance from the parent plant.

Syncarp a fused carpel.

Synsepalum sepals which are fused together.

Tap root the primary root of non-fibrous root systems derived directly from the radicle; characteristic of dicotyledonous plants.

Tender not hardy.

Tepal a member of the perianth, used when sepals and petals cannot be distinguished.

Terrarium a sealed transparent vessel for growing plants.

Terrestrial ground-living.

Transpiration the loss of water vapour by plant tissues, especially through the pores (stomata) of the leaves.

Trifoliate composed of three leaflets.

Truncate with a base or apex which is abruptly squared off.

Tuber a swollen underground stem used for food storage.

Tubercle a small swelling or bump.

Turion a short shoot or scaly sucker produced from an underground stem or tuber.

Umbel a usually flat-topped inflorescence arranged like the spokes of an umbrella.

Velamen the outer covering on the aerial roots of orchid species.

Viscid gelatinous, sticky.

Viviparous the production of young plants, bulbils or leafy buds on a parent plant.

Xerophyte a plant adapted to grow in arid environments.

Zygote the cell formed by the fusion of the male and female gametes.

GENERA AND FAMILY NAMES

Recent taxonomic research into the inter-relationships of monocotyledons has resulted in a comprehensive re-definition at family level; this has particularly affected Liliaceae. The new family names are included here with the old name retained in parentheses. *Lilium* itself and many other genera still validly remain in Liliaceae in its new, strict sense.

Abromeitiella	Bromeliaceae
Acanthocalycium	Cactaceae
Actinidia	Actinidiaceae
Adiantum	Adiantaceae
Aechmea	Bromeliaceae
Aeonium	Crassulaceae
Agave	Agavaceae
Aldrovanda	Droseraceae
Allemanda	Apocynaceae
Aloe	Aloeaceae
	(Liliaceae)
Alstroemeria	Alstroemeriaceae
Amaranthus	Amaranthaceae
Ananas	Bromeliaceae
Annona	Annonaceae
Antigonon	Polygonaceae
Aporocactus	Cactaceae
× *Aporophyllum*	Cactaceae
Arachis	Leguminosae
Arisaema	Araceae
Aristolochia	Aristolochiaceae
Asplenium	Aspleniaceae
Astrophytum	Cactaceae
Babiana	Iridaceae
Beaumontia	Apocynaceae
Begonia	Begoniaceae
Bessera	Alliaceae
	(Liliaceae)
Billardiera	Pittosporaceae
Billbergia	Bromeliaceae
Blechnum	Blechnaceae
Bomarea	Alstroemeriaceae
Borzicactus	Cactaceae
Bougainvillea	Nyctaginaceae
Brassavola	Orchidaceae
Brassia	Orchidaceae
Brocchinia	Bromeliaceae
Brodiaea	Alliaceae
	(Liliaceae)
Byblis	Byblidaceae
Camellia	Theaceae
Canarina	Campanulaceae
Canna	Cannaceae
Carica	Caricaceae
Carnegiea	Cactaceae
Cattleya	Orchidaceae
Cephalocereus	Cactaceae

Cephalotus	Cephalotaceae
Ceratonia	Leguminosae
Ceropegia	Asclepiadaceae
Chamaecereus	Cactaceae
Chlidanthus	Amaryllidaceae
Chlorophytum	Anthericaceae
	(Liliaceae)
Citrus	Rutaceae
Cleistocactus	Cactaceae
Clerodendrum	Verbenaceae
Clianthus	Leguminosae
Clitoria	Leguminosae
Cobaea	Cobaeaceae
Cochlioda	Orchidaceae
Cocos	Palmae
Coelogyne	Orchidaceae
Coffea	Rubiaceae
Conophytum	Aizoaceae
Corchorus	Tiliaceae
Cotyledon	Crassulaceae
Crassula	Crassulaceae
× *Crindonna*	Amaryllidaceae
Crinum	Amaryllidaceae
Cryptanthus	Bromeliaceae
Cyathea	Cyatheaceae
Cyclamen	Primulaceae
Cymbidium	Orchidaceae
Cyperus	Cyperaceae
Cyphomandra	Solanaceae
Cyrtanthus	Amaryllidaceae
Cyrtomium	Aspidiaceae
Darlingtonia	Sarraceniaceae
Davallia	Davalliaceae
Dendrobium	Orchidaceae
Dicksonia	Dicksoniaceae
Didymochlaena	Aspidiaceae
Dionaea	Droseraceae
Diplazium	Athyriaceae
Drosera	Droseraceae
Drosophyllum	Droseraceae
Drynaria	Polypodiaceae
Eccremocarpus	Bignoniaceae
Echeveria	Crassulaceae
Echinocactus	Cactaceae
Echinocereus	Cactaceae
Echinofossulocactus	Cactaceae
Echinopsis	Cactaceae
Eichhornia	Pontederiaceae
Encyclia	Orchidaceae
Epidendrum	Orchidaceae
Epiphyllum	Cactaceae
Espostoa	Cactaceae
Eucharis	Amaryllidaceae
Eucomis	Hyacinthaceae
	(Liliaceae)
Euphorbia	Euphorbiaceae
Fascicularia	Bromeliaceae
Faucaria	Aizoaceae

Ferocactus	Cactaceae
Ficus	Moraceae
Freesia	Iridaceae
Gasteria	Aloeaceae
	(Liliaceae)
Genlisea	Lentibulariaceae
Gloriosa	Colchicaceae
	(Liliaceae)
Gossypium	Malvaceae
Graptopetalum	Crassulaceae
× *Graptoveria*	Crassulaceae
Greenovia	Crassulaceae
Guzmania	Bromeliaceae
Gymnocalycium	Cactaceae
Habranthus	Amaryllidaceae
Haemanthus	Amaryllidaceae
Hardenbergia	Leguminosae
Hatiora	Cactaceae
Haworthia	Aloeaceae
	(Liliaceae)
Heliamphora	Sarraceniaceae
Hemionitis	Hemionitidaceae
Hibbertia	Dilleniaceae
Hibiscus	Malvaceae
Hippeastrum	Amaryllidaceae
Homeria	Iridaceae
Hoya	Asclepiadaceae
Huernia	Asclepiadaceae
Hymenocallis	Amaryllidaceae
Ipomoea	Convolvulaceae
Ixia	Iridaceae
Jasminum	Oleaceae
Kadsura	Schisandraceae
Kalanchoe	Crassulaceae
Kennedia	Leguminosae
Lachenalia	Hyacinthaceae
	(Liliaceae)
Laelia	Orchidaceae
Lapageria	Philesiaceae
	(Liliaceae)
Lapeirousia	Iridaceae
Lawsonia	Lythraceae
Lemboglossum	Orchidaceae
Leucocoryne	Alliaceae
	(Liliaceae)
Lilium	Liliaceae
Litchi	Sapindaceae
Lithops	Aizoaceae
Littonia	Colchicaceae
	(Liliaceae)
Lobivia	Cactaceae
Lophophora	Cactaceae
Lycaste	Orchidaceae
Lycoris	Amaryllidaceae
Lygodium	Schizaeaceae
Mammillaria	Cactaceae
Mandevilla	Apocynaceae
Mangifera	Anacardiaceae

Masdevallia	Orchidaceae	*Phoenix*	Palmae	*Sparaxis*	Iridaceae
Maurandya	Scrophulariaceae	*Pinguicula*	Lentibulariaceae	*Sprekelia*	Amaryllidaceae
Melocactus	Cactaceae	*Platycerium*	Polypodiaceae	*Stapelia*	Asclepiadaceae
Microlepia	Dennstaedtiaceae	*Pleione*	Orchidaceae	*Stenomesson*	Amaryllidaceae
Moraea	Iridaceae	*Plumbago*	Plumbaginaceae	*Stephanotis*	Asclepiadaceae
Musa	Musaceae	*Polianthes*	Agavaceae	*Streptanthera*	Iridaceae
Mutisia	Compositae	*Polypodium*	Polypodiaceae	*Strongylodon*	Leguminosae
Myrtillocactus	Cactaceae	*Pteris*	Pteridaceae	*Sutherlandia*	Leguminosae
Neoregelia	Bromeliaceae	*Punica*	Punicaceae	*Swainsona*	Leguminosae
Nepenthes	Nepenthaceae	*Pyrostegia*	Bignoniaceae	*Tacitus*	Crassulaceae
Nephrolepis	Oleandraceae	*Quercus*	Fagaceae	*Tecophilaea*	Tecophilaeaceae
Nerine	Amaryllidaceae	*Quesnelia*	Bromeliaceae	*Tetrastigma*	Vitaceae
Nidularium	Bromeliaceae	*Quisqualis*	Combretaceae	*Thunbergia*	Thunbergiaceae
Notocactus	Cactaceae	*Rebutia*	Cactaceae	*Tibouchina*	Melastomataceae
Odontoglossum	Orchidaceae	*Rhipsalis*	Cactaceae	*Tigridia*	Iridaceae
Olea	Oleaceae	*Rossioglossum*	Orchidaceae	*Tillandsia*	Bromeliaceae
Oncidium	Orchidaceae	*Rumohra*	Davalliaceae	*Trachelospermum*	Apocynaceae
Opuntia	Cactaceae	*Sandersonia*	Colchicaceae	*Trapa*	Trapaceae
Ornithogalum	Hyacinthaceae		(Liliaceae)	*Trichocereus*	Cactaceae
	(Liliaceae)	*Sansevieria*	Dracaenaceae	*Tritonia*	Iridaceae
Oryza	Gramineae		(Liliaceae)	*Utricularia*	Lentibulariaceae
Osmunda	Osmundaceae	*Sarracenia*	Sarraceniaceae	*Vallota*	Amaryllidaceae
Pachyphytum	Crassulaceae	*Sauromatum*	Araceae	*Veltheimia*	Hyacinthaceae
Pandorea	Bignoniaceae	*Schlumbergera*	Cactaceae		(Liliaceae)
Paphiopedilum	Orchidaceae	*Sechium*	Cucurbitaceae	*Vriesea*	Bromeliaceae
Parodia	Cactaceae	*Sedum*	Crassulaceae	*Watsonia*	Iridaceae
Passiflora	Passifloraceae	*Selenicereus*	Cactaceae	*Zantedeschia*	Araceae
Pelargonium	Geraniaceae	*Senecio*	Compositae	*Zephyranthes*	Amaryllidaceae
Pellaea	Sinopteridaceae	*Simmondsia*	Simmondsiaceae	*Zingiber*	Zingiberaceae
Persea	Lauraceae	*Solandra*	Solanaceae	*Zygopetalum*	Orchidaceae
Petrea	Verbenaceae	*Sollya*	Pittosporaceae		
Phalaenopsis	Orchidaceae	*Sophronitis*	Orchidaceae		

Illustration Acknowledgements

Gillian Beckett: pages 1, 18 (above), 21, 22, 26, 30, 37 (below), 39, 42, 48, 49 (below), 51, 53 (left and right), 54 (above), 55 (right), 56 (below), 60 (below), 61, 62, 121 (below), 160, 172, 177 (below), 178, 180, 181, 182, 183, 186, 193, 197, 200 (below), 201, 205, 209 (above), 211; K. Beckett: 49 (above), 202; J. K. Burras: 85, 86; B. Fearn: 23, 32, 35, 37 (above); H. Gaulton: 18 (below); S. Jury: 134; Sue Minter: 118; D. Philcox: 98, 104, 106; D. L. St Romaine: 5, 9, 36; Harry Smith: 110; Joyce Stewart: 144 (right), 145, 150 (right) 155.

Original artwork by Lyn Cawley: 14, 15, 16, 17, 42, 43, 45, 47, 68, 69, 77, 94, 95, 114, 115, 116, 117, 126, 128 (below), 142, 143, 166, 168, 169, 189.

All other illustrations by kind permission of the Trustees of the Royal Botanic Gardens, Kew.

INDEX

Page numbers in *italics* refer to illustrations